"THE MAID" AND "THE HANGMAN"

FOLKLORE STUDIES: 21

"The Maid" and "The Hangman"
Myth and Tradition in a
Popular Ballad

ELEANOR LONG

UNIVERSITY OF CALIFORNIA PRESS
BERKELEY · LOS ANGELES · LONDON
1971

UNIVERSITY OF CALIFORNIA PUBLICATIONS
FOLKLORE STUDIES: 21

ADVISORY EDITORS
BERTRAND BRONSON, ALAN DUNDES, WOLFRAM EBERHARD
WAYLAND HAND, JAAN PUHVEL, S. L. ROBE, D. K. WILGUS

Approved for publication September 19, 1969
Issued May 7, 1971

UNIVERSITY OF CALIFORNIA PRESS
BERKELEY AND LOS ANGELES
CALIFORNIA

❖

UNIVERSITY OF CALIFORNIA PRESS, LTD.
LONDON, ENGLAND

ISBN: 0-520-09144-2
LIBRARY OF CONGRESS CATALOG CARD NUMBER: 79-628704

TO
ARTHUR GILCHRIST BRODEUR
UNDER WHOSE TUTELAGE AND WITH WHOSE ENCOURAGEMENT
THIS STUDY WAS ORIGINALLY CONCEIVED

ACKNOWLEDGMENTS

As ANY folklorist knows, when an Unpromising Heroine sets out to perform an Impossible Task she has need of Extraordinary Helpers of specialized abilities—sometimes a great number of them. I should like to acknowledge some portion of my own obligation to such Helpers here:

To Judah Bierman, Carl E. W. L. Dahlstrom, Arthur Gilchrist Brodeur, William A. Matthews, and Franz H. Bäuml, who taught me the value of close textual analysis.

To Wayland D. Hand, who introduced me to international folklore scholarship.

To Anne Hinckley and other staff members of the Reference Department of the Research Library, and to Marjorie Griffin, secretary, Jeannine Talley, Marina Bokelman, and other fellow students at the Center for the Study of Comparative Folklore and Mythology, all of whom facilitated my work at the University of California, Los Angeles, through innumerable acts of kindness cheerfully performed.

To Edith Fowke, John Robb, and Jan P. Schinhan, whose replies to requests for information were prompt and generous.

To James Orville Smith, whose resourcefulness was taxed to the utmost in typing the original manuscript.

To Mrs. Richard Kluckhohn of the University of California Press, whose skillful blue pencil has done much to make "the crooked straight, and the rough places plain" in the final revision.

To A. L. Lloyd and the British Broadcasting Company Archive; Rae Korson and the Library of Congress Music Division; Edmund Berkeley, Jr., and the University of Virginia Library; and James Delargy and the Irish Folklore Commission Archive, who graciously placed their facilities at my disposal and furnished many a valuable text thereby.

For permission to reproduce the tunes appearing in chapter iv, I am deeply greatful to the American Folklore Society, publishers of the *Journal of American Folklore;* to the English Folk Song and Dance Society, publishers of the *Journal of the Folk Song Society;* to Donal O'Sullivan, editor of the *Journal of the Irish Folk Song Society;* to the Duke University Press, publishers of *The Frank C. Brown Collection of North Carolina Folklore;* to Arthur Palmer Hudson, editor of *Folk Tunes from Mississippi;* to the Oxford University Press, publishers of *English Folk Songs from the Southern Appalachians,* edited by Cecil Sharp and Maud Karpeles; to J. J. Augustin, Incorporated, publishers of *Ballads and Songs from Ohio,* edited by Mary O. Eddy; to the H. W. Gray Company, publishers and copyright holders of *Lonesome Tunes,* edited by Loraine Wyman and Harold Brockway; to the Wilkinson Folk Song Manuscripts Division of the University of Virginia Library; and to the Harvard University Press, publishers of *South Carolina Ballads,* edited by Reed Smith.

There is no way adequately to thank all the informants and collectors responsible for preserving the traditions from which these tunes were selected, but some measure of the debt may be inferred from the variant sources furnished in chapter iii.

Finally, to the giant whose shoulders proved to be as broad as they were firm while this study was being prepared in its original form as a doctoral dissertation, D. K. Wilgus. The ground upon which he stands may, I hope, be fortified in turn by a pebble or two to be gleaned from it.

Needless to say, I am wholly responsible for any errors or shortcomings that have persisted in spite of the best efforts of the Helpers named above. When all gifts have been bestowed, and all obstacles cleared away, the Unpromising Heroine must still face the Dragon on her own!

Dublin, 1970   E. L.

CONTENTS

LIST OF TABLES

ABBREVIATIONS

AA	*American Anthropologist*
AaT	Antti Aarne and Stith Thompson, *The Types of the Folktale (FFC* 184)
AAW	*Aus allen Weltteilen*
ABAW (P-H)	*Abhandlungen, Bayerische Akademie der Wissenschaften, phil.-hist. Klasse*
ACUT (H)	*Acta et Commentationes Universitatis Tartuensis (Dorpatensis) B. Humaniora*
AFP	*American Folk-Song Publications*
AR	*Archiv für Religionswissenschaft*
AS	*American Speech*
BBC	British Broadcasting Company, Archive
BLAM	*Boletino latino-americano de musica*
CFSB	*Colorado Folklore Society Bulletin*
CFQ	*California Folklore Quarterly*
Child	Francis James Child, *The English and Scottish Popular Ballads*
DA	Mitford Matthews, *A Dictionary of Americanisms on Historical Principles*
DAE	W. A. Craigie and J. R. Hulbert, *A Dictionary of American English on Historical Principles*
DAS	Harold Wentworth and Stuart Berg Flexner, *A Dictionary of American Slang Based Upon Historical Principles*
DGF	Svend Grundtvig, et al., *Danmarks gamle Folkeviser*
DJV	*Deutsches Jahrbuch für Volkskunde*
DKAW (P-H)	*Denkschriften, Kaiserliche Akademie der Wissenschaften, phil.-hist. Klasse*
DOST	W. A. Craigie and A. J. Aitken, *A Dictionary of the Older Scottish Tongue*
DR	*Dalhousie Review*
DSL	Karl Wander, *Deutsches Sprichwörterlexicon*
DVM	John Meier, et al., *Deutsche Volkslieder mit ihren Melodien, I. Balladen*
DW	Jakob Grimm, et al., *Deutsches Wörterbuch*
EC	*Essays in Criticism*
EDD	Joseph Wright, *The English Dialect Dictionary*
EDSL	John Jamieson, *An Etymological Dictionary of the Scottish Language*
EETS	*Early English Texts Society Publications*
EIHC	*Essex Institute Historical Collections*
EMU	*Ethnologische Mitteilungen aus Ungarn*
Erk-Böhme	Ludwig Erk and Franz Magnus Böhme, *Deutscher Liederhort*
FA	*Folklore Americano*
FF	*Folkminnen og Folktankar*
FFC	*Folklore Fellows Communications*
FFMA	*Folklore and Folk Music Archivist*
FJ	*Folk-Lore Journal*
HDA	E. Hoffmann-Krayer and Hanns Bächtold-Stäubli, *Handwörterbuch des deutschen Aberglaubens*
HDM	Lutz Mackensen and Johannes Bolte, *Handwörterbuch des deutschen Märchens*
HF	*Hoosier Folklore*
HR	*Hispanic Review*
IFC	Irish Folklore Commission, Archive
ITS	*Irish Texts Society Publications*
JAF	*Journal of American Folklore*
JAIHS	*Journal of the American-Irish Historical Society*
JDAI	*Jahrbuch des deutschen archäologisches Instituts*
JEFDSS	*Journal of the English Folk Dance and Song Society*
JEGP	*Journal of English and Germanic Philology*
JFI	*Journal of the Folklore Institute*
JFSS	*Journal of the Folk-Song Society*
JGLS	*Journal of the Gypsy Lore Society*

JIFMC	*Journal of the International Folk Music Council*
JIFSS	*Journal of the Irish Folk-Song Society*
JMULS	*Journal of the Malta University Literary Society*
JPE	*Journal of Political Economy*
JSFO	*Journal de la Société Finno-Ougrienne*
JVF	*Jahrbuch für Volksliedforschung*
KFR	*Kentucky Folklore Record*
KHM	Jakob and Wilhelm Grimm, *Kinder- und Hausmärchen*
Laws	G. Malcolm Laws, Jr., *Native American Balladry* (A–I) and *American Ballads from British Broadsides* (J–Q)
LC-AFS	Library of Congress Music Division, Archive of Folk Song
LC-AMD	Library of Congress, Art-Music Division
LC-AV	Library of Congress Music Division, Audio-Visual Department
LCJ	*Louisville* (Kentucky) *Courier-Journal*
MAFS	*Memoirs of the American Folklore Society*
MED	Hans Kurath and Sherman S. Kuhn, *Middle English Dictionary*
MF	*Midwest Folklore*
MLQ	*Modern Language Quarterly*
MNW	E. Verwijs and J. Verdam, *Middelnederlandsch Woordenboek*
MP	*Modern Philology*
MQ	*Musical Quarterly*
MWQ	*Mid-West Quarterly*
NDEW	H. S. Falk and Alf Torp, *Norwegisch-dänisches etymologisches Wörterbuch*
NED	James Murray, et al., *A New English Dictionary on Historical Principles*
NEHGR	*New England Historical and Genealogical Register*
NQ	*Notes and Queries*
NYFQ	*New York Folklore Quarterly*
NZM	*Neue Zeitschrift für Musik*
PAFS (B)	*Publications of the American Folklore Society, Bibliographical Series*
PFS	*Publications of the Folk-Lore Society*
PIU (F)	*Publications of Indiana University, Folklore Series*
PMLA	*Publications of the Modern Language Association*
PQ	*Philological Quarterly*
PSE	*Princeton Studies in English*
PSP	*Percy Society Publications*
PTFS	*Publications of the Texas Folklore Society*
PUCLALL	*Publications of the University of California at Los Angeles in Languages and Literatures*
PUK (H)	*Publications of the University of Kansas, Humanistic Series*
RA	*Revue archéologique*
Roscher	W. H. Roscher, *Ausführliches Lexicon der griechischen und römischen Mythologie*
SAWW (P-H)	*Sitzungsberichte, Akademie der Wissenschaften zu Wien, phil.-hist. Klasse*
SFQ	*Southern Folklore Quarterly*
SGRS	Otto von Reinsberg-Düringsfeld and Ida Düringsfeld, *Sprichwörter der germanischen und romanischen Sprachen*
SIM	*Sammelbände der internationalen Musikgesellschaft*
SN	*Studia Norvegica*
SR	*Saltire Review*
SVF	*Studien für Volksliedforschung*
TASJ	*Transactions, Asiatic Society of Japan*
TFSB	*Tennessee Folklore Society Bulletin*
TSL	*Tennessee Studies in Literature*
UCLA-CWF	University of California at Los Angeles, Archive of California and Western Folklore
UCLA-WKF	University of California at Los Angeles, Western Kentucky Folklore Archive

UO-RG	University of Oregon, Robert W. Gordon Archive
UR	*Ungarische Revue*
USCB	*University of South Carolina Bulletin*
USUN	*University Studies of the University of Nebraska*
UVL-M	University of Virginia Library, Manuscript Division
VMKAW (L)	*Verslagen en Mededeelingen, Koninklijke Akademie van Wetenschappen, Afdeeling Letterkunde*
WF	*Western Folklore*
WMQ	*William and Mary Quarterly*
ZV	*Zeitschrift für Volkskunde*

I

PURPOSE AND METHOD

FEW TRADITIONAL ballads of the Western world have been discussed more extensively on an international scale than has the one represented in Francis James Child's standard British collection as no. 95, and entitled by him "The Maid Freed from the Gallows." In addition to Child's own far-reaching and pioneering annotation of this ballad's pan-European tradition,[1] special studies on the same comparative basis were published in 1919 by H. Grüner-Nielsen in relation to the Danish version "Faestemand løskøber Faestemø" (*DGF* 486);[2] in 1934 by Erik Pohl with emphasis upon the German "Die Losgekaufte" (Erk-Böhme 78);[3] and in 1957 by Iivar Kempinnen, focusing upon the Finnish "Lunastettava neito."[4] A more limited but highly illuminating treatment of the Italian version, "La Donna Rapita" or "Scibilia Nobili," appeared in Giovanni Bronzini's *La Canzone Epico-lirica nell'Italia Centro-Meridionale* in 1966.[5]

The Anglo-American version of the ballad has also received considerable attention from English and American scholars since the publication of Child's collection. Their emphasis, however, has been somewhat different from that placed by the European investigators just named, who concentrated upon the questions of differentiating the ballad's types and determining their genetic relationships. Except for a few brief and relatively modest studies of the possible origin or archetypal form of individual ballad traditions like those limited to Child 95 which have been contributed by Anne Gilchrist and Lucy E. Broadwood in 1915,[6] A. H. Krappe in 1941,[7] and Ingeborg Urcia and Tristram P. Coffin in 1966 and 1967,[8] English and American folklorists have tended to inquire into the origins and functions of folklore materials only to the degree that general theory might be served.[9] In consequence, the individual ballad has commonly been relegated to an ancillary role: variants are isolated from their traditional contexts for the purpose of illustrating theoretical principles formulated a priori by the investigator. The ballad known as "The Maid Freed from the Gallows" figures in just this way in treatises supporting, as the climate has been favorable, several theses: that all folklore materials are survivals of ancient solar myth; that ballads take their origin from the communal compositions of dancing throngs; that folklore materials embody symbols that, if not necessarily solar, have universal meaning more or less intuitively accessible to the scholar; that ballads originated as snatches of sung verse systematically interpolated into prose narrative (the *cantefable*); and that the folklore materials of isolated groups of persons constitute in themselves accurate and reliable evidence for defining the social and emotional attitudes of such groups.

Sabine Baring-Gould was the first to publish a version of the ballad in *cantefable* form,[10] the story he printed in 1866 consisting of three major narrative units. In the first, a little man dressed all in gold presented two girls with golden balls and warned them that they would be hanged if they should lose them. This episode, although it bears tenuous resemblances to Germanic legendry and to other narrative settings for the ballad with which I am concerned, is significantly

1

idiosyncratic in relation to its analogues.[11] In the second episode, one of the girls lost her ball and her sweetheart went in search of it. These two motifs are to be found in the *Kinder-und Hausmärchen der Brüder Grimm,* the first as the opening formula for Tale 1, "The Frog Prince," and the second as the body of Tale 4, "The Youth Who Went Forth to Learn Fear."[12] The ballad stanzas conclude the story:

> Stop! Stop! I think I see my mother coming.
>
> Oh, mother, hast brought my golden ball,
> And come to set me free?
>
> I've neither brought thy golden ball,
> Nor come to set thee free,
> But I have come to see thee hung
> Upon this gallows tree.
>
> Stop! Stop! I think I see my father coming.
>
> Oh, father, hast brought my golden ball,
> And come to set me free?
>
> I've neither brought thy golden ball,
> Nor come to set thee free,
> But I have come to see thee hung
> Upon this gallows tree.
>
> Stop! Stop! I think I see my sweetheart coming.
>
> Oh, sweetheart, hast brought my golden ball,
> And come to set me free?
>
> Aye, I have brought thy golden ball,
> And come to set thee free,
> I have not come to see thee hung
> Upon this gallows tree.

Only the first portion of this narrative has no specific analogue in traditional or literary materials. Thirty years later, Baring-Gould was to assert that it was precisely this portion that invested the whole with significance:

The story is almost certainly the remains of an old religious myth. The golden ball which one sister has is the sun, the silver ball of the other sister is the moon. [In the text as it was printed, both balls were of gold.] The sun is lost; it sets, and the trolls, the spirits of darkness, play with it under the bed, that is, in the house of night, beneath the earth.[13]

From this interpretation all consideration of the content of both traditional tales and the ballad is effectively excluded. Later proponents of the doctrine of folk-symbolism gave the ballad stanzas somewhat more attention, at the same time offering a new perspective on the golden ball and its meaning. According to Miss Gilchrist and Miss Broadwood, "The story is plainly allegorical, the golden ball— in other versions a gold key (cf. old ballad, David Herd's MSS: 'Oh, if my love was a coffer of gold / And I was the keeper of the key')—signifying the maiden's honor, which when lost can only be restored by one person—her lover. Gold seems from early times to have been the symbol of integrity. A circle of gold—like the silken snood of the Scottish maiden—appears in Danish ballads as the virgin's insignia."[14] (According to Julius Krohn, the Danish ballads referred to reflect a custom that "probably originated in Sweden, where in the Middle Ages the unmarried women, at least those of the nobility, wore such ornaments on all festive occasions.")[15]

Earlier, Miss Gilchrist had not found the allegory quite so plain. "In the 'Lady Maisry,' 'Prickly Bush,' and 'Golden Ball' class of ballads the *motif* is that of *ransom*. The victim is at war with her kindred, and in a position of dire peril and disgrace—abandoned by her relatives and in imminent danger of being burnt or hanged—a situation from which the lover—and only he—can, and will, deliver her, by restoring her lost honor or paying the ransom demanded in vain from her kith and kin."[16] A contradiction is inherent in this analysis: the girl is described as demanding ransom from the very "kith and kin" who are themselves her immolators in Child 65 "Lady Maisry" and with whom she is "at war" because of her offense. But the 1915 report happily resolved the contradiction by forgetting that the *"motif"* had ever been *"ransom"*—thus, of course, like Baring-Gould forsaking the ballad text for the allegory.

This thesis was endorsed by Dorothy Scarborough[17] and by Phillips Barry, who found a resemblance between the lost golden ball of the *cante-fable* and the ring and brooch figuring in medieval Irish adaptations of the tale of "The Ring of Polycrates" (AaT 736A);[18] by James Reeves, who agreed with Gilchrist and Broadwood that the "prickly bush" of a refrain accompanying some variants of the ballad "represents a fatal love-entanglement";[19] by Ingeborg Urcia, who accepted the implications of extratextual materials published by Child in concluding that the ballad's subject was a wayward girl, and by Tristram Coffin, who unearthed evidence that golden balls might at some time actually have been used as intrauterine contraceptive devices (see n. 8).

With the enthusiastic support of Francis B. Gummere,[20] George Lyman Kittredge concerned himself not with folk symbolism but with the theory that the popular ballad originated in the improvisation of a communal throng—a theory to which a text of "The Maid Freed from the Gallows" quite different from those chosen by the symbolists lent itself admirably. Kittredge's exemplar was collected in the United States, and its ransom was plainly "gold and fee," with no golden balls, keys, or prickly bushes in evidence.

> "Hangman, hangman, howd yo hand,
> O howd it wide and far!
> For theer I see my feyther coomin,
> Riding through the air.
>
> "Feyther, feyther, ha yo brot me goold?
> Ha yo paid my fee?
> Or ha yo coom to see me hung,
> Beneath the hangman's tree?"
>
> "I ha naw brot yo goold,
> I ha naw paid yo fee,
> But I ha coom to see yo hung
> Beneath tha hangman's tree."
>
> "Hangman, hangman, howd yo hand,
> O howd it wide and far!
> For theer I see my meyther coomin,
> Riding through the air.

"Meyther, meyther, ha yo brot me goold?
Ha yo paid my fee?
Or ha yo coom to see me hung,
Beneath tha hangman's tree?"

"I ha naw brot yo goold,
I ha naw paid yo fee,
But I ha coom to see yo hung
Beneath tha hangman's tree."

"Hangman, hangman, howd yo hand,
O howd it wide and far!
For theer I see my sister coomin,
Riding through the air.

"Sister, sister, ha yo brot me goold?
Ha yo paid my fee?
Or ha yo coom to see me hung,
Beneath tha hangman's tree?"

"I ha naw brot yo goold,
I ha naw paid yo fee,
But I ha coom to see yo hung
Beneath tha hangman's tree."

"Hangman, hangman, howd yo hand,
O howd it wide and far!
For theer I see my sweetheart coomin,
Riding through the air.

"Sweetheart, sweetheart, ha yo brot my goold?
Ha yo paid my fee?
Or ha yo coom to see me hung,
Beneath tha hangman's tree?"

"O I ha brot yo goold,
And I ha paid yo fee.
And I ha coom to take yo froom
Beneath tha hangman's tree."

Kittredge's analysis is a dramatic one.

Suppose now that "The Hangman's Tree" is a new ballad, sung for the first time by the impro-
vising author. The audience are silent for the first two stanzas, and until the first line of the third
has been finished. After that, they join in the song. So inevitable is the course of the narrative,
so conventionally fixed the turn of the phraseology, that they could almost finish the piece by
themselves if the author remained silent . . . "The Hangman's Tree" . . . is a survival of an archaic
type specimen, in full vigor of traditional life.[21]

In a footnote, Professor Kittredge offered to substitute "reversion to" for "survival of"; but he enunciated what may be regarded as the rallying cry for Anglo-
American ballad scholarship as a whole when he added, "We are here concerned
not with 'The Hangman's Tree' itself, but with what it stands for."

For Joseph Jacobs and Martha Beckwith, "what it stands for" became yet
another theory concerning the ballad as a genre. In their opinion, its original
form was the *cante-fable*, and ballad stanzas grew out of rhythmically structured
elements occurring at the most dramatic moments in a prose narrative.[22] Their

versions of "The Maid Freed from the Gallows" did little to substantiate the new claim, however. Jacobs relied upon the idiosyncratic and amalgamated text that Baring-Gould had by his own confession composed;[23] Miss Beckwith's text, collected in Jamaica, featured a heroine who had done "something against the rule and regulation of her royalty" and was ransomed neither by the restoration of a lost ball nor by "gold and fee," but by "gold and silver." Perhaps because of the difficulties created by such textual discrepancies, but more probably because of the shift of scholarly attention away from the subject of origins (to be discussed below), the theory has attracted few adherents, although Herbert Halpert and Kenneth Porter briefly revived it in 1941, 1942, and 1957.[24]

Finally, a new focus upon folklore materials as products and reflections of specific cultures led to studies like those of Dan Ben-Amos and Roger Abrahams, both of whom were as successful as their predecessors in finding certain texts of "The Maid Freed from the Gallows" useful for illustrative purposes.[25] Examining the "cultural background" as an "operative element" in the structure of ballads, Ben-Amos showed that "the conflict here is between the role of the father as the protector of his daughter and his functioning in the particular situation of the ballad" ("Situation-Structure," p. 169); "The Maid Freed from the Gallows," therefore, achieves its highest point of tension in the third stanza and fails to build to a satisfactory climax. The situation is even less aesthetically desirable in an Irish analogue (Laws L11 "The Gallows"),[26] where "the conflict appears to be between love and an unstable moral value like public opinion." Abrahams also chose to juxtapose cultural context and ballad content. Developing the thesis that the male protagonists in Anglo-American balladry are essentially passive, weak willed, and lacking in heroic qualities, he noted approvingly that "only in 'The Maid Freed from the Gallows' does the lover actively come in to free his maid." To the psychology of the American folk, then, could be attributed the phenomenon that "in well over half the American variants there is either a reversal of sexes, and the savior is a girl, or there is no indication of the sex of either the condemned or the sweetheart."[27]

Abrahams was by no means the first to puzzle over this phenomenon. Child thought that the appearance of a male victim in some British texts might be "a modern turn to the story, arising from the disposition to mitigate a tragic tale" (Child, III, 516). Arthur Kyle Davis attempted to relate it to "the 'Southern chivalry' which has made it difficult to convict a woman in the south."[28] Russell Ames, William A. Owens, and John Greenway expressed varying degrees of concern over what seemed to them to be a predilection for a male victim peculiar to the American Negro.[29] Cecil Sharp and Dorothy Scarborough, however, dismissed the problem of *why* their informants preferred to sing about a condemned man rather than a condemned woman by simply assuming that they had not done so, even when specifically informed otherwise.[30]

All such attempts to explain the ballad situation direct their attention more to the customs and attitudes of those who sing ballads than to the ballad materials themselves (whether it is nineteenth-century sentimentalists, Americans, Southerners, or Negroes who are so distinguished), and the approach thus manifested is fundamentally no different from that of the application of purely literary standards to ballad texts.[31] The common assumptions are that the texts chosen for examination are representative of a corpus that has been adequately (although intuitively) defined by the investigator, and that criteria extrapolated by him from any arbitrarily selected discipline may be applied with valid results. The possibility that neither assumption is trustworthy is tacitly denied: in this instance, the "norms" taken for granted by Ben-Amos and Abrahams both in regard to the sex of the victim, and in regard to the order in which the relatives appear, are far from being susceptible of empirical proof.

The innately casual attitudes toward folk art displayed by the scholars under discussion here have not gone unchallenged. As early as 1887, Moses Gaster took members of the English Folklore Society to task in a lecture on "The Modern Origins of Fairy Tales." His subject was the then-popular search for the origins of folklore materials; but the force of his argument is clearly applicable in other areas.

The faults inherent in every new undertaking, viz. of mixing the elements promiscuously and attributing to every branch of the new study the same origin, was conspicuously felt in the new study of folklore. Once a theory was adopted, say for customs or myths, it was immediately applied to superstitions, tales or charms, as if they were all of the same age and derived from the same source. This *general* explanation is still in force, although, as I think, each branch of folklore should be studied separately, endeavouring to prove the origin of each independently of the other; afterwards we may try to ascertain the relationship which exists between each.[32]

In 1928, Archer Taylor found it necessary to deplore what he called the psycho-analytic method of selecting random versions for closer study, and asked that his colleagues adopt Grundtvig's system of painstaking comparison of variants before venturing upon theoretical or aesthetic judgments.[33] In 1950 Tristram Coffin asserted that "the greatest bulk of the Child scholarship of the future must, of necessity, center about the examination and correlation of the material already published and collected. This being the case, it is important that we be not deceived by the 'freedoms' taken in the past when such freedoms may have been justified by the scarcity of the material."[34] Four years later, John Greenway protested that, for the most part, "symbolism in the ballad exists only in the eyes of the beholder," and urged that "looking through these ballads for a common denominator ... be the first step in interpreting a symbolic concept."[35]

D. K. Wilgus characterized the practice of generalizing on a noncomparative basis as "Shooting Fish in a Barrel": his article published under that title in 1958 suggested that those who drew conclusions about the culture of the American folk from the condition of Child ballads collected in the United States might do well to examine contemporary British materials, which revealed precisely the same patterns.[36] Commenting upon the situation in 1961, MacEdward Leach expressed the belief that the influence of cultural anthropology upon folklore scholarship was responsible for American reluctance to engage in comparative studies, but insisted that without such studies no valid generalizations about either ballads or cultures could be formulated.[37] (Unwittingly, he illustrated his own thesis by describing "The Maid Freed from the Gallows" as a degenerate form of a tale about a girl kidnapped by pirates and held for ransom.) A statement by George Herzog in 1938 showed that the influence was beginning to be operative in that period: although he warned against "militant provincialism" in ballad study, he also confessed that "the general and fundamental problems of origin and ultimate derivation" were "extremely elusive," and asserted that "every scrap of folksong found in use today may be looked upon as a living document of a special phase of contemporary life."[38] Recent positions taken by Greenway, Richard Dorson, and Melville Jacobs reveal to what extent the "living document of a special phase of contemporary life" has ousted "general and fundamental," but "elusive," concerns among American specialists in folklore.[39] That the phenomenon is not limited to the American scene is indicated by a protest similar to Leach's, but three years earlier, from Anna Birgitta Rooth, whose concern was for the comparative study of Indo-European myth in European universities.[40]

It is not surprising, then, that in 1964 it was still possible for W. Edson Richmond to report that "the scores of studies for which Professor Taylor called [see n. 33] have not appeared. . . . Indeed, perhaps the most vexing problem in ballad study today is the amount of unsupported, speculative writing that has been indulged in by many who have written to prove hypotheses of which they were unduly fond, by many who love ballads not wisely but too well."[41]

The purpose of my study is at least partially to redress the balance in relation to the popular ballad, "The Gallows Tree." This title has been used in preference to the prejudicial appellations "The Maid Freed from the Gallows" and "The Hangman's Tree," both of which involve identification with problematical elements in the ballad's tradition, the sex of the victim, and the physical setting of the ballad situation. The study must be described as partial because a complete analysis of the ballad's European tradition is regrettably not feasible within the scope of this monograph; for that portion of the investigation (chaps. vi, vii) recourse must be had to such published texts as are accessible and to the findings of scholars who have made comprehensive studies of the materials.

Five aspects of the tradition are considered. First, a collection of 250 texts recovered from oral tradition in the British Isles, the United States, and Australia is analyzed on the basis of recurrent verbal traits. Second, the melodic tradition associated with those texts is examined in the 108 tunes that were similarly collected.[42] Third, an inquiry is made into the traditional history of the symbols connected with "The Gallows Tree." Fourth, investigations of its European analogues are reviewed; and fifth, proposals concerning the ultimate origin of the complex are considered.

My method is based upon the geographical-historical principles first formally described by Kaarle Krohn in 1926, although the techniques involved had been observed in the practices of such folklorists as Reinhold Köhler and Emanuel Cosquin for many years previous to that date and had been outlined earlier by Antti Aarne.[43] The chief characteristics of the method have been clearly enunciated by Walter Anderson and W. Edson Richmond:

1. The investigator must assemble all the variants known to exist of the narrative in question.
2. He must, without prejudice, compare all these variants carefully, trait by trait.
3. He must always keep in mind the date and the location of each variant.[44]

As Richmond observed, rigorous standards are sometimes difficult to maintain.

All the variants known to exist may not be accessible while the study is being carried on; precise information concerning date and place is frequently lacking or untrustworthy. It is also questionable whether it is possible truly to free oneself from subjective prejudice in classifying and analyzing motifs. Anderson dramatized this last hazard in an ingratiating anecdote:

It was in the summer of the year 1911, and I was sitting in a railroad car traveling from Copenhagen to Berlin. I had just added to my previously collected twenty Danish variants of "Kaiser und Abt" twenty-one more, and now tried, according to my esteemed models (*e.g.*, Gaston Paris), to arrange them neatly in redactions and subredactions. I was bitterly disappointed: according to the combinations of persons a variant would belong to one group, according to the combinations of questions to another, according to the formulation of a particular question to a third, according to its answer a fourth, and so on. The groups cut across each other like the circles made by several stones thrown into calm water. I struggled and struggled; but all was in vain—nothing came of it.[45]

Significantly, however, Anderson was able to add that "it was on this railway journey that I first realized the importance of the principle of multiple transmission." His struggle against frustration led to the formulation of a theory that could be tested and verified in the study about which the anecdote was told: stability in folklore materials is maintained largely because each individual involved in their transmission hears the materials not once but many times and not from a single source but from many of them. Similar theoretical contributions can be ascribed to other geographical-historical studies. Anna Birgitta Rooth's *The Cinderella Cycle* shows the "archetypal" or normative form of a story to be an achieved one rather than the original.[46] Holger Nygard's *The Ballad of Heer Halewijn* demonstrates the phenomenon also commented upon by Marta Pohl and Lajos Vargyas,[47] that North Germanic and Scottish traditions tend to preserve (or, more frequently, to introduce) supernatural elements omitted from their Continental and English counterparts (a phenomenon that casts some doubt upon Nygard's own conclusion that the "supernatural" version of "Heer Halewijn" is of necessity the oldest); Nygard's study testifies as well to the fact that ballad relationships can often be traced through the retention of minor and no longer meaningful traits. Jan-Ojvind Swahn's *The Tale of Cupid and Psyche* clearly identifies cultural and linguistic oikotypes[48] not by the method described as psychoanalytical by Taylor, but in terms of their idiosyncratic manipulations of a common original theme.[49] Despite objections ranging from the complexity of the demands made upon the investigator to the fundamental irrelevance of the results so obtained,[50] the likelihood that useful folklore theory will continue to be, and indeed can only be, generated by the geographical-historical approach remains a strong one.

The organization of the materials in my study, however, departs from conventional procedures in one respect: geographical and chronological considerations have been subordinated to those of verbal correspondences. Ballad texts may, of course, be classified in many different ways, and classification by verbal traits is difficult in that the vicissitudes of transmission almost guarantee that no clear lines of demarcation can be drawn on the basis of one feature which will not do violence to the traditional pattern of another, as Anderson's remarks so vividly illustrate. Pan-European studies normally base their differentiation of versions upon geographical distribution; but often this is merely a convenient way of differentiating on the basis of the languages in which those versions are communicated. Such distinctions are frequently, though not inevitably, accurate indexes to textual variation where a number of such geographic-linguistic "bundles" are involved.

Anglo-American tradition, however, is characterized by several unique factors that render a geographical organization highly inappropriate. First, the language differentiation that underlies the patterning of geographical distribution in European oral traditions is absent. Texts collected in Australia, Ireland, Montana, and North Carolina draw upon the same common stock of English and Scottish words. Dialectical variation is minimal and not regionally defined: the text quoted above in illustration of George Lyman Kittredge's theory of communal composition is purportedly Yorkshire in dialect, but was collected in North Carolina after having been learned in Virginia. Regional and national variation based *solely* upon linguistic differences, therefore, is nonexistent.

Second, the United States and the Caribbean Islands have been settled by a highly mobile people. It is often forgotten, when images are conjured up of the bearers of folk tradition, that the lower classes of England, Scotland, and Ireland began to move to the Western Hemisphere early in the seventeenth century, and that few members of these classes remained permanently in the area where they were first located as indentured servants or poorly paid free laborers. The twentieth-century record is recent enough to be self-evident: two world wars and a severe economic depression resulted in massive migrations within the boundaries of the United States. But the same restlessness is manifested in the records of the colonies and of the nineteenth century. While a general movement from east to west is most obvious, the continuous traffic taking place between south and north and from the mainland to the offshore islands is not to be overlooked.[51] To classify oral traditions in terms of geographical location in the face of this kind of shifting folk population would be fruitless, as is readily revealed in an examination of the differences between variants of any single item in such a regional collection as that of Frank C. Brown in North Carolina.

Third, mass culture dissemination, in the form of chapbooks, songbooks, published collections, concert performances, school instruction, and phonograph records, has figured significantly in Anglo-American traditions since the nineteenth century. Variants promulgated in this way may or may not have a profound effect upon the tradition, but their influence cannot be localized.

To these pragmatic objections may be added a fourth, closely bound up with the more theoretical aspects of classification. The disadvantage of grouping versions according to their geographical distribution is that it becomes extraordinarily difficult to locate and identify variants with translingual and transcontinental textual affiliations. Lines of transmission, either within a linguistic family or across the barriers that are too frequently assumed to be imposed by language and territory, are quite unlikely to emerge from such an organization of materials. In contrast, when texts are arranged according to significant verbal traits not only textual relationships but also any regional or linguistic oikotypes that do exist are clearly made manifest.

Using a modified version of Vladimir Propp's schematic approach to the folktale,[52] therefore, I analyzed the texts according to the verbal units found in the first two stanzas. Those units were translated into letter-number formulas: for example, the presence of a person addressed in line 1, stanza 1 is indicated by a capital letter (*A*); the title by which he is addressed by a small letter (*d* for "hangman," *a* for "Judge"); followed if necessary by a distinctive number (*Aa1* representing "Lord Judge," *Aa2*, "justice of the peace," and so on). It thus became possible to represent these two stanzas in a single straight line: any given text could without extraordinary difficulty be reconstructed by referring to the schema, while a large number of texts could be easily compared.

In this fashion it was determined that the single most important feature of the ballad in Anglo-American tradition was the injunction found in the first line; closely following it in significance were the terms of the ransom asked and the title of the executioner. Using these three formulas as criteria, it was possible to distinguish five versions of the ballad in Anglo-American tradition, each of which is rather generously distributed along the geographical-historical continuum: a "hold your hand" group, represented as group A, table 1; a "slack the rope—pay my fee" group (group B, table 2); a "Lord Judge—gold and silver" group (group C, table 3); a "hold the rope—set me free" group (group D, table 4); and a "golden ball—pardon from the king" group, characterized by the obtaining of the victim's release not by cash payment but by means of the restoration of a lost object or a royal pardon (group E, table 5). These tables will be found following discussion and analysis of each group. Each table is accompanied by its own bibliography of variants furnishing all available data regarding informant, date and place of collection, and number of reprints.

Because "The Gallows Tree" has been frequently pressed into service on behalf of a priori assumptions, it constitutes a particularly appealing subject for investigation. Some theoretical questions can be immediately proposed:

1. How relevant to the meaning of a ballad are its narratives and refrains? How close is the relationship between these elements and variant texts?

2. Which textual elements have the greatest stability, which the greatest tendency to variation? Which are most useful in establishing relationships between variants and types?

3. To what degree is oral tradition influenced by (a) immediate cultural context, (b) mass culture vehicles such as printed materials, phonograph recordings, and other "official" means of dissemination, (c) massive innovations by creative individual singers within the oral tradition?

4. Is there reliable correspondence between textual and melodic traditions?

5. Which features of a narrative song (the basic idea, the rhythmical pattern, verbal commonplaces) are likely to survive transmission across linguistic barriers?

To most, if not quite all, of these questions, answers have already been suggested by such studies as Archer Taylor's *Edward and Sven i Rosengård*,[53] Nygard's *The Ballad of Heer Halewijn*, Bertrand Bronson's "Mrs. Brown and the Ballads,"[54] and "The Interdependence of Ballad Tunes and Texts,"[55] and by the patient works of detection performed by Phillips Barry in the *Bulletin of the Folk-Song Society of the Northeast* and D. K. Wilgus in the *Kentucky Folklore Record*.[56] If my study serves further to illuminate some of their conclusions, I consider its purpose fulfilled and its methodology justified.

II

THE SCHEMA

THE SCHEMA devised for classifying and analyzing the texts of the ballad under consideration consists of nine major headings (rubrics XYZ, and A–H) and four subsidiary ones (rubrics "yonder" and I–K). The first is the sex of the protagonist. In approximately half of the variants no sex is indicated, although occasionally it may be inferred from stipulations occurring in variants very closely related on other textual grounds. For example, in the English group accompanied by a "prickly bush" refrain (A7, A14, A16–20, A22, A24, A29, A32–36), four informants specified that the victim was male; since none specified a female, and since a male is also specified in another English variant (A21) that corresponds closely to some members of the group although it lacks the refrain, it is probable that the entire group represents a tradition in which a man is rescued by his sweetheart. Some variants establish the victim's sex within the ballad text, usually in the form of the relatives' response "no, daughter," or "oh, son." This is represented in the schema by Ya or Za. Another group utilizes proper names, as is shown in the schema by the presence of Zb or Ab. Finally, sex is frequently attributed by extratextual materials, in the form of "crossing" ballads[1] (A8–9, A11, A13–14, C31–32, C35–43, C45–46), the embedding of the ballad texts in a prose narrative (A25, C12–13, C48, E1–2, E7, E14, E19–20), or a description of the ballad situation furnished by the informant (A5, A12, A18, A21, A30, B26, B28, B80, C25, C47, C52, D6, D10–12, D16, D40, E3–5, E12–13). Such attribution is indicated in the group tables by Ia, Ib, and Ic, respectively.

Four major rubrics have been utilized for the exposition of the ballad's opening stanza. The rubric A refers to the title of address with which it normally begins; B, to the command or request made by the victim, usually consisting of a transitive verb (Ba) and its object (Bb). A third category, Bc, indicates that the title of address follows, rather than precedes, the injunction; this phenomenon occurs in eleven texts in group A (2–3, 8–10, 13–15, 20, 22, 27), eight texts in group B (21–28) fifteen in group C (1–7, 27, 34, 37–38, 40–43), and two in group E (21–22). Rubric C accounts for the third line of the stanza, which rationalizes or explains the request with a statement varying in specific content, but to the general effect that the victim is aware of the approach of a potential savior. The rhyme scheme is represented by D.

The second stanza of the ballad constitutes the victim's appeal for ransom, either in cash or in a limited number of variants in the form of restoration of a stolen or lost object. I did not think it necessary to show the entire sequence of relatives, which varies from zero (when only one person is called upon for ransom, represented in the schema by the absence of Ea) to a list comprising a large extended family. The rubric E, therefore, shows only the first and last potential rescuer to appear. Although the classic sequence is presumed to be father-mother-brother-sister-sweetheart, approximately one-sixth of the variants initiate the sequence with "mother" (Ea2); less frequently, "brother," "grandmother," "sister," or "friend" is the first to appear. Variation in the ultimate

11

position is normally limited to the appellation used for the beloved, although substitutions here are also not unknown. I was surprised to find a rubic (EC) necessary for failure to obtain help from anyone; when Tristram Coffin reported such a story type,[2] he had located no variant in which it occurred, but my investigation has yielded several. Rubrics A–E may be distinguished from variant designations because they will always be accompanied by qualifying small letters (Ba, Ec); variant designations will consist simply of capital letter and arabic numeral (A16, C3).

Other significant second-stanza features are the form of the verb, ranging from the demand "Give me" to the question "Have you come?" (Fa); the precise terms of the ransom (Fb); the nature of the third line, which is sometimes explanatory (Ga–e), sometimes an alternative question (Gf-h); and the ultimate phrase of the fourth line (H). No provision has been made in this stanza for specifying the presence or absence of rhyme, since it is readily ascertainable from combinations of Fb and H; instead, subheadings represent variations in the form of qualifying adjectives or prepositions.

The presence of borrowed materials is attested under rubric I, as described earlier. J indicates that a refrain accompanies the text; the content will be furnished in the discussion. Variants followed by K were reported as game songs.

The word "yonder" presented a special problem. It occurs in nearly one-third of the assembled texts, but its position varies from the third line ("yonder comes my father") to the final line ("yonder gallows tree"). In order to render its presence visible, the symbol "o" was adopted; the placing of "o" indicates the position of "yonder" in the text in question.

In the discussion to follow, the word "variant" is used interchangeably with the word "text" to refer to a unique form of the ballad sung by a specific person. "Version" and "type" are used both for forms possessing distinctive narrative features and for those in which the distinction can be made only on the basis of verbal patterns (e.g., "slack the rope" and "hold the rope"). "Tradition" refers to any idea or narrative pattern that is perpetuated primarily through oral and unofficial channels; "traditional" is used to distinguish materials that have demonstrably been so perpetuated over a relatively broad chronological and geographical continuum from those whose distribution is restricted and directly traceable to learned or "mass culture" sources.[3]

Because of the fluidity of textual components, both within and among major groupings, texts are furnished only schematically; *Normalformen,* arrived at by the process of inductive analysis, are found in the conclusions to chapter iii.

SCHEMA

XYZ SEX OF PROTAGONIST

    X Indeterminate

    Y Female

    Ya Female, indicated by "daughter" in relatives' response

    Z Male

    Za Male, indicated by "son," "sir," or "boy" in relatives' response

    Zb Male, indicated by "George" or "John"

A   INITIAL ADDRESS

    a To magistrate

        1 Judge, Lord Judge

        2 Justice [variation: "Justice of the peace"]

        3 Jury

        4 [Lord] Joshua

        5 Lord James

        6 Johnnie Law

        7 "old man"

    b To victim [or bystander]

        1 George

        2 John, Johnnie

        3 Johnson

    c To jailer

    d To hangman

    e To "ropeman"

    f To "captain"

    g To "boys"

    h To "Mr. Brakeman"

    i To "Handsel"

B   INJUNCTION (LINES 1–2)

    a Verb

        1 hold [up]

        2 stay

        3 slack [up]

        4 spare

        5 stand

        6 wait [variation: "Go away"]

        7 take a while [variation: "Tarry a while"]

        8 stop

        9 idiosyncratic

    b Object

        1 hand[s]

        2 head

        3 rope[s]

        4 life

        5 line[s]

        6 tongue

        7 idiosyncratic

    c Injunction precedes designation of addressee

C   QUALIFICATION (LINE 3)

    a Verb

        1 I see [variations: "I think I see," "I believe I see," "I spy"]

  2 I hear [variations as above]
  3 here comes [variation: "until . . . comes"]
  b participle
    1 coming
    2 riding
    3 walking
    4 rocking
    5 traveling
    6 wandering
    7 rambling
    8 lumbering
    9 tumbling
    10 other
  o "Yonder"
    1 yonder comes
    2 I looked over yonder [variation: "Look over yonder"]
    3 on yonder hill

D   RHYME (LINE 4)

  a Line 4 "-ile"
    1 mile
      a line 2 "while"
      b line 2 "-ee"
    2 stile
      a line 2 "while"
      b line 2 "-ee"
  b Line 4 "-ee"
    1 sea [variation: "see"]
      a line 2 "while"
      b line 2 "-ee"
    2 me
      a line 2 "while"
      b line 2 "-ee"
  c Line 4 idiosyncratic or lacking
      a line 2 "while"
      b line 2 "-ee"

o   "YONDER" (LINE 4)

  a Line 4 "-ile": "yonder stile"
  b Line 4 "-ee": "over yonder stile to me"
  c Line 4 idiosyncratic or lacking: "yonder hill"

E   APPEAL FOR RANSOM

  a Initially directed to
    1 father
      a "father's face"

    2 mother
        a "mother's voice"
    3 brother
    4 sister
    5 grandmother
    6 friend
    7 sweetheart
  b Finally directed to
    1 true love
    2 lover, love
    3 sweetheart
    4 dear old [variation: "little"] girl
    5 darling
    6 husband, wife
    7 Warenston, Willie, Edward, Charlie, Jack
    8 mother
    9 grandmother
    10 baby
    11 social worker
    12 beggar man
    13 brother
  c Not granted
    1 sweetheart refuses
    2 sweetheart's reply lacking

F   INJUNCTION OR QUERY (LINES 5–6)

  a Verb
    1 injunction
        a Some of [variation: "a little of," "any"]
        b Give me [variation: "bring me"]
        c Find
    2 have you
        a got, any
        b brought [me, my, any]
        c come [with]
        d found
    3 did you bring [variation: "come to bring"]
  b Object
    1 gold [variation: "golden store"]
    2 fee
    3 silver
    4 money
        a "white money"
    5 golden ball
    6 comb
    7 jewels

    8 key

    9 silken cloak

   10 to pay [variation: "have you paid"]

      a fee

      b fine

      c fare

      d way

   11 to . . . free

      a set me

      b buy me [variation: "have you bought me"]

      c bring me [variation: "have you brought me"]

      d pay me [variation: "have you paid me"]

   12 [in final stanza] "pardon from the king/queen"

G   ALTERNATIVE QUERY OR QUALIFICATION (LINE 7)

  a To keep

    1 me from

    2 my body from

      a cold clay ground [variation: "sod," "grave"]

      b earth [variation: "grave"]

  b To save

    1 me from [variation: "my life"]

    2 my body from

      a cold clay ground [variation: "sod," "grave"]

      b earth

  c To take me off

  d For I have stolen a . . . cup

    1 golden [variation: "golden key"]

    2 silver

  e For I am going to be hanged

  f Or have you [variation: "are you"]

    1 come

      a to see me hanged [variation: "hang," "hanging"]

      b to see me hung

      c to see me die

    2 traveled many [a, long] mile[s]

    3 walked many [a, long] mile[s]

  g Or did you

    1 come [variation: "this long, long way"]

      a to see me hanged [variation: "hang," "hanging"]

      b to see me hung

      c to see me die

  h Or is it your intention

      a to see me hanged [variation: "hang," "hanging"]

      b to see me hung

      c to see me die

o   "Yonder" (line 7)

    a   To keep ... "yonder" grave
    b   To save ... "yonder" grave

H   Final Words (line 8)

    a   Final word "tree"
       1   gallows
       2   hangman's [variation: "**hanging**"]
       3   willow [variations: "weeping," "mellow"]
       4   other generic or qualitative [oak, sorrowful, sycamore, scarlet, **Tyburn**, lonesome, maple, juniper, shady, shameful, decidal, cypress]
       5   "beneath"
    b   Final words "shall be"
    c   Final words "shall see"
    d   Final word "pole"
       1   gallows
       2   hangman's
       3   willow
       4   raspel
    e   Final word "line" [variation: "twine"]
       1   gallows
       2   hangman's
    f   Final word idiosyncratic
       1   gallows

o   "Yonder" (line 8)

    a   Final word "tree": "yonder" [variation: "yon," "beyond," "under"]
    b   Final word "pole": "yonder"
    c   Final word idiosyncratic: "yonder"

IJK   Additional Rubrics

    I   Borrowed narrative or lyrical materials
       a   "Crossing" ballad
       b   Prose narrative
       c   Explanation or description of situation by informant
       d   Migratory stanzas

    J   Refrain

    K   Game

III

THE TEXTS

GROUP A

GROUP A is based upon an injunction in the first line to "hold" or "stay" the executioner's hand. Three subgroups can be readily distinguished: in one (A1–A12) the victim's ransom is in the form of "gold and fee" (Fb1, 2); in the second (A13–A28) it is "gold" and "silver" or "money" (Fb1, 3 or Fb1, 4); and in the third it is simply "gold" (Fb1). Geographical distribution is wide; in these forms, the ballad has been collected in areas ranging from Kent and Somerset in the south to Durham in the north of England, in Scotland, in Australia, in Jamaica, and in the American states of North Carolina, Missouri, Tennessee, and Florida.

Textual components are discussed in the order in which they appear in the table. First to be considered is the sex of the victim. Of the thirty-seven ballad variants in the group, eight specify that a female is to be rescued from the gallows; of these, five (A8–11, A13) are from Scotland, one (A12) from Tennessee, one (A31) from North Carolina, and one (A25) from Jamaica. Variants A12 and A25 show textual affiliations with the Scottish texts in other respects: A12 in its "gold and fee" ransom, found in all Scottish variants in this group except A13, and in its designation of the victim's lover by a proper name (Eb7); A25 in its use of a first-stanza participle "traveled" (Cb5) and ransom in the form of "gold and silver," corresponding to A13's "traveled" and "gold and white monie."

Three Scottish texts (A9, A11, A13) were recovered "crossed" with variants of Child 173 "Mary Hamilton" (Child 173E, F, and X), a narrative song in which a girl is condemned and executed for having murdered her illegitimate infant. In one of these (Child 173X), the "Gallows Tree" stanzas are so modified that the lover does not offer to rescue her (Ec1). It is clear that the ballad situation could not have originated in the "Hary Hamilton" context. A13, in contrast, shares with A8, A10, A12, and A31 the identification of the victim's sex by the incorporation of the word "daughter" in the text (Ya), and A8 has been augmented by a nuncupative curse upon the victim's relatives which is characterized by such incorporations:

"Gae hame, gae hame, father," she says,
"Gae hame, and saw yer seed;
And I wish not a pickle of it may grow up,
But the thistle and the weed.

"Gae hame, gae hame, gae hame, mother,
Gae hame and brew your yill;
And I wish the girds may a' loup off,
And the Deil spill a' yer yill.

"Gae hame, gae hame, gae hame, brother,
Gae hame and lie with yer wife;
And I wish that the first news I may hear
That she has tane your life.

18

> "Gae hame, gae hame, sister," she says,
> "Gae hame and sew yer seam,
> I wish that the needle-point may break,
> And the crows pyke out your een."

This nuncupative curse also occurs in most variants of Child 96 "The Gay Goshawk," and in a broadside ballad entitled "I'll O'er the Bogie wi' Him";[1] it has not, however, been recovered from English, as opposed to Scottish, tradition. Gilchrist and Broadwood argued ("Children's Game-Songs," p. 235) that it was related to an English game-song tradition in which a girl refuses to mourn at the news of the deaths of her relatives but responds to word of her lover's death, a tradition that has European analogues and can be dated at least to the twelfth century.[2] As the nuncupative curse appears in these Scottish exemplars, however, it conforms precisely to a tradition that is equally ancient, but one that occurs regularly in all Finnish variants of the "Gallows Tree" tradition and sporadically in those of other northern countries. Julius Krohn showed in 1892 that it was to a Finno-Ugric source, entering the Scandinavian version no earlier than the late seventeenth century, that all "Gallows Tree" variants manifesting the curse must have been indebted (see chap. i, n. 15).

Scottish texts featuring "daughter" may or may not be linked directly with the "curse" tradition; but to the predilection for supernatural interpretations shared by Scots and northern Germanic peoples (see chap. i, n. 47) can be added here a predilection for female protagonists. In A10 occurs yet another example, this time in the form of a refrain:

> O, the broom, the bonny broom,
> The broom of the Cauthery Knowes,
> I wish I were at home again,
> Milking my ain daddy's ewes!

As Child noted (IV, 192), the tune to which this refrain was sung throughout Britain was "remarkably popular" during the seventeenth and eighteenth centuries. The ballad story that normally accompanied it (see Child 217 "The Broom of Cowdenknowes" and notes) was as irrelevant to the "Gallows Tree" situation as that of "Mary Hamilton": a girl finds herself pregnant after yielding to a casual stranger who returns in time to save her from disgrace, with neither life jeopardy nor ransom figuring in the ballad situation.

In contrast, English variants in this group show a marked preference for male victims. Two of the American texts identifying their protagonists as "George" (A4, A5) can be traced to the mispronunciation of "Judge" which is unmistakably evident in the British Broadcasting Company's phonograph recording of A16; and the "son" of A28, also from America, may justifiably be regarded as a remodeling of "daughter." But there remain the "John" of A2 (from Australia) and A7 (from Wiltshire, England) and the "Johnson" of A27 (from North Carolina, as are the other American texts under discussion) as evidence that such modifications are not purely accidental. Variant A28 also addresses the executioner as "Johnnie Law," which serves as an indication that they are derived from an original text featuring "Judge" in the same postverbal position (Bc) that it holds in the Scottish texts with female protagonists.[3] The four variants from England lacking "Judge" but specifying a male victim through explanatory material (Ic) or through the pronoun "he" (A18, A21, A24, A34) agree in this respect with A14, also from England, and A14 shares "Judge" with the Scottish texts.

According to Erik Pohl, the "Judge" to which our attention has thus been directed is a secondary development, since the "I see" (CaI) of the third line of the first stanza suggests an out-of-doors, not a courtroom, locale (*"Losgekaufte,"* p. 45). "Hangman" (Ad) occurs in fifteen of these texts, "Judge" in only six. To those six, however, may be added the corruptions to "George" and "John" noted above, and "Judge" appears regularly in the earliest texts of record (A1, A8, A9, A10, A11, A13, dating from the late eighteenth and early nineteenth centuries), twice in the form of "Justice" (Aa2). Similarly, with a single exception (A24), "hangman" texts have either "hold your hand" (Ba1b1) or "stay your hand" (Ba2b1); the texts postulated as corrupt have "hold up your head" (A2), "stand there" (A7), "hold your tongue" (A8), "take a while" or "stay a while" (A16), "stand back" (A27), and "pass your hands" (A28).

Anna Birgitta Rooth's study of the Cinderella cycle showed that its most widely known form in Europe was not the original one. In 1911 Friedrich Ranke found that the most conservative variants of a popular German legend were not those most coherent and widely disseminated, but the rare and relatively illogical texts, and that the original account had been best preserved in a remote Alpine region.[4] As early as 1864, moreover, J. G. von Hahn had cited illustrative materials in parallels between motifs in classical Greek legend and modern German popular tales (e.g., learning to speak animal languages from a grateful snake) and, conversely, motifs in medieval Germanic saga and modern Balkan tales (e.g., a sleep-producing thorn).[5] In a seminal essay in 1927 Archer Taylor asserted that "confused versions may represent a transitional state between an obscured and partially understood *Urform* [original form] and a better-ordered, more intelligible, but later form" ("Precursors," p. 489), and in 1932 demonstrated the process by which this happens in the history of another German legend, adding that "a detail concerning which stories told on opposite sides of the area agree is very likely to represent a trait which belongs to the very oldest levels in the history of the story."[6] Data have since been gathered by Y. L. Cahan and Max Weinreich showing that Yiddish traditions in Slavic countries preserve traits from German materials of three hundred years earlier;[7] Lajos Vargyas (*Medieval History*) has found the same kind of relationships between verbal traits in Hungarian and in French narrative songs. Walter Anderson described the procedure that must be followed in analyzing such data in metaphorical terms: "We lay the variants upon each other, so to speak, and hold them up to the light: then out of the confusion of individual variants the contours of the original form appear in bold relief."[8]

Despite the logicality and consistency of the "hangman, hold your hand" formulation, therefore, the presence, distribution, and condition of "Judge"-related texts suggests that an *Urform* be sought which would account for them, from the "hold your hand, Lord Judge" of A10, A14, and A15 to the "stand back, stand back, pretty little Johnson" of A27.

The third textual element is the injunction. "Hand" is even more common in these texts than is "hangman"; twenty-two variants take it as the object of the verb.

Here, however, the pattern that emerges when the variants are held up to the light is similar to that of "Judge," "Justice," "George," and "John": A2 and A5 have "hold up your head," A8 has "hold your tongue." Examination of the traditional ballads in the Child collection shows that "hold your tongue" is widely distributed as a commonplace in Scottish balladry; it occurs in variants of fifty-two ballads.⁹ Since only a handful of these texts are from English tradition, and since a great many of them are associated with "daughter" or another family appellation such as is characteristic of Scots-Scandinavian materials, we may be certain that both traits are of Scottish provenance.

Of much more limited currency is "hold your hand." In addition to "The Gallows Tree," it is featured in four English ballads of broadside or minstrel tradition: Child 128 "Robin Hood Newly Revived," Child 150 "Robin Hood and Maid Marian," Child 158 "Hugh Spencer's Feats in France," and Child 231 "The Earl of Errol." The appearance in Scots tradition of the formula is more assured: it is found in variants of Child 37 "Thomas Rymer," Child 39 "Tam Lin," Child 46 "Captain Wedderburn's Courtship," Child 65 "Lady Maisry," Child 103 "Rose the Red and White Lily," Child 157 "Gude Wallace," Child 173 "Mary Hamilton," Child 182 "The Laird o Logie," Child 206 "Bothwell Bridge," Child 209 "Geordie," Child 231 "The Earl of Errol," Child 244 "James Hatley," Child 254 "Lord William," and Child 280 "The Beggar-Laddie," or fourteen variants in all.

Of particular concern in relation to "Gallows Tree" texts is a phenomenon observable in Child 254. In each of the three "Lord William" variants published by Child, "hold your hand" alternates with "stand," the injunction found in the deteriorated "Judge" texts of "The Gallows Tree"; the injunction is echoed in Child 73 (I-text), and is found as "stay still" in Child 257 (B-text). "Hold your hand" is manifestly intrusive in the Scots variants listed above. When the data are held up to the light, they show the very strong probability that the "stay thy hand" of A29 and A20–23 is a formulation that originated in the text of this ballad and was modified in Scotland either to "hold your hand" (under the influence of the endemic commonplace "hold your tongue") or to "stay" or "stand" as corrupt forms. "Stand" exerted a very slight but traceable influence in turn upon such Scottish variants as Child 73I, 257B, and 254A, B, and C;¹⁰ A24's "Hangman, stand 'ere a while" transforms the probability into a demonstrable certainty.

The "pass your hands" of A28 is phonetically somewhat like the "peace for a little while" of A1, the text selected by Child as his A-variant and widely reprinted. Since A28 also has the "methinks" of that text, there can be small doubt that this variant is indebted to the source as printed, at least so far as the first stanza is concerned. Noticeable, however, is the corruption of "Judge" to "Johnny Law," as well as the difference in the ransom specified.

Finally, two American texts (A26, A31) add "wait" to their regular injunctions (Ba6). Such an injunction occurs regularly in Scandinavian tradition;¹¹ but Child 254C also alternated "hold your hand" with "wait," and "away, away" occurs as an injunction in Scottish variants of Child ballads in precisely the same sporadic fashion that "stand" does, this time in Child 53 "Young Beichan," Child 64 "Fair Janet," Child 83 "Child Maurice," Child 110 "The Knight and the Shepherd's Daughter," Child 178 "Captain Car," and Child 231 "The Earl of Errol."

As both Erik Pohl and H. Grüner-Nielsen pointed out, there are strong logical reasons for doubting that the English ballad about a person saved from hanging by the payment of cash is derived directly from the Scandinavian ballad about a person saved from kidnaping by pirates by the sale of specifically enumerated personal possessions. My survey of Child's materials tends to verify their contention on phonological grounds: if "The Gallows Tree" did circulate in Britain with a first-line "stay thy hand, Lord Judge" before the first text was recorded in writing as "good Lord Judge, peace for a little while" (A1), its effect upon surrounding tradition is the form of "stay," "stand," and "wait" might have been predicted. The reciprocal influence of "hold thy tongue" upon the phrase is equally easy to account for.

The standard third line for the first stanza in this group is "I think I see my father coming" (Ca1b1). One English, one Scottish, and three American variants (A1, A10, A6, A26, A28) add "riding" (Cb2); the Australian A2 has "walking" (Cb3); the Scottish A8 and A9 have "wandering"; the English A14 has "tumbling"; and A13 and A25, one from Scotland and one from Jamaica, have "traveling," as was noted previously. "Yonder" occurs in line 3 of three Scottish texts (A10, A11, A13), as represented in the table by Co, but in line 4 of fifteen English variants (A7, A15–20, A22, A24, A29, A32–36), where it is regularly associated with "stile" (Da2a). "Stile" is found in no Scottish or American text, and may be considered a late development. Since "yonder comes" is not universal in Scots tradition, and since "yonder" appears with "tree" in the second stanza (Hao) in two American and one Scots text (A3, A13, A37), we may conjecture that although the word was probably featured in the original text, its position was not in the first stanza.

In five texts in this group the regular sequence of relatives differs from the others in that the victim's mother is first to arrive (Ea2). The substitution is associated with "George" and "Johnson" in two American variants (A4, A27), with "hangman" in two English ones (A35, A36), both of which depart from the tradition represented in variants otherwise closely related to them. A16 and A17 initiate the sequence with "sister," and A28 with "friend."

Requests for ransom take three basic forms: "some of" or "a little of, give me"; "have you any"; and "have you brought" or "did you bring." The last (Fa2b, c, Fa3) occurs in twenty variants, the first (Fa1) in three, and the second (Fa2a) in eleven. But, just as an original "Judge" can account for "George," "John," and "hangman," and "stay thy hand" for "hold your hand," "stand," and "wait," so "have you any" suggests itself as the most logical starting point for both "some of" and "have you brought."

Probably the most interesting textual feature in the stanza, however, is the nature of the ransom. Nine variants ask for "gold and fee" (Fb1, 2), and two American texts (A3, A6) for "gold to pay my fee" (Fb1, 10a), each with "hold your hand." The "gold to set me free" of A29–37, therefore, appears to be a simple rhyming alternative, and the "silver" and "money" (Fb3, 4) of A13–28 to be secondary accretions. "Fee" in the sense of movable property other than gold was a commonplace in Middle English, losing this sense during the seventeenth century;[12] it persisted in the formula "gold and fee" in variants of thirty-one ballads in the Child collection.[13] As Knut Liestøl pointed out in a study of Scottish-Norwegian traditional relationships, the formula is equally commonplace in the balladry of Norway.[14]

But "fee" in the sense of a charge fixed by law for services rendered is not only the sole meaning recognized in North America[15] (which might otherwise account for the rationalization "pay my fee" in variants from that part of the world); it occurs in Child ballad variants even more frequently than does "hold your tongue," and with the same Scottish preponderance that was recorded for that common-place formula. Of the fifty-seven ballads featuring "fee" in the sense of "charge for services," twenty—almost all Scottish—use the formula "pay a fee."[16] This for-mula, therefore, must also be regarded as one of considerable status in Scottish tradition.

Nor may "gold and silver" be regarded merely as the modernization of an archaic expression. The earliest known English use of "gold and fee," in an eleventh-century translation of the New Testament, reads "gold *ne seolfer* ne of whether this may be a literary or at least an urban tradition; but "gold and silver," fifteen are English,[18] two Irish (Child 12 "Lord Randal" and Child 93 "Lamkin"), and thirteen Scottish. The fact that "gold and silver" appears fifty-seven times in the Roxburghe collection of broadside ballads[19] raises the question of whether this may be a literary or at least an urban tradition; but "gold and money" occurs in variants of nine Child ballads,[20] "gold and white monie" in eighteen.[21]

It is clear, therefore, that no simple lines of genetic relationship may be drawn from "fee" to "set me free." "Silver," "money," and "white money" are as ubiqui-tous in Anglo-Scots ballad tradition as is "gold and fee" in Scotts-Norwegian. When the texts in group A are considered as a whole, however, both "gold and fee" and "gold to set me free" are found to be almost invariably associated with "hold your hand": "gold and fee" with "Judge" and its corrupted forms, "gold to set me free" with "hangman." "Gold and silver to set me free" and "gold and money to set me free" occur not only in "hold your hand" texts (A13–15, A18, A19), but in all "stay your hand" variants except for the fragment A23 and the hesitating A29, and in the only "hangman" texts (A20, A22) in which the verb phrase precedes the name of the person addressed (Bc), the pattern that is norma-tive in "Judge" texts. An original text featuring "stay your hand, Lord Judge," and "gold and silver to set me free" is indicated.

Nineteen variants in this group follow the plea for ransom with the alterna-tive query "or have you come," or "or did you come" (Gf, Gg). Of those remain-ing, eight have "to keep me [my body] from the grave [ground]" (A1, A15, A16, A17, A19, A22, A24, A28). The indebtedness of A28 to A1 is corroborated here, but the intervening variants show that the indebtedness is not perfect; A1 is the only such text that does not have "gold and silver" or "gold and money" as the ransom (see n. 22). Six have "to save me," three (A8, A11, A13) in that form, two with "gold and fee." "Save my body" is combined with "gold and fee" (A7, which also has "John, stand here"); "gold and money" (A18, with "hold your hand"); and "gold and silver" (A25, the Jamaican *cante-fable* featuring the female victim and "traveling" of A13).[22] The Australian A2 combines "or have you come" with "to take me off this Tyburn tree" (Gc), which provides as much evidence as may be necessary that "to keep me" and "to save me" belong to the same stratum of the tradition as does the "Judge" from which its "John" was derived—a stratum in which the gallows setting, with its "hangman" and "or have you come," had not yet appeared. The same may be said of A1's "yonder grave" (Go).

The pattern of I-elements in this group suggest that little relationship exists between narrative settings and the ballad's traditional situation. Child 173 "Mary Hamilton" furnished one such setting; the *fable* of A25 furnishes another, in which a girl is to be hanged for violating "the rule and regulation of her royalty" and is bought off the gallows (the text specifies a hangman, not a judge) with gold and silver. But A14 is similarly "crossed" with Child 155 "Little Sir Hugh," and features "silver and gold and jewels" together with a judge. And the informants who furnished texts A5, A18, and A21 shared with A14 the conviction that the protagonist was a male (Ic); one of them called him "George" (suggesting an antecedent "Judge"), and the other two featured "gold and money" in the ransom (suggesting an antecedent "gold and silver").

The last component to be discussed is the refrain sung with thirteen of these texts. (The refrain "O, the broom of Cauthery Knowes," attached to A10, has already been mentioned as one that, probably together with its tune, was popularly attached to more than one narrative song.) This one has several variant forms, of which the most common is

> Oh, the prickly bush,
> It pricked my heart full sore,
> And if ever I get out of the prickly bush,
> I'll never get in any more.

This formulation has been collected both independently (A38, A39, A40) and with the "Gallows Tree" text in Wiltshire, Buckinghamshire, Somerset, and Dorset in southern England. A variation, "Oh, the prickly holly bush," was also sung in Dorset (A16);[23] another, "O the briery bush," in Somerset (A29). A second version runs

> O the prickly briers,
> That prick my heart full sore,
> If I ever get free from the gallows tree,
> I'll never get there any more.

This one is localized in Somerset and Wiltshire (A18, A19, A20). It is regularly associated with "gold and silver" or "gold and money"; the "prickly holly bush" version also has "gold and silver," as does one variant to which the most common form of the refrain is attached (A14). With a third line corresponding to that of the most common refrain, however, it occurs in two Somerset variants (A32, A33) asking for "gold to set me free." Variant A14, with "prickly bush," is "crossed" with "Little Sir Hugh" and features "gold and silver and jewels to set me free"; A41, with "prickly brier," is attached to a Child 155 text without benefit of "Gallows Tree" stanzas. Variant A34, with "prickly bush," was sung in a concert series by the ballad popularizer Plunkett Greene during the last quarter of the nineteenth century.[24] Variants with the refrain in the form of "prickly bush," therefore, are traceable to this mass culture influence; the "prickly brier" refrain, specially adapted to the ballad situation in A18, A19, and A20, led an independent existence before becoming part of the "Gallows Tree" tradition, and may have done so through the medium of its association with "Little Sir Hugh." The singer of A29 reflects awareness of a dual tradition not only in her hesitation between "hold your hand" and "stay your hand" (Ba1, 2), but also in her combining of the traditional and the mass culture versions of the refrain in "briery bush."

Both refrains associated with texts in this group, then, are demonstrably secondary and the association contrived. In spite of Cecil Sharp's belief that "there is no feature that is more characteristic of the popular ballad than the refrain,"[25] the more cautious observations of Gordon Hall Gerould and Joseph W. Hendren that refrains tend to be nonessential and superadded have been borne out.[26]

The influence of mass culture dissemination in this instance is mixed. Popularization not only of the refrain but also of the formulas "hangman, hold your hand" and "gold to set me free" is evident, particularly in the closely related Somerset and Dorset variants A32–A36. It is equally evident, however, that another version of the refrain, attached to more conservative texts, thrived relatively well on its own, and that few singers of the ballad in England failed to modify their texts in various ways. Furthermore, the pattern of distribution of A34's elements indicates that its composer drew upon extant tradition at least as much as he contributed to it.

These findings corroborate those of other investigators. Walter Anderson denied that the influence of printed or literary material was likely to be any greater upon folk tradition than that of other sources: "Often it is great—almost one hundred percent, at other times much less. . . . But the oral variants agree with each other item for item in the most important aspects, and contradict the printed text that has been experienced only once."[27] Hinrich Siuts called attention to the readiness with which traditional singers adapt familiar materials to new orientations,[28] as probably occurred with "hangman," "hold your hand," and the "prickly brier" refrain before the complex received support by virtue of its concert version. William Bascom summed up the principle involved as follows: "Innovations which are incompatible with the pre-existing patterns are rejected. This is not a mystical process of culture which operates independently of individuals, but the result of the fact that individuals judge everything in terms of their previous experience."[29]

Discussion of the place of commonplace verbal formulas, narrative settings (whether in songs or in prose), and refrains in the tradition of "The Gallows Tree" inevitably leads to the classic question of whether the traditional mechanism of the ballad singer is one of improvisation upon an idea, utilizing the singer's own stock of formulas and subsidiary themes, or one of memorization, with improvisation occurring only as a consequence of forgetting or rejecting portions of the memorized material. Following Albert Lord and Milman Parry, James H. Jones recently asserted that the former was true, and that such features in individual variants reflect the tradition of the singer, not of the ballad.[30] From this point of view, it could be argued that "The Gallows Tree" was recomposed throughout

TABLE 1
Texts, Group A

Text no.	Sex of protagonist	Initial address	Injunction (lines 1-2)			Qualification (line 3)		Rhyme (line 4)	"Yonder" (line 4)	Appeal for ransom			Injunction (lines 5-6)		Alternative qualification (line 7)	"Yonder" (line 7)	Final words (line 8)	"Yonder" (line 8)	Borrowed materials	Refrain	Game
			Verb	Object	Precedes	Verb	Participle			Initial	Final	Not granted	Verb	Object							
1	X	Aa1	Ba1			Ca1	b1,2	Da2a		Ea1	b1		Fa1a	b1,2	Ga2	o	Ha1				
2	Zb	Ab2	Ba1	b2	c	Ca1	b1,3	Da1a		Ea1	b1		Fa2b	b1,2	Gc,f1b		Ha4	o			
3	X	Aa7	Ba1	b1	c	Ca1	b1	Dc,a		Ea1	b3		Fa2b	b1,10a	Gf1b		Ha1				
4	Zb	Ab1	Ba1	b1		Ca1	b1	Da1		Ea2	b3		Fa2b	b1,2			Hf				
5	Zb	Ab1	Ba1	b2		Ca1	b1	Da1a		Ea1		c1	F	b1			Ha5,2		Ic		
6	X	Ad	Ba1	b1		Ca1	b1,2	Dc	o	Ea1	b3		Fa2b	b1,10a	Gf1b		Ha1			♩	
7	X	Ab2	Ba5			Ca1	b1	Da2a		Ea1	b3		Fa2b	b1,2	Gb2a		Ha1				
8	Ya	Aa1	Ba1	b6	c	Ca1	b1,6	Da1a		Ea1	b1		Fa2b	b1,2	Gb1		Ha1		Ia		
9	Y	Aa2	Ba1	b1	c	Ca1	b1,6	Da1a		E		c1	Fa2b	b1,2	Gg1a		Ha		Ia	♩	
10	Ya	Aa1	Ba1	b1	c	Co1	b1,2	Da1a		Ea1		c2	Fa2a	b1,2	Gg1a		Ha1				
11	Y		Ba1	b1		Co1	b1	Db2a		Ea1	b7		Fa1a	b1,2	Gb1		Ha1		Ia		
12	Ya	Ad	Ba9	b3		Ca1	b1	Db	o	Ea1	b7		Fa2b	b1,2	Gf1a		Ha1	o	Ic	♩	
13	Ya	Aa2	Ba1	b1	c	Co1	b5	Da1a	o	Ea1	b7		Fa1b	b1,4a	Gb1		Hb		Ia		
14	Z	Aa1	Ba1	b1	c	Ca1	b1,9	Da2a	o	Ea1	b1		Fa2b	b3,1,7,11a	Gf1b		Ha1		Ia	♩	
15	X	Aa1	Ba1	b1	c	Ca1	b1	Da2a	o	Ea1	b1		Fa2b	b1,4,11a	Ga2a		Ha1			♩	
16	X	Aa1	Ba2,7			Ca1	b1	Da2a	o	Ea4	b2		Fa2a	b1,3,11a	Ga2a		Ha1			♩	
17	X					Ca1	b1	D2	o	Ea4	b3		Fa2a	b1,3,11a	Ga2a		Hf				
18	Z		Ba1	b1		Ca1	b1	Db2		Ea2	b3		Fa2a	b1,4,11b	Gb2a		Ha1		Ic	♩	
19	X		Ba1	b1		Ca1	b1	Db2	o	Ea1	b3		Fa2a	b1,4,11d	Ga2a		Ha1			♩	
20	X	Ad	Ba2	b1	c	Ca1	b1	Dc,a		Ea1		c2	Fa2a	b1,4a,11a	Gg1b		Ha1		Ic	♩	
21	Z								o	Ea1	b3		Fa2a	b1,4,11a	Gf1b		Ha1				
22	X	Ad	Ba2	b1	c	Ca1	b1	Da2a		Ea1	b1		Fa2b	b1,3,11a	Ga2a		Ha1		Ic	♩	
23	X	Ad	Ba2	b1		Ca1	b1														
24	Z	Ad	Ba…																		

No.																	
26....	X	Ad	Ba3,6		Ca1	b1,2	Da1a		Ea1	b2	Fa2c	b3,1,4,11b	Gf1b	Ha4		Ic	J
27....	Zb	Ab3	Ba5	c	Ca1	b1	Da1a		Ea2	b8	Fa2b	b1,3,10d	Gf1a	Hc			
28....	Za	Aa6	Ba9	b1	Ca1	b1,2	Da1a		Ea6	b1	Fa2b	b4,1,3	Ga2b	Ha1			
29....	X	Ad	Ba1,2	b1	Ca1	b1	Da2a	o	Ea1	b1	Fa2a	b1,11a	Gg1b	Ha1		Ic	
30....											F	b11a	Gg1a	Ha1	o		
31....	Ya	Ad	Ba1,6	b1	Ca1	b1	Da1a		Ea1	b3	Fa2b	b1,11b	Gf1a	Ha4			J
32....	X	Ad	Ba1	b1	Ca1	b1	Da2a	o	Ea1	b1	Fa2a	b1,11a	Gf1b	Ha1			J
33....	X	Ad	Ba1	b1	Ca1	b1	Da2a	o	Ea1	b1	Fa2a	b1,11a	Gf1b	Ha1			J
34....	Z	Ad	Ba1	b1	Ca1	b1	Da2a	o	Ea2	b3	Fa2b	b1,11a	Gf1b	Ha1			J
35....	X	Ad	Ba1	b1	Ca1	b1	Da2a	o	Ea2	b3	Fa2b	b1,11a	Gg1a	Ha1			J
36....	X	Ad	Ba1	b1	Ca1	b1	Da2a	o	Ea1	b1	Fa2b	b1,11c	Gf1a	Ha1			
37....	X													Ha4		Ia	
38....																	J
39....																	J
40....																	J
41....																	J

its tradition from materials at hand: a commonplace "hold your hand," the commonplaces "gold and fee" and "gold and silver," the situations of the heroines in Child 173 and Child 217, and so on. But the evidence of the texts tends to support Albert B. Friedman's rebuttal of Jones's thesis.[31] Not only have commonplace formulas been shown to be intrusive upon the ballad text to the same degree that they are commonplace (well though they may be preferences of individual singers), but the narrative settings and refrains are equally intrusive and secondary. Miss Beckwith, whose attempt to fix the origin of narrative song in manifestations like A25 was overly ambitious, quite rightly pointed out that its creator adapted the material as he received it to the style of his own culture's art ("Jamaica," p. 457); my textual analysis showed beyond doubt that details in the ballad itself had been memorized with considerable accuracy. Whether creatively of this kind is operative, or whether, as Vargyas proposed, "inflation of the preliminaries" is largely due to misunderstanding or forgetting of the original circumstances (*Medieval History*, p. 264), the basic stability and regular patterns of modifications of these texts make it unmistakably clear that the tradition thus far established originated in a single recognizable text and has been perpetuated by a memorial, not an improvisatory, process.

SOURCES OF VARIANTS: GROUP A (TABLE 1)
(For Full Citations, See Bibliography)

A1. Reverend P. Parsons, Wye, Kent, 1770 (reported by Bishop Percy; Child A-text).
Sargent and Kittredge, *Ballads*, 1932, pp. 200–201.
Reed Smith, *South Carolina*, p. 83.
Reed Smith, *Survivals*, p. 53.
Numerous other reprints.

A2. Anderson F. Bennett, Queensland, Australia, 1924 (LC-AFS, Gordon MS 1565).
R. W. Gordon, *Adventure Magazine*, July 23, 1926, pp. 128–129, 189.
Reed Smith, *South Carolina*, p. 85.

A3. William Lewis, Anderson County, Missouri, 1927 (reported by Randolph, *Ozark Folksongs*, I, 143–144).
Randolph, *Ozark Life*, 6 (1930), 34.
Bronson, *Traditional Tunes*, II, 464–465.

A4. Monroe Ward, Watauga County, North Carolina, 1936 (reported by Belden and Hudson, *North Carolina*, II, 146).

A5. Steve Church, North Carolina, 1941 (reported by Schinhan, *Music*, pp. 78–79).

A6. Emma Backus, North Carolina, n.d. (claimed to have been "brought over to Virginia before the Revolution"; reported by W. W. Newell, Child, V, 296).
Sargent and Kittredge, *Ballads*, 1932, pp. xxv–xxvi.
Hutchison, "Sailors' Chanties," p. 22.
C. Alfonso Smith, "Ballads surviving," pp. 114–115.
Reed Smith, *South Carolina*, p. 82.
Reed Smith, *Survivals*, p. 54.

A7. G. Wirrall, Marlborough, Wiltshire, 1908 (reported by Gilchrist and Broadwood, "Children's Game-Songs," pp. 228–229).
Reeves, *Circle*, pp. 184–185.
Bronson, *Traditional Tunes*, II, 455.

A8. Unidentified informant, Scotland, n.d. (reported by John Leyden; Child I-text, Child, IV, 481). Sargent and Kittredge, *Ballads*, 1932, pp. 201–202.

A9. Unidentified informant, Scotland, n.d. (Child 173 "Mary Hamilton" X-text, Child, IV, 511–512).

A10. Widow McCormick, Dumbarton, Scotland, n.d. (reported by William Motherwell; Child B-text).

A11. Unindentified informant, Scotland, 1802–1803 (reported by W. F. Skene; Child D-text; Child 173 "Mary Hamilton" F-text; see also Child, V, 246–247).

A12. Mrs. Haun, Cocke County, Tennessee, 1937 (reported by Haun, "Cocke County," pp. 99–102). Coffin, "Unusual Texts," pp. 180–181.

A13. Unidentified informant, Scotland, n.d. (reported by Peter Buchan; Child E-text; Child 173 "Mary Hamilton" E-text).

A14. Reverend Edmund Venables, Buckinghamshire, 1883 (reported as learned from Woburn nursemaid; Venables, "Lancashire Ballad," p. 275; Child C-text).
Venables, "Folk Song," p. 86.
Broadwood and Fuller-Maitland, *English County Songs*, p. 113.

A15. Unidentified informant, Hampshire, 1907 (reported by Reeves, *Circle*, p. 184).

A16. Walter C. Lucas, "The Prickly Bush," Sixpenny Handley, Dorset, n.d. (Columbia KL-206).
Bronson, *TraditionalTunes*, II, 456.
Lucas, BBC 9467 (12 EH 54495).
Lucas, LC-AFS 9917A.

A17. Ted Keen, North Marston, Buckinghamshire, 1952 (recorded by Seamus Ennis; Keen, BBC 18140).

A18. Relative of Dr. George Birkbeck Hill, Somerset, 1888 (reported by Nutt, "Old Ballad," p. 144).

A.19. Dr. George Birkbeck Hill, Somerset, 1890 (Child J-text; Child, IV, 481).

A20. Tim Fox, Bampton, Wiltshire, 1923 (reported by Williams, *Upper Thames*, p. 283).

A21. J. Bandinel, Durham, 1895 (reported as having been learned eighty years earlier; Bandinel, "Folk Song," p. 118).

A22. Robert Little, Wiltshire, 1923 (reported by Williams, *Upper Thames*, pp. 281–282). According to Mr. Little, this version was very popular with the Gypsies of his region.

A23. Alden Mace, Southwest Harbor, Maine, 1928 (reported by Barry, Eckstorm, and Smyth, *Maine*, p. 207).

A24. Fred Hewlett, Mapledurwell, Hampshire, 1955 (recorded by Bob Copper; Hewlett, BBC 21859).

A25. Thomas Willliams, Jamaica, 1924 (reported by Beckwith, "Jamaica," pp. 465–475).
Reed Smith, *Survivals*, pp. 59–61.
Leach, *Ballad Book*, pp. 298–299.
Friedman, *Viking Book of Folk Ballads*, pp. 134–136.
Numerous other reprints.

A26. Ruth Simmons, Florida, n.d. (reported by Morris, *Florida*, pp. 297–298).

A27. "Minnie Lee," Pamlico County, North Carolina, 1927 (reported by Belden and Hudson, *North Carolina*, II, 148).

A28. Student at Davidson College, North Carolina, 1927 (reported by Davis, *Virginia*, pp. 380–381).

A29. Mrs. Overd, Langport, Somerset, 1909 (reported by Sharp and Marson, *Somerset,* V, 54).
Sharp, *One Hundred Songs,* p. 42.
Reed Smith, *South Carolina,* pp. 83–84 (refrain only).
Bronson, *Traditional Tunes,* II, 467.
Zoder and Zoder, "Das Volkslied," pp. 397–398.

A30. William Andrews, Lancashire and Cheshire, 1882 (Andrews, "Lancashire Ballad," p. 269; Child Gb-text).

A31. Cora Clark, Avery County, North Carolina, 1929 (reported by Henry, *Southern Highlands,* pp. 95–97).
Bronson, *Traditional Tunes,* II, 470–471.

A32. Unidentified informant, Langport, Somerset, 1883 (reported by Reeves, *Idiom,* pp. 153–154).

A33. Reverend D. M. Ross, Langport, Somerset, 1908 (reported by Bronson, *Traditional Tunes,* II, 469–470).

A34. Heywood Sumner, Somerset, 1893 (reported by Broadwood and Fuller-Maitland, *English County Songs,* p. 112; Child K-text, Child, V, 233).
Fuller-Maitland, "Folk Song," p. 119.
Bronson, *Traditional Tunes,* II, 455.

A35. H. Way, Dorset, 1906 (reported by Gilchrist and Broadwood, "Children's Game-Songs," pp. 230–231).

A36. Julia Scaddon, "The Prickly Bush," Chidcock, Dorset, 1952 (Caedmon Records TC-1145B [12-inch LP]).
Scaddon, BBC 18694.

A37. John Duncan, Mitchell County, North Carolina, 1922 (reported by Belden and Hudson, *North Carolina,* II, 147).

A38. W. Major, Flambere, Somerset, 1910 (reported by Bronson, *Traditional Tunes,* II, 455).

A39. Betsy Pike, Somerton, Somerset, 1906 (reported by Bronson, *Traditional Tunes,* II, 468).

A40. Mrs. Timms, Buckland, Somerset, 1909 (reported by Bronson, *Traditional Tunes,* II, 452).

A41. W. Hainworth, England, 1895 ("Folk Song," p. 119).

GROUP B

With ninety-three variants, characterized by the injunction to "slack the rope," group B is by far the largest in the collection. Like group A, it can be divided into subgroups: a first (B1–28) in which the appeal for ransom is routinely for "gold to pay my fee" (Fb1, 10a); a second characterized by the presence of "yonder" in the third line of the first stanza (Co) together with "traveled" (Cb5) and "free" (Fb11) in some variants (B29–34); a third (B35–51) featuring the substitution of "I looked over yonder" (Co2) for "yonder comes" and "pay my fine" (Fb10b) for "pay my fee"; a fourth (B63–73) asking for "money" (Fb4) rather than "gold"; and a fifth (B74–93) with "gold to set [bring, pay] me free."

"Daughter" appears only twice in this group: B32 (with "wait," "yonder comes," and "gold to bring me free") and B74 (also with "wait" and "free"). A total of thirty-seven variants have "son" (Za), seventeen of them in the subgroup featuring "I looked over yonder." Variant A28, with "Johnnie Law" and "pass your hands," shared this trait, which can by now be regarded with certainty as a remodeling of "daughter" parallel to the remodeling of "yonder comes" in this subgroup. Of the texts lacking this kind of sexual attribution, three (B14, B31, B79) specify a female victim, and ten (B2, B17, B18, B26, B28, B55, B69, B80, B83, B84) a male. Only one of the variants specifying a female (B14) has "gold to pay my fee," and only two specifying a male (B69, B83) have "set me free."

Six texts in the group (B50, B51, B62, B78-80) address a "ropeman" (Ae) instead of a "hangman" (Ad), two in conjunction with "gold to set me free" and "beneath the tree" (Ha5). This complex must be considered secondary to the "hangman" tradition; but since B50 and B62 correspond in other respects to a type featuring "pay my fine," it may be conjectured that the combination "ropeman—set me free—beneath the tree" originated in a different context. Three variants have "jailer" (Ac), again with "free" (B91, B92), although one (B90) is fragmentary. Since B90 is alone in manifesting the "slack the rope" injunction, the other two having "hold the key" and "lengthen the rope," independent derivation is again to be inferred. Correspondence with A10 in "yonder comes" and "riding" so far as B91 is concerned suggests that "jailer" may be added to the list of corruptions of "Judge."

Like "pay my fee," "slack the rope" appears at first sight to be an Americanism. It is not entered as such, however, in either Craigie and Hulbert's *Dictionary of American English on Historical Principles* or Matthew's *Dictionary of Americanisms on Historical Principles,* while the *NED* records the use of "slack" as a transitive verb, primarily in Scotland, beginning in the sixteenth century.[32] Consultation of the Child corpus offers evidence of the same kind manifested for the existence of "stand," "stay," and "away!" in Scottish ballad tradition, if not even more conclusive: in Child 251 "Long Johnny More," the hero, who is about to be hanged, sees his uncle approaching and cries,

> Ye're welcome here, my uncle dear,
> Ye're welcome unto me;
> Ye'll loose the knot and slack the rope,
> And set me frae the tree.[33]

In spite of the massive conformity of the Scottish texts published by Child (with "daughter," "hold your hand, Lord Judge," and "gold and fee"), as well as the conspicuous absence of "The Gallows Tree" from other Scottish collections,[34] the testimony of intrusions upon the texts of Child 251 and Child 254 cannot be easily dismissed. There is no empirical way to account for them except by the existence in Scotland of versions of this ballad featuring "stay thy hand" (probably with "gold and silver to set me free") and "slack the rope" (probably with "gold to pay my fee") before either "stand" or "slack the rope" entered American tradition. Furthermore, although "wait" occurs in this group with "slack the rope" four times (B3, B72, B74, B75), once with "son" and once with "daughter," and with "swing the rope" (in the form of "tarry") once (B33), it stands alone in conjunction with "yonder" in B32 and B34, one of which has a third-line "walking" and "bring me free," the other the "traveling" that linked A13 and A25. B32 also has "daughter"; the two texts in group A featuring "wait" (A26, A31) both had "set me free." An original "hangman, wait a while," with "daughter," "yonder comes," and "gold and silver to set me free" is indicated; that it would have been in conflict with a "hold your hand, Lord Judge—gold and fee" development on the one hand, "hangman, slack the rope—gold to pay my fee" on the other, both with male protagonists, may be inferred from the dominant preferences outside the tradition represented by Child's texts.

Twenty-nine texts in this group have the participle "riding" (Cb2) in line three of the first stanza, as did five in group A; seven, "traveling" (Cb5); twenty-three, "walking" (Cb3); and two "rocking" (Cb4), recognizable as a corruption of "walking." "Riding" thus dominates the tradition both geographically (England, Scotland, and the United States) and textually ("hold your hand," "slack the rope," "fee," and "silver"). "Traveling" continues to be limited and therefore indicative of relationships between variants; "walking," encountered in a single Australian variant in group A, was associated there with "hold up your head, dear John" and "gold and fee," and may be conjectured to be a modification of "traveling" in Scottish tradition.

First stanza rhyme in this group is universally "while-mile" with the exception of B3, B12, and B13, which have "and a few more minutes for me" in line 2. In seventeen variants the victim's mother is the first to arrive, in one (B39) his brother, in another (B81) his sister, and in two (B48, B52) his sweetheart (in B48 it is his mother who effects the rescue).

Variant B1 is unusual in its close relationship to group A text featuring "some of" (Fa1), "gold and fee" (Fb1, 2), and "to keep me" (Ga). Like B2–4, B6–9, B16, B32, and B38, it also has "yonder tree"; and like A28, it resembles Child's A-text to a suspicious degree.[35] But A16 had "some of" with "gold and silver to set me free"; A15, A19, A22 had "to keep me" with variations of that ransom pattern; and "to save me" occurred in A7, A8, A11, A13, A18, and A25. While the singer of B1 may have been exposed to the Child collection, therefore, her combining of material from the printed source with "hangman, slack the rope" is consistent with the tendency discussed earlier in connection with mass media influence. The wording of the second stanza thus demonstrates both the original position of "yonder," and that "to keep me" is antecedent to "or have you come" in the third line of the stanza. The text of A1 runs, "To keep my body from yonder grave, / And my neck from the gallows tree,"[36] changed by B1 to "will keep me from hanging on yonders gallows tree." It was proposed in connection with group A texts that neither Scottish "yonder comes" nor English "yonder stile" was likely to have been present in the original text; in B1, presuming its at least partial dependence upon A1, we can see precisely how American variants acquired "yonder tree" (as did one Scottish text, A13), and deduce that "yonder" migrated to other lines in the text as the alternative question supplanted "to keep me" or "to save me" in the victim's appeal.

A different situation obtains in regard to variants B35–B52. The text for B41 was published together with its tune in a parlor songbook in 1916; B42 and B45 were reported as having been learned from teachers in the Kentucky Settlement Schools; B40 is a phonograph recording issued in 1919. The complex is a distinctive one, with "I looked over yonder," "gold to pay my fine," and a truncated second stanza combined with a refrain,

> Oh, you won't love and it's hard to be beloved,
> And it's hard to make up your mind;
> You've broke the heart of many a true love,
> True love, but you won't break mine.

With schoolrooms, the printed page, and the phonograph combining forces to fix the tradition, it is not surprising that B43 and B46 are faithful replicas of B41, B42, and B45.[37] What is remarkable is that they are the only variants in the group of which this is true. Texts B35–37 follow B40 in retaining "to pay my fee," but the first two restore the missing two lines in Stanza II as well; B39, B44, B48, and B49 do the same in conjunction with "pay my fine." Distribution of the refrain is extraordinarily limited in comparison to that of "The Prickly Bush" in England, where the association antedated any mass media support. Texts B53–57, 59–60 have "pay my fine," but abandon "I looked over yonder." Even under the most favorable conditions, then, nontraditional influences can be seen to exert only minimal control.

Variants B21–28 offer a final example of possible nontraditional influence. In the schema, Bc represents a text in which the verb phrase precedes the title of the person addressed; in group A this syntax was characteristic of variants in which "Judge" or a derivation of "Judge" occurred (the two exceptions, A20 and A22, both had "stay your hand, hangman"). In these texts, it occurs as "slack the rope, hangman"; two of them are phonograph recordings of relatively recent date, and one of them, B21, reportedly collected in West Virginia in 1902 or 1903, was repeatedly reprinted in scholarly and semischolarly publications beginning in 1907. Except for B28, the conformity of these texts to each other is as massive as their inverted syntax is unique; it is safe to conclude, in the absence of the patterns established elsewhere (A1, A28, and B1; A34 and other "prickly bush" variants; B44 and other "pay my fine" variants), that the "tradition" here is a "literary" one.

Even "literary" traditions, however, are not without their special appeal. The phonograph recording B24 ends with the sweetheart's refusal to pay the necessary ransom; such a denouement has traditional support in one variant "crossed" with Child 173 (A9), and in a fragmentary text from North Carolina (A5). Another phonograph recording, B26, betrays familiarity with the Child collection in an explanatory stanza,

> You stole the bishop's golden ball,
> You stole his silver key,
> And I have come to see you hung
> Upon the gallows tree.[38]

Its composer is not likely, however, to have been familiar with a Hottentot version of "The Gallows Tree" paralleling a second explanatory stanza:

> You would not dust my feather bed,
> Nor brew me a spot of tea,
> So I have come to see you hung
> Upon the gallows tree.

In the Hottentot tale, a girl is bewitched because she has been rude to a stranger. As she asks in succession her grandparents, the family servants, and her parents for assistance, they reply, "Haven't I asked you for a drink of water?" "Haven't I asked you to prepare the milk for me?" "Haven't I asked you to straighten the house?"[39]

Such parallels illustrate what Robert L. Rands and Carroll L. Riley have defined as the "complex demand" aspect of the theory of convergence.[40] In substantive opposition to the principle of archaic survivals discussed earlier in this chapter, exponents of convergence argue that similar cultural situations are likely to produce similar artifacts without benefit of either a common origin or transmission from one to the other.[41] Rands and Riley go further in asserting that once the nucleus of a trait cluster (e.g., the ballad situation) has been established, certain secondary traits will tend to recur spontaneously and independently of either direct communication or cultural similarities, in response to the demands of the trait cluster itself. Two such responses are attested here: given the condition of jeopardy, the motifs of failure to obtain rescue and justification for the refusal to rescue are potential in the situation, and may be expected to recur in popular and traditional, as well as in sophisticated, exemplars.

A third sophisticated text, B28, was collected in Los Angeles, California, one year after the Watts ghetto had exploded in an orgy of rioting and looting which resulted in charges of theft against nearly 3000 persons.[42] It furnishes a narrative *incipit*:

> I broke into that big, white store,
> And there I got a gun,
> I shot and fought but I was caught,
> They got me on the run.

The rescuer in this version is neither sweetheart nor mother, but a social worker, and the ballad concludes with the comment,

> Now I get that white man's check,
> I get it all the time,
> And my own brother couldn't save me
> From the gallows twine.

In spite of its topicality and implied social commentary, B28 reveals a broader knowledge of the "Gallows Tree" tradition than do other "slack the rope, hangman" variants. Its request for ransom is in the form of "silver to pay my fine," rhyming with "gallows twine," so that it is related to the Settlement School variants of group B on the one hand, and to "gold and silver" variants of group A on the other.

Variants B54 and B86 exhibit a feature that is rare in the "Gallows Tree" tradition in comparison to borrowed or invented narrative materials: the migratory lyrical stanza. In B54 this is a circumlocution for "never":

> The blackest crow that ever flew
> Will surely turn white,
> If ever I prove false to thee
> Bright day shall turn to night.[43]

B86 combines two traditions, one of them an American ballad commonplace of Welsh derivation:

> Through the pine, through the pine,
>   where the sun never shines,
> And shiver when the cold wind blows.
> I've killed no man, and I robbed no train,
> I have done no hanging crime.[44]

The "slack the rope" group has furnished valuable evidence in several respects. With the aid of Child 254, these texts demonstrate that "The Gallows Tree" circulated in the British Isles during the eighteenth century to a greater degree and in a greater variety of forms than published collections or the variants of group A would indicate. They dramatically reinforce the conclusions drawn from group A that refrains are neither meaningful nor primary in the ballad's tradition and that mass media dissemination affects oral tradition only to the extent that the mass media version itself is based upon oral tradition. Finally, two variants suggest that the principle of convergence may be applicable to folklore materials in terms of the structure of the materials rather than in terms of cultural context: that alterations in the order of appearance of the victim's relatives are due to this kind of convergence seems highly probable.

SOURCES OF VARIANTS: GROUP B (TABLE 2)
(FOR FULL CITATIONS, SEE BIBLIOGRAPHY)

B1. Mrs. [Stone] Maxie, Campbell County, Virginia, 1914 (reported by Davis, *Virginia*, p. 377).

B2. Grace Baker, Maryville, Tennessee, 1932 (reported by G. Anderson, "East Tennessee," pp. 48–49).

B3. Essie Wallace Yowell, Campbell County, Virginia, 1914 (reported by Davis, *Virginia*, pp 366–267).

B4. Roy Pierce, Carter County, Tennessee, 1938 (reported by Perry, "Carter County," pp. 154–156).

B5. Roy Pierce, Carter County, Tennessee, 1938 (reported by Perry, "Carter County," p. 304). Bronson, *Traditional Tunes*, II, 471–472.

B6. Mr. and Mrs. Crockett Ward, Galax, Virginia, 1940 (recorded by John A. and Ruby T. Lomax; Ward, LC-AFS 4083 B2).

B7. Mrs. Crockett Ward, transcribed by Mr. Crockett Ward (LC-AFS, Fields M. Ward MSS, III 12).

B8. Mrs. I. L. Stowe, Texas, n.d. (reported by Owens, *Texas*, pp. 46–47).

B9. Jean Holeman, North Carolina, 1922 (reported as learned forty-five years earlier from Negro servant Maria McCauley; Belden and Hudson, *North Carolina*, II, 147, and Schinhan, *Music*, p. 78).

B10. Henry Cooper, North Carolina, 1924 (reported by L. W. Chappell, *Roanoke*, pp. 35–36). Bronson, *Traditional Tunes*, II, 461.

B11. Flora Stafford Swetnam, Kentucky, n.d. (reported by Hudson, *Mississippi*, p. 114).

B12. Mrs. James Sprouse (later became Mrs. Williamson), Campbell County, Virginia, 1915 (reported by Davis, *Virginia*, pp. 370–371).

B13. Mrs. [Lynch] Creasey, Campbell County, Virginia, 1916 (reported by Davis, *Virginia*, pp. 377–378).

B14. Henry Belk, Union County, North Carolina, 1919 (reported by Belden and Hudson, *North Carolina*, II, pp. 146–147).

B15. Charlie Poole and His North Carolina Ramblers, "Hangman, Hangman, Slack That Rope," 1928 (Columbia Records 15318-D [146772]).

TABLE 2
TEXTS, GROUP B

Text no.	Sex of protagonist	Initial address	Injunction (lines 1–2) Verb	Object	Precedes	Qualification (line 3) Verb	Participle	Rhyme (line 4)	"Yonder" (line 4)	Appeal for ransom Initial	Final	Not granted	Injunction (lines 5–6) Verb	Object	Alternative qualification (line 7)	"Yonder" (line 7)	Final words (line 8)	"Yonder" (line 8)	Borrowed materials	Refrain	Game
1....	X	Ad	Ba3	b3		Ca1	b1	Dc		Ea1	b1		Fa1a	b1,2	Ga1		Ha1	o			
2....	Z	Ad	Ba3	b3		Ca1	b1,3	Da1a		Ea1	b1		Fa2b	b1,10a	Gf1b		Ha1	o			
3....	X	Ad	Ba3,6	b3		Ca2	b1	Da1b		Ea1	b2		Fa3	b1,10a	Gg1b		Ha1	o			
4....	X	Ad	Ba3	b3		Ca2	b1,2	Da1a		Ea1	b3		Fa2b	b1,10a	Gf1b		Ha1	o			
5....	X	Ad	Ba3	b3		Ca1,2	b1,2	Da1a		Ea2											
6....	X	Ad	Ba3	b3		Ca1	b2	Da1a		Ea1	b3		Fa2c	b1,10a	Gf1a		Ha1	o			
7....	X	Ad	Ba3	b3		Ca1	b2	Da1a		Ea1	b3		Fa2c	b1,10a	Gf1a		Ha3	o			
8....	X	Ad	Ba3	b3		Ca1	b1,2	Da1a		Ea1	b1		Fa3	b1,10a	Gf1a		Ha3	o			
9....	X	Ad	Ba9,3	b3		Ca1	b1,2	Da1a		Ea1	b3		Fa3	b1,10a	Gf1b		Ha5,3	o			
10...	X		Ba3	b3		Ca2	b10	Da1a		Ea1	b2		Fa2b	b1,10a	Gf1b		Ha1				
11...	Za		Ba3	b3		Ca2	b1	Da1b		Ea1	b1		Fa2b	b1,10a	Gf1a		Ha1				
12...	X	Ad	Ba3	b3		Ca1	b1	Da1b		Ea1	b5		Fa3	b1,10a	Gf1a		Ha1				
13...	Y	Ad	Ba3	b3		C	b2	Da1		Ea1	b1		Fa2a	b1,10a	Gg1b		Hf				
14...	Za	Ad	Ba3	b3		Ca1	b1,3	Da1a		Ea1	b1		Fa3	b1,10a	Gf1b		Ha1				
15...	Za	Ad	Ba3	b3		Ca1	b3	Da1a		Ea2	b1		Fa3	b1,10a	Gf1b		Ha1				
16...	Z	Ad	Ba3	b3		Ca1	b3	Da1a		Ea1	b3		Fa3	b1,10a	Gg1b		Ha1	o			
17...	Z	Ad	Ba3	b3		Ca1	b3	Da1a		Ea1	b3		Fa2b	b1,10a	Gg1a		Ha1				
18...	Za	Ad	Ba3	b3		Ca1	b1	Dc		Ea1	b3		Fa2b	b1,10a	Gg1a		Ha1				
19...	Za	Ad	Ba3	b5		Ca1	b1	Dc		Ea2	b3		Fa2b	b1,10a	Gg1b		Ha1				
20...	X	Ad	Ba3	b5		Ca1	b1,2	Da1a		Ea1	b1		Fa2b	b1,10a	Gf1a		Ha1				
21...	X	Ad	Ba3	b3	c	Ca1	b1,2	Da1a		Ea1	b2		Fa2b	b1,10a	Gf1a		Ha1				
22...	X	Ad	Ba3	b3	c	Ca1	b1,2	Da1a		Ea1			Fa2b	b1,10a			Ha1				
23...	X	Ad	Ba3	b3	c	Ca1	b2	Da1a		Ea1		c1	Fa2b	b1,10a							
24...	X	Ad	Ba3	b3	c	Ca1	b1,2	Da1a		Ea1	b1		Fa2b	b1,10a	Gf1a		Ha1				
25...	X	Ad	Ba3	b3	c	Ca1	b1,2	Da1a		Ea1	b1		Fa2b	b1,10a	Gf1a		Ha1				
26...	Z	Ad	Ba3,9	b3	c	Ca1	b1,2	Da1a		Ea1	b1		Fa2b	b1,10a	Gf1b		Ha1		Io		

No.																
29....	X	Ad	Ba3	b3	Col	b1	Dala	Ea1	b1	Fa2b	b1,10a	Gf1b	Ha1			
30....	Za	Ad	Ba9	b3	Col	b5	Dala	Ea1	b3	Fa2b	b1,11b	Gf1b	Ha1			
31....	Y	Ad	Ba3	b3	Col	b5	Dala	Ea2	b1	Fa3	b1,11b	Gf1b	Ha4	o		
32....	Ya	Ad	Ba6		Col	b3	Dala	Ea2	b1	Fa2b	b1,11c	Gf1b	Ha1			
33....	X	Ad	Ba9,7	b3	Col		Da	Ea2	b2	Fa2a	b1					
34....	X	Ad	Ba6		Col	b5	Dala	Ea1								
35....	Za	Ad	Ba3	b3	Co2	b1,3	Dala	Ea1	b3	Fa2b	b1,10a	Gf1a	Ha1	o		J
36....	Za	Ad	Ba3	b3	Co2	b1,3	Dala	Ea1	b1	Fa2b	b1,10a	Gf3	Ha2			J
37....	Za	Ad	Ba3	b3	Co2	b1,3	Dala	Ea1	b1	Fa2b	b1,10a		Ha1			J
38....	Za	Ad	Ba3	b3	Co2	b3	Dala	Ea1	b1	Fa2b	b3,1	Gf1b	Hd2			J
39....	Za	Ad	Ba3	b3	Col	b3	Dala	Ea3	b1	Fa2b	b1,10b	Gf1b	He1			J
40....	Za	Ad	Ba1	b3	Co2	b1,3	Dala	Ea1	b3	Fa2b	b1,10a		Ha1			J
41....	Za	Ad	Ba3	b3	Co2	b1,3	Dala	Ea1	b3	Fa2b	b1,10b		He1			J
42....	Za	Ad	Ba3	b3	Co2	b1,3	Dala	Ea1	b3	Fa2b	b1,10b		He1			
43....	Za	Ad	Ba3	b3	Co2	b1,3	Dala	Ea1	b3	Fa2b	b1,10b		He1			
44....	Za		Ba3	b3	Co2	b1,3	Dala	Ea1	b1	Fa2b	b1,10b	Gf1b	He1			
45....	Za	Ad	Ba3	b3	Co2	b1,3	Dala	Ea1	b3	Fa2b	b1,10b		He1			
46....	Za	Ad	Ba3	b3	Co2	b1,3	Dala	Ea1	b3	Fa2b	b1,10b		He1			
47....	Za	Ad	Ba3	b3	Co2	b1,3	Dala	Ea1	b3	Fa3	b1,10b		He1			
48....	Za	Ad	Ba4	b5	Co2	b1,4	Dala	Ea7	b8	Fa3	b1,10b	Gg1b	He1			
49....	Za	Ad	Ba3	b3	Co2	b1,2	Dala	Ea1	b1	Fa3	b1,10b	Gg1a	He1			
50....	Za	Ae	Ba3	b3	Co2	b1,3	Dala	Ea1	b3	Fa2b	b1,10b		Hf1			
51....	Za	Ae	Ba3	b5	Co2	b3	Dala	Ea1	b3	Fa2b	b1,10b		He1			J
52....	X	Ad	Ba3	b3	Ca3	b1	Dala	Ea7	c2	Fa3	b1,10b	Gg1b	He1			
53....	X	Ad	Ba3	b3	Ca3	b1,2	Dala	Ea2	b3	Fa3	b1,10b	Gg1a	He1		Id	
54....	Z	Ad	Ba3	b3	Cal	b3	Dala	Ea2	b1	Fa3	b1,10b		He1			
55....	X	Ad	Ba3	b3	Ca3	b1	Dala	Ea1	b3	Fa3	b1,10b					
56....	X	Ad	Ba3	b3	Ca3	b1	Dala	Ea2	b1	Fa2b	b1,10b	Gf1b	He1			
57....	Za	Ad	Ba3	b3	Cal	b5	Dala	Ea1	b3	Fa2b	b1,10b	Gf1b	He1			
58....	Za	Ad	Ba3	b3	Cal	b5	Dala	Ea1	b3	Fa2b	b1,10a	Gf1a	Ha1			
59....	X	Ad	Ba3	b3	Ca3	b1	Dala	Ea1	b1	Fa2b	b1,10b	Gf1b	He2			
60....	Za	Ad	Ba9	b3	Cal	b1	Dc a	Ea1	b3	Fa2b	b1,10b	Gf1b	Ha1			
61....	Za	Ag	Ba3	b3	Cal	b1	Dala	Ea1	b1	Fa3	b1,10b	Gg1a	He1			
62....	X	Ae	Ba3	b3	Cal	b1	Dc a	Ea1	b3	Fa3	b1,10c	Gg1a	Ha1			
63....	X	Ae	Ba8,3	b5	Cal	b1	Dala	Ea1	b1	Fa3	B4,10b	Gg1c	He2			
64....	Za	Ad		b3	Cal	b1,2	Dala	Ea1	b2	Fa2a	B4,10a	Gf1b	Ha1			

TABLE 2—Continued

Text no.	Sex of protagonist	Initial address	Injunction (lines 1-2) Verb	Injunction (lines 1-2) Object	Injunction (lines 1-2) Precedes	Qualification (line 3) Verb	Qualification (line 3) Participle	Rhyme (line 4)	"Yonder" (line 4)	Appeal for ransom Initial	Appeal for ransom Final	Appeal for ransom Not granted	Injunction (lines 5-6) Verb	Injunction (lines 5-6) Object	Alternative qualification (line 7)	"Yonder" (line 7)	Final words (line 8)	"Yonder" (line 8)	Borrowed materials	Refrain	Game
65	X	Ad	Ba3	b3		Ca1	b1,2	Da1a		Ea1			Fa2b	b4,10a	Gf1b		Ha1				
66	X	Ad	Ba3	b3		Ca1	b1	Da1a		Ea2	b1		Fa2b	b4,10a	Gf1b		Ha1				
67	X	Ad	Ba3	b3		Ca1	b1,2	Da1a		Ea2											
68	X	Ad	Ba3	b3		Ca1	b1,2	Da1a		Ea2	b3		Fa2b	b1,11a	Gf1a		Ha2				
69	Z		Ba3	b3		Ca1	b1,2	Da1a		Ea1											
70	X	Ad	Ba3	b3		Ca1	b1,2	Da1a		Ea1	b1		Fa2b	b4,1,10a	Gf1a		Ha1				
71	Za	Ad	Ba3,6	b3		Ca1	b1,5	Da1a		Ea1	b1		Fa2b	b4,10a	Gf1a		Ha2				
72	Za	Ad	Ba3,6	b3		Ca1	b1,5	Da1a		Ea1			F	b4							
73	Ya		Ba3,6	b3		Ca1	b1	Dc a		Ea1	b2		Fa3	b1,11b	Gg1b		Ha4				
74	X	Ad	Ba3,6	b3		Ca1	b1	Da1a													
75	Za	Ad	Ba3,6	b3		Ca1	b1,2	Da1a		Ea1	b1		Fa2b	b1,11a	Gf1b		Ha3				
76	Za	Ad	Ba3	b3		Ca1	b1	Da1a		Ea1	b1		Fa3	b1,11a	Gf1b		Ha3				
77	X	Ad	Ba3	b3		Ca1	b1	Da1a		Ea1	b3		Fa2a	b1,11a	Gg1b		Ha5,3				
78	Y	Ae	Ba3	b3		Ca1	b1	Da1a		Ea1	b1		Fa2a	b1,11a	Gg1b		Ha5,4				
79	Z	Ae	Ba3	b3		Ca2	b1	Dc a		Ea1											
80	Z	Ae	Ba3	b3		Co3	b1	Da1a					Fa2a	b1,11a	Gf1b		Ha5,4		Ic		
81	Za	Ad	Ba4	b3		Ca1	b1	Da1a		Ea4	b3		Fa2a	b1,11a	Gf1b		Ha5,1				
82	Za	Ad	Ba4	b3		Ca1	b1	Da1a		Ea2	b3		Fa2c	b11a			Ha4				
83	Z	Ad	Ba3	b3		Ca1	b1	Da1a		Ea1	b1		Fa2c	b10a	Gf1b		Ha1				
84	Z	Ad	Ba9	b3		Ca1	b1,2	Da1a		Ea1	b3		Fa3	b1,11a	Gg1b		Ha4				
85	X	Ad	Ba9	b3		Ca1	b1,4	Da1a		Ea1,2	b1		Fa3	b1,11a	Gg1b		Ha1				
86	Za	Ad	Ba3			Ca1	b1,3	Da1a		Ea1	b1		Fa3	b1,11c	Gg1b		Ha1				
87	X	Ad	Ba3	b3		Ca1	b1,2	Da1a		Ea1	b3		Fa3	b1,11c	Gg1b		Ha1		Id		
88	Za	Ad	Ba3	b3		Ca2	b1,2	Da1a		Ea2	b5		Fa3	b1,11d	Gg1b		Ha4		Id		
89	X		Ba3	b3		Ca1	b1	Da1a		Ea2											
90	X	Ac	Ba3	b3		Ca2		Da1a		Ea2											
91	Za	Ac	Ba1	b7		Co1	b1,2	Da1a		Ea1	b1		Fa3	b1,11d	Gg1b		Ha4				
92	X	Ac	Ba9	b3		Ca1	b1,2	Da1a		Ea1	b3		Fa2c	b1,10b,11a	Gf1b		Ha4				
93	X	Ad	Ba3	b3		Ca1		Da1a													K

B16. Miss Carrie Rakes, Franklin County, Virginia, 1939 (reported by Raymond H. Sloan; UVL-M).

B17. Mrs. Alice Wagoner, Franklin County, Virginia, 1939 (reported by Raymond H. Sloan; UVL-M).

B18. Hattie Quinn, Franklin County, Virginia, 1940 (reported by Raymond H. Sloan; UVL-M).

B19. Almeda Riddle, "The Hangman," Arkansas, 1959 (Prestige/International Records INT 25009).

B20. Almeda Riddle, "The Hangman," Rhode Island, 1964 (Vanguard Records VRS-9183/VSD 79183).

B21. Unidentified "illiterate mountaineer," Jager, West Virginia, 1903 (reported as received from Reed Smith by Kittredge, "Two Popular Ballads," p. 56).
   Reed Smith, *South Carolina*, pp. 144–146.
   Sandburg, *Songbag*, p. 72.
   Smith and Rufty, *American Anthology*, pp. 37–38.
   Reed Smith, "La balada tradicional," pp. 275–284.
   Botkin, *American Folklore*, pp. 822–824.

B22. John West, Gibson County, Indiana, 1935 (reported by Brewster, "Traditional Ballads," p. 312; identical with B21).
   Brewster, *Indiana*, pp. 125–127.

B23. Unidentified informant, Tennessee, n.d. (reported by Marie Campbell, "Gallows Tree," p. 95).

B24. Harry Jackson, "The Hangman's Song," 1959 (Folkways Records FH 5723 [12-inch LP]).

B25. Carroll Wayne Parker, Ola, Arkansas, 1958 (recorded by Max Hunter; Parker, LC-AFS 11,908 A11).

B26. "Jimmie Driftwood" [James Morris], "Slack Your Rope," 1958–1959 (RCA Victor Records LPM 1994 [12-inch LP]).

B27. Jane Hurd, Trumann, Arkansas, 1967 (reported by Jeannine Talley; UCLA-CWF).

B28. Unidentified informant, Los Angeles, California, 1966 (reported by Janeen Johnston; UCLA-CWF).

B29. Young man named Richards, Logan County, West Virginia, 1916 (reported by Cox, *South*, p. 116).

B30. Mrs. E. E. Chiles, Jefferson County, Missouri, 1916 (reported as learned sixteen years earlier from housemaid Elsie Ditch; Belden, *Missouri*, p. 67).
   Kittredge, "Ballads and Songs," p. 320.
   Bronson, *Traditional Tunes*, II, 469.

B31. E. C. Morgan, Knoxville, Tennessee, 1939 (reported as having been learned in Kentucky; Duncan, "Hamilton County," p. 81).

B32. Elizabeth Snyder, Hamilton County, Tennessee, 1939 (reported as having been learned in North Carolina; Duncan, "Hamilton County," pp. 77–79).

B33. Unidentified informant, Sea Islands, North Carolina, n.d. (reported by Parsons, *Sea Islands*, pp. 189–191).
   Reed Smith, *South Carolina*, p. 88.
   Barry, Eckstorm, and Smyth, *Maine*, p. 212.
   Bronson, *Traditional Tunes*, II, 467.

B34. Belvia Hampton, North Carolina, n.d. (reported by Schinhan, *Music*, p. 79).

B35. Mrs. Walter, North Carolina, n.d. (reported by Belden and Hudson, *North Carolina*, II, 144–145).

B36. Jean Ritchie, Kentucky, 1951 (reported by Ritchie, *Singing Family,* p. 153; Ritchie, Folkways Records FA 2301 [12-inch LP]).
    Bronson, *Traditional Tunes,* II, 462.
    Ritchie, LC-AFS 10,089 A9 (recorded by Duncan Emrich).

B37. May Kennedy McCord, Springfield, Missouri, 1897, 1938 (reported by Randolph, *Ozark Folksongs,* I, 145).
    Bronson, *Traditional Tunes,* II, 472.
    McCord, LC-AFS 5334 B1 (recorded by Vance Randolph).

B38. Miss Etta Kilgore, Wise County, Virginia, 1939 (reported by Emory L. Hamilton; UVL-M).

B39. Jeannie Hall, Arkansas, 1930 (reported by Randolph, *Ozark Folksongs,* I, 144–145).

B40. Bentley Ball, "The Gallows Tree," 1919 (Columbia Records A3084).

B41. Lucy Ann Cook, Harlan County, Kentucky, n.d. (reported by Wyman and Brockway, *Lonesome Tunes,* pp. 44–47).
    Reed Smith, *South Carolina,* p. 84.
    Reed Smith, *Survivals,* p. 55.
    Pound, *American Ballads,* pp. 31–33.
    Cambiaire, *Mountain Ballads,* pp. 15–16.
    Bronson, *Traditional Tunes,* II, 461–462.

B42. Children in Pine Mountain Settlement School, Harlan County, Kentucky, 1916 (reported by Wells, *Ballad Tree,* pp. 115–116).

B43. Clara Callahan, North Carolina, n.d. (reported by Scarborough, *Song Catcher,* pp. 197–198).

B44. Mary Ann Short, Kentucky, 1917 (reported by Sharp and Karpeles, *Southern Appalachians,* I, 211).

B45. James Still, Hindman Settlement School, Kentucky, n.d. (reported by Trout, "Greetings," December 19, 1957).

B46. James Taylor Adams, Big Laurel, Virginia, 1938–1939 (reported by Henry, Southern Highlands, pp. 97–98).
    LC-AFS, WPA MSS, Virginia Songs and Rhymes, Ballads W11671, as obtained from H. H. Fuson.
    Adams, UVL-M.

B47. J. Tom Miles, 1938–1939, as obtained from *Arcadian Magazine,* Eminence, Missouri, 2 (June, 1932), 4 (LC-AFS, WPA MSS, Missouri Songs and Rhymes, Ballads W7360).

B48. Mrs. C. A. Brackett, Hamilton County, Tennessee, 1938 (reported by Duncan, "Hamilton County," pp. 79–80).

B49. Unidentified informant, Hillsborough County, Florida, 1917 (reported by Davis, *Virginia,* p. 381).

B50. "Two little mountain girls in Kentucky" (reported by Thomas, *Devil's Ditties,* pp. 164–165).

B51. Lenore C. Kilgore, Big Laurel, Virginia, 1939 (reported by James Taylor Adams; UVL-M).

B52. "Lengthy, a Tennessee boy" (reported by Sandburg, *Songbag,* p. 385).

B53. Nell Caldwell, Logan County, West Virginia, 1928 (reported by Cox, *West Virginia,* pp. 29–30).

B54. Mrs. J. H. Humphries, Craig County, Virginia, 1932 (reported by Davis, *More Virginia,* pp. 224–226).

B55. John W. Bevins, Wise County, Virginia, 1942 (reported by James M. Hylton; UVL-M).

B56. Nancy E. Pearson (collector), Giles County, Virginia, 1917 (reported by Davis, *Virginia,* p. 328).

B57. Alice Stanchfield, 1969, reported as learned from stepfather Oscar Thompson (see D40; reported by Arthur G. Brodeur, Berkeley, California).

B58. Mrs. Cordelia Bentley, Esserville, Virginia, 1939 (reported by Emory L. Hamilton; UVL-M).

B59. Unidentified informant, Alleghany County, Virginia, 1915 (reported by Davis, *Virginia*, p. 380).

B60. Esther Finlay Hoevey, New Orleans, Louisiana, n.d. (reported by Scarborough, *Negro Folk-Song*, pp. 41–42).

B61. Bradley Browning, Arjay, Kentucky, 1937 (recorded by Alan and Elizabeth Lomax; Browning, LC-AFS 1387 A2 and B1).

B62. "Old woman," Harrison County, Mississippi, 1916 (reported by Davis, *Virginia*, pp. 381–382)

B63. Edwin Swain, Florida, n.d. (reported by Scarborough, *Negro Folk-Song*, p. 39).
Bronson, *Traditional Tunes*, II, 452–453.

B64. L. C. Welch, Louisville, Kentucky, 1958 (reported as learned from Polly Ann Sheffy, Virginia, 1900; Trout, "Greetings," January 30, 1958).

B65. Mrs. J. L. Long, Virginia, 1918 (reported by Bronson, *Traditional Tunes*, II, 453).

B66. Mrs. Laura Donald, Dewey, Virginia, 1918 reported by Sharp and Karpeles, *Southern Appalachians*, I, 212).
Bronson, *Traditional Tunes*, II, 471.

B67. Mrs. Lawson Grey, Virginia, 1918 reported by Bronson, *Traditional Tunes*, II, 454).

B68. Mrs. Molly E. Bowyer, Villamont, Virginia, 1918 reported by Sharp and Karpeles, *Southern Appalachians*, I, 213).
Bronson, *Traditional Tunes*, II, 454).

B69. Mrs. Pearl Brewer, Pocahontas, Arkansas, 1958 (recorded by Max Hunter; LC-AFS 11,905 B4).

B70. Bob Bradley, Blue Ridge, Virginia, 1918 (reported by Bronson, *Traditional Tunes*, II, 454).

B71. May Kennedy McCord, Springfield, Missouri, 1952 (recorded by Anne Grimes; McCord, LC-AFS 11,457 A1).

B72. Mrs. [Holland] Maxie, Franklin County, Virginia, 1914 (reported by C. Alfonso Smith, "Ballads Surviving," p. 119.
Scarborough, *Negro Folk-Song*, p. 42.
Reed Smith, *South Carolina*, p. 87 (first stanza only).
Davis, *Virginia*, pp. 367–369.
Bronson, *Traditional Tunes*, II, 458.

B73. Mrs. James York, Iredell County, North Carolina, 1939 (reported by Schinhan, *Music*, p. 81).

B74. Jesse Harvey, Poplarville, Mississippi, n.d. (reported by Hudson, "Ballads and Songs," p. 106).

B75. Belvia Hampton, North Carolina, n.d. (reported by Schinhan, *Music*, p. 77).

B76. Carrie Hess, West Virginia, 1916 (reported by Cox, *South*, pp. 116–117).

B77. Mrs. Walter Gilley, Tennessee Industrial School, n.d. (reported by McDowell and Lassiter, *Memory Melodies*, p. 22).

B78. Flora Hood, West Virginia, 1890, 1916 (reported by Cox, *South*, pp. 117–118).

B79. Hazel K. Black, West Virginia, n.d. (reported by Cox, *South*, p. 118).

B80. B. B. Chapman, West Virginia, 1924 (reported by Josiah Combs; UCLA-WKF, Josiah H. Combs Collection of Songs and Rhymes).

B81. Walter H. Keener, West Virginia, 1947 (reported by Musick, "West Virginia," pp. 42–44).

B82. Jo Wilburn, Fayetteville, Arkansas, 1958, as learned from friend whose grandmother learned it in southern Illinois (recorded by Mary C. Parker; Wilburn, LC-AFS 12,050 B17).

B83. Mr. Joliffe, Northampton County, Virginia, 1921 (reported by Davis, *Virginia,* pp. 375–376).

B84. Hobart Smith, Saltville, Virginia, 1942 (recorded by Alan Lomax; Smith, LC-AFS 6723 B1).

B85. Flora Havens, Blount County, Tennessee, 1932 (reported by G. Anderson, "East Tennessee," pp. 46–48).

B86. Lizzie Dills, Kentucky, n.d. (reported by Fuson, *Kentucky Highlands,* pp. 113–114).

B87. J. A. Wyatt, King William County, Virginia, 1922 (reported by Davis, Virginia, pp. 378–379).

B88. Unidentified informant, North Carolina, n.d. (Isabel Rawn, collector; reported by Belden and Hudson, *North Carolina,* II, 144).

B89. Jane Brown, Canton, Ohio, n.d. (reported as having been learned in Georgia; Eddy, *Ohio,* pp. 62–63).
     Bronson, *Traditional Tunes,* II, 459.

B90. Effie Mitchell, Burnsville, North Carolina, 1918 (reported by Sharp and Karpeles, *Southern Appalachians,* I, 213).
     Bronson, *Traditional Tunes,* II, 460.

B91. Bertha Fooshe, Chickasaw College, Pontotoc, Mississippi, 1928 (reported by Alice M. Child, "Folk Ballads," pp. 43–44).

B92. Julia Harn, Florida, n.d. (reported as learned from Bob Miller [cf. C21, also reported as having been learned from Miller]; Morris, *Florida,* p. 298).

B93. Ethel Perry Moore, Lincoln County, Nebraska, n.d. (reported by Botkin, *Play-Party Song,* p. 62).

GROUP C

Group C, characterized by an injunction to "wait," either alone or in combination, includes three subgroups: in the first, the person addressed in line 1 is "Joshua," and the appeal is for "gold and silver to pay my fee" (Aa4, Fb1, 3, 10a); in the second, a "hangman" is addressed and the appeal may be for "money to pay my fee" (as in B63–66, B71–73) or "gold to set me free" (as in A29–37); in the third, the appeal is for "silver and gold" (Fb3, 1) and the address may be to either "hangman" or "Judge."

Variants 1–11 constitute the first subgroup. The third line in the second stanza of their texts offers an explanation for the victim's situation: "For I have stolen a golden [silver] cup" (Gd). "Have you any" (Fa2a) occurred in eleven group A variants (A10, with "gold and fee"; A16–20, A22, and A24, with "gold and silver" or "gold and money" "to set me free"; and A29, A32, and A33, with "gold to set me free"). It also occurred in seven variants in group B (B14, with "gold to pay my fee," B33, with "yonder comes" and "gold," B64, with "money to pay my fee," and B78–82, with "gold to set me free"). In these texts it is normative, and may on the basis of this distribution be considered antecedent to "some of" and "have you brought" ("have you brought" being regular with "hangman," "some of" with "gold and fee"). "For I have stolen a golden cup" may therefore be regarded as an interpolation substituting for "to keep my body from yonder grave," from the same early stratum, and not for the alternative question that was to replace it in later versions.

Also characteristic of variants 1–11 are "daughter," the combined injunction "hold your hand and wait" (with "hold your hand" preceding "Joshua"), "I think I hear" (Ca2), a first-stanza rhyme in "-ee" (Db), and a final line "hanging it will be" or "hanged I shall be" (Hb). Conscious and massive innovation, as in the case of the "prickly bush" concert version and the Settlement School version, is evident. Although the cup theft rationalization is explicable enough in terms of the "complex demand" phenomenon discussed in connection with group B, traditional support for the narrative motif in which an innocent person is condemned to death for theft after a golden cup has been purposely secreted among his belongings is as old as the biblical story of Joseph and his brethren,[45] and is attested in broadside balladry of the seventeenth and eighteenth centuries.[46] The innovator, therefore, drew the "story" from other traditional materials as did the creators of the "crossed" versions combined with Child 173 and Child 155 and the Jamaican *cante-fable* (A25); elements drawn from within the "Gallows Tree" tradition are "hold your hand, Lord Judge" (with yet another phonological corruption of "Judge"), "wait," "gold and silver," and "to pay my fee." Apparently peculiar to the innovative text are "I think I hear," "-ee" rhyme in the first stanza, and "hanging it shall be" in the second.

These variants were all collected in the United States, eight from North Carolina, one each from Tennessee, Virginia and West Virginia; there is no record or indication that mass media intervention was involved in their dissemination. A singular opportunity is afforded, therefore, to compare the influence of such a version with that of those utilizing the concert hall, the schoolroom, or the phonograph for their promulgation. In addition to these closely conforming and memorized exemplars, B3, B4, B6, B10, B11, B80, B89, C15, C16, C46 have "I think I hear" (Ca2); (in the singing of B6 by a husband and wife, the wife's "I think I hear" is audible although the husband's preference for "I think I see" is manifest both in this instance and in his transcription of B7). Variants B3, B12, and B13, all from Virginia, and A18 and A19, both from Somerset, have "for me" in Stanza I, the American variants with "gold to pay my fee" and the English with no title of address, "hold your hand," and "money," A19 "to pay me free"; C15, C16, C17, and C18 have fourth lines ending in "see" or "sea"; A14, from Buckinghamshire, with "hold your hand, Lord Judge," "silver and gold," has "hanging it shall be"; A27, with "stand back, little Johnson" and "gold and silver," has "hanging you shall see," as does C18.

The idea of theft has been preserved only in C18, where the cup has been replaced by a comb and rescue is obtained by its restoration, and in C19, where the information concerning the crime is relegated to the relatives' reply (as it was in relation to the "bishop's golden ball" and "silver key" in B26). Variant C25, which preserves nothing of the text, describes such a putative crime in a prose commentary.

From these data it may be inferred that massive innovations originating in oral tradition have roughly the same effect upon subsequent tradition as do those originating in more sophisticated settings and sponsored by mass media. The evidence of the English and American "for me" texts indicates that the fourth line of the present subgroup may be secondary ("rambling o'er the sea," rhyming with "wait a while and see"); it also indicates, as did the presence of the verbs "stand," "stay," and "wait" in Child 251 and others, "slack the rope" in Child 254, and as does the "hanging it shall be" of A14, that yet another version was at some time extant in the British Isles. A further and inescapable conclusion is that Walter Anderson's theory of multiple transmission, a phenomenon corresponding in substance if not in detail with what Cecil Sharp preferred to describe as "selection" and Phillips Barry as "communal recreation,"[47] is correct. The interplay of what might be regarded as insignificant details shows that the majority of the singers of the variants thus far examined knew and drew upon more than one version of the text. In contrast C15 and C16 display the same precise verbal correspondence that was apparent in a few exemplars of the "prickly bush" group, the Settlement School group, and the "slack the rope, hangman" group; a correspondence that can be accounted for only by direct and probably visual memorization.

The relationship of the two remaining groups offers a further opportunity to test all four of the above assertions. Variant C40, with "go away, Mr. Judge," no sequence of relatives, ransom by "silver and gold," and an alternative query, "have you walked these long, long miles to see me hung from the hangman's pole," is a commercial recording in which the "Gallows Tree" stanzas are incorporated into a "blues ballad" in which a jealous lover shoots his rival.[48] The effect of the recording is clear in C37–43, the most impressive record thus far of "nontraditional" dissemination. Fragmentary materials in other versions of the ballad suggested the prior existence of a text featuring "daughter," "hangman, wait a while," and "gold and silver to set me free," and variants C19–29 present just such a pattern except for the omission of "silver" from the ransom. Variants C31–36, three of which are also "crossed" with the "blues ballad," and one of which was reported as first heard in Scotland in the nineteenth century, furnish corroborative evidence, with "yonder comes," the order of "silver" and "gold" reversed, and a new rhyme furnished in "pole." Perhaps the most dramatic testimony, however, is offered by the collection in 1962 of variant C27, similar to C26 in respect to ransom. C26 has "pay my bond so free"; C27 has "pay my bondage free." On the basis of the pronunciation of "bondage" in C27 ("b" being a very soft labial almost indistinguishable from "m," and "d" and "g" very nearly elided), both may be considered phonological corruptions of "money to pay me free" as in A19. As published in Child's collection (J-text), A19 reads "hold up thy hand"; the text of C27, however, agrees both with the fragments "hangman, stay thy hand" of A23 (from Maine) and "hangman, wait a while" of C28 (from Devonshire) and with the "Stay thy hand, hangman" tradition represented by A20 and A22, which have "gold and white money" and "gold and silver" "to set me free." Like C26, it also features "daughter." In this complex of variants, ranging in date from the mid-nineteenth century to the second half of the twentieth, and geographically from the English Midlands to Maine to Arkansas, can unmistakably be seen the relationships between "stay thy hand," "hold thy hand," and "wait," and between "silver," "money," and "bond." A historical development emerges in which "Judge" becomes "hangman," "stay thy hand" becomes either "hold thy hand" or "wait," "silver" either becomes "money" and subsequently drops out or takes the antecedent position to make a rhyme word of "gold," and "daughter" is introduced, in that chronological order. (It may be noted that while C27 addresses a "hangman," the victim asks him to stay his hand and to "leave me here in this jail," implying the survival of the court-room setting similarly attested by other American texts featuring "Judge" or "jailer.")

The "blues ballad" version, to which Tristram Coffin may have been the first to call attention,[49] has been included in an intensive study of Laws I4 by Marina Bokelman; her M.A. thesis shows that the "crossing" in C31, C32, and C36 is independent of that manifested in variants C37–43. It can be concluded, therefore that the phenomenon is the by now familiar one of an oral tradition borrowed from and reinforced by, but not supplanted by, a mass media version.[50] The utilization in C33 of the qualifying term "raspel" (a word borrowed from the Dutch and corresponding to English "rascal," and in usage in the British Isles but not in the United States)[51] together with "money" instead of "silver," combines with the evidence just discussed to attest the presence of the complex with all its variations in the British Isles during the nineteenth century as well as in the United States in the twentieth.

A second *cante-fable* from Jamaica (C48) is rooted in the same tradition; although its ballad text is severely eroded, its heroine asks first for silver, then for gold. The narrator of the tale exhibits concern for rationality and coherence in fixing the cause of the impending execution and ordering the sequence of relatives. In his tale, a variant of AaT 403 "The Cruel Stepmother," a mistreated stepdaughter leaves home to work at caring for a sailor's livestock and is spied upon by her stepmother and stepsister. When they secretly feed the sailor's horses green grass and the horses die in consequence, the heroine is sentenced to death in punishment for not fulfilling her task. Since it is a parent who is responsible for her predicament, father and mother are not asked for ransom, and the appeal is limited to her sister, brother, and lover.

The idea salient in the narrative from which variants 1–11 are derived—that the victim is innocent of the crime of which he or she stands accused—is present here and in C12 and C13, two more *cante-fables* from the Bahama Islands. The heroine of C12 finds a watch and is accused by her stepmother of stealing it. In C13, "Jane" finds a gold thimble shortly before her employer loses one, with the same consequence. It may be suspected, therefore, that C2's "they say I've stolen a silver cup" (unique for the group) represents the situation as it was originally conceived. Variants C12 and C13 also have the configuration previously noted only in A2, "to take me off the . . . tree,"[52] which was then argued to be another indication of the priority of the courtroom setting, with its "to keep me from . . . the gallows tree," over that of the gallows itself, with "or have you come to see me hanged." Since C47, with "silver and gold," has "to keep me from" in correspondence with B1, and both A2 and B1 have "gold and fee" as the terms of ransom, the argument is supported by these variants, with the corollary that "gold and silver" antedates "gold and fee." Variant C49, the only American text outside the "crossed" group C37–45 to preserve "Judge" in an uncorrupted form, combines

TABLE 3
TEXTS, GROUP C

Text no.	Sex of protagonist	Initial address	Injunction (lines 1-2) Verb	Injunction Object	Injunction Precedes	Qualification (line 3) Verb	Qualification Participle	Rhyme (line 4)	"Yonder" (line 4)	Appeal for ransom Initial	Appeal Final	Appeal Not granted	Injunction (lines 5-6) Verb	Injunction Object	Alternative qualification (line 7)	"Yonder" (line 7)	Final words (line 8)	"Yonder" (line 8)	Borrowed materials	Refrain	Game
1	Ya	Aa4	Ba1,6	b1	c	Ca2	b1,7	Db1b		Ea1	b1		Fa2a	b1,3,10a	Gd1		Hb				
2	Ya	Aa4	Ba1,6	b1	c	Ca2	b1,8	Db1b		Ea1	b1		Fa2a	b1,3,10a	Gd2		Hb				
3	Ya	Aa4	Ba1,6	b1	c	Ca2	b1,7	Db1b		Ea1	b1		Fa2b	b1,3,10a	Gd1		Hb				
4	Y	Aa4	Ba1,6	b1	c	Ca1	b10	Db1b		Ea1	b1		Fa2b	b1,3,10a	Gd1		Hb,a3				
5	Y	Aa4	Ba1,6	b1	c	Ca1	b10	Db1b		Ea1	b3		Fa2a	b1,3,10a	Gd2		Hb	o			
6	Za	Aa4	Ba6		c	Ca2	b10	Db1b		Ea1	b1		Fa3	b1,3,10a	Gd2		Hb				
7	X	Aa4	ba1,6	b2	c	Ca2	b6	Db1b		Ea1	b1		Fa2b	b1,3,10a	Gd2		Hb				
8													Fa2a	b4,1,10a	Gd2		Hb				
9													Fa2a	b1,3,10a	Gd2		Hb				
10	Y,Z	Aa4	Ba1	b1		Ca1	b10	Db1		Ea1	b3		Fa2a	b1,3,11b			Ha1	o			
11	Y	Aa4	Ba6			Ca2	b1,5	Db1b		E	b1		Fa2a	b1,3	Gf1a		Ha1	o			
12	Y					Ca3				Ea2	b2		Fa2a	b1,3	Gc		Ha1		Ib		
13	Y					Ca3				Ea6	b7		Fa3	b1,3	Gc		Ha1		Ib		
14	X	Ad				Ca2				Ea1	b2		Fa3	b4,10a	Gb1		Ha1				
15	X	Ad	Ba1			Ca2	b1,7	Db1a		Ea1			Fa2b	b4,10a			Ha4	o			
16	X	Ad	Ba1	b3		Ca1	b1,7	Db1a		Ea1			Fa2b	b3,1,4,10a			Ha4	o			
17	X	Ad	Ba1,6	b3		Ca1	b10	Db1b		Ea2	b2		Fa2b	b6,11a	Gf1a		Ha2				
18	Ya	Ad	Ba3	b3		Ca1	b5	Db b		Ea1	b2		Fa2b	b1,11b	Gf2		Hc				
19	Ya	Ad	Ba1,6			Ca1	b1,5	Da1a		Ea1	b3		Fa2b		Gf1b / Gd1		Ha4 / Hb				
20	Ya	Ad	Ba6			Ca1	b5	Da1a		Ea1	b3		Fa2a	b1,11b	Gf1b		Ha4	o			
21	Z	Ad	Ba1,6	b3		Ca1	b1,3	Da1a		Ea1	b3		Fa2c	b1,11a	Gf1b		Ha1				
22	Ya	Ad	Ba6			Ca3		Da1a		Ea1	b3		Fa2a	b1,11a	Gf1b		Ha4	o			

K

No.																	
25....	Ya	Ad	Ba6			Ca1	b5	Da1a	Ea1	b1		Fa2b	b1,11c	Gf1b		Ha4		Ia
26....	Ya	Ad	Ba6		c	Ca3	b2	Da1a	Ea1	b2		Fa3	b1,11d	Gf1b		Ha5,4		Ia
27....	Ya	Ad	Ba6,2	b1		Ca1	b1	Db	E	b8		Fa3b	b1,11d	Gg1a		Ha4		Ia
28....		Ad	Ba6															
29....	Ya	Ad	Ba8,6	b3		Co1	b5	Da1a	Ea1	b2		Fa3	b1	Gg1a		Hd3		Ia
30....												F	b1			Hd3		
31....	Z	Ad	Ba6			Co1	b1	Da1a	Ea1	b3		Fa2b	b3,1	Gf1b		Hd2		Ia
32....	Z	Ad	Ba6			Co1	b1	Da1a	Ea1	b4		Fa3	b3,1	Gf1b		Hd2		Ia
33....	X				c	Ca1	b1	Dc	Ea1			Fa3	b4,1	Gg1b		Hd4		
34....		Ad	Ba6			Ca1	b1	Da1a	Ea1	b3		Fa3	b3,1	Gg1b		Hd2	o	Ia
35....	Z								E	b3		Fa2b	b3,1	Gf1a		Hd2	o	Ia
36....	Zb	Ad	Ba6			Ca1	b1	Da1a	E	b4		Fa2b	b3,1	Gg1a		Hd2		Ia
37....	Za	Aa1	Ba6		c	Ca1	b3	Da1a	E	b4		Fa2b	b3,1	Gf3		Hd2		Ia
38....	Za	Aa1	Ba6		c	Ca1	b1,3	Dc	E	b4		Fa2b	b3,1	Gf3		Hf		Ia
39....	Za	Aa1	Ba6			Ca1	b3	Da1a	Ea2	b4		Fa2b	b3,1	Gf3,c		Hd2		Ia
40....	Za	Aa1	Ba6		c	Ca1	b1	Da1a	E	b4		Fa2b	b3,1	Gf3		Hd2		Ia
41....	Za	Aa1	Ba6		c	Ca1	b3	Da1a	E	b4		Fa2b	b3,1	Gf3		Hd2		Ia
42....	Za	Aa1	Ba6		c	Ca1	b3	Da1a	E	b4		Fa2b	b3,1	Gf3		Hd2		Ia
43....	Za	Aa1	Ba6		c	Ca1	b3	Da1a	E	b4		Fa2b	b3,1	Gf3		Hd2		Ia
44....											c2			Gf3		Ha2		
45....	Za	Aa1				Ca2	b2		E	b4		Fa2b	b3,1	Gg3		Hd2		Ia
46....	Z	Ad	Ba6					Da1a	E	b4		Fa3	b3,1	Gg1a		Hd2		Ia
47....	Y								Ea2	b		Fa3	b3,1	Ga1		Hd1		Ic
48....	Y								Ea4	b2		Fa3	b3,1			Hf		Ib
49....	Za	Aa1	Ba1	b3		Co1	b1	Da1a	Ea1	b1		Fa2b	b1,4,11a	Gf1b		Ha4	o	
50....	X		Ba1,6	b3		Ca1	b1	Da1	Ea1			Fa2b	b3,1	Gf1b		Ha5,3		
51....	X								Ea1			Fa2b	b3,1			Ha4		
52....	Z	Ad	Ba1			Ca1	b1	Da1a	Ea6	b13		Fa1b	b3,1	Ga1		Hd1		Ic

"yonder comes" and "gold and money to set me free" with "hold the rope," a manifest intrusion.

Finally, C47 furnishes a possible example of "complex demand" similar to those discussed earlier. As has been indicated, its ballad text is independent of other "silver and gold" variants, although it has the "did you bring" found in A25, C7, C13, C14 (with "gold and silver") B3, B8, B9, B12, B13, B15–17, B31, B49, B53–55, B61–63, B74, B77; B85–91 (with "gold to set me free"); C23, C24, C26 (with "gold to set me free"); C29 (with "gold"); C32–34, C36, C45, C46 (with "silver and gold"). In the narrative setting for C47 (mother coming first, friend last) the usual sequence of refusals followed by acquiescence is reversed: all the members of the family offer all they have and only the friend refuses. This syndrome occurs in certain versions of the ballad found in eastern Europe; a single example from Serbian tradition will suffice for illustrative purposes.

> Jowo wandered onto the Guards' scaffold,
> The rotten wood broke under him,
> He fell, and his arm was broken.
> Quickly they called the healing-woman,
> A *Wila* from the mountain-forest.
> She asked a great deal for healing him!
> From his mother her white right hand,
> From his sister her braided locks,
> And her pearl necklace from his wife.
>
> His mother gave her white hand,
> His sister gave her braided locks,
> But his wife gave not her necklace.
> "I'll not, by God, give my pearl necklace,
> It was given me by my father."
> Then the *Wila* from the mountain was angry,
> And she poisoned Jowo's wound.
> Jowo died,—alas, poor mother![53]

SOURCES OF VARIANTS: GROUP C (TABLE 3)
(FOR FULL CITATIONS, SEE BIBLIOGRAPHY)

C1. Mrs. Sarah Buckner, North Carolina, 1916 (reported by Sharp and Karpeles, *Southern Appalachians*, I, 208–209).
Bronson, *Traditional Tunes*, II, 460.

C2. T. Jeff Stockton, Tennessee, 1916 (reported by Sharp and Karpeles, *Southern Appalachians*, I, 208).
Bronson, *Traditional Tunes*, II, 460.

C3. Harold Staats, Tug Fork, West Virginia, 1921 (reported by Cox, *South*, pp. 118–119).

C4. Mrs. Lena Bare Turbyfill, Elk Park, North Carolina, 1939 (recorded by Herbert Halpert; Turbyfill, LC-AFS 2844 B).

C5. Bascom Lamar Lunsford, Leicester, North Carolina, as learned from Henry Marlor, Boyd's Cove, Madison County, North Carolina, 1949 (recorded by Duncan Emrich; Lunsford, LC-AFS 9474 A3).

C6. Nate Marlor, Boyd's Cove, Madison County, North Carolina, 1936 (recorded by Sidney Robertson; Marlor, LC-AFS 3169 A).

C7. Pauline Herman, Newton, North Carolina, n.d. (reported by Bascom Lamar Lunsford; Herman, LC-AMD).

Herman, UO-RG.

C8. Mrs. Laurel Jones, Burnsville, North Carolina, 1918 (reported by Sharp and Karpeles, *Southern Appalachians*, I, 213).

Bronson, *Traditional Tunes*, II, 464.

C9. Frank Profitt, Wautauga County, North Carolina, 1939 (reported by Schinhan, *Music*, pp. 79–80).

C10. Joe Wells, Esserville, Virginia, 1939 (reported by Emory L. Hamilton; UVL-M).

C11. Sina Boone, North Carolina, 1918 (reported by Sharp and Karpeles, *Southern Appalachians*, I, 213).

C12. "Recca," Mangrove Cay, Andros Islands, n.d. (reported by Parsons, *Andros Islands*, pp. 153–154).

Reed Smith, *South Carolina*, pp. 90–91.

Bronson, *Traditional Tunes*, II, 472–473.

Numerous other reprints.

C13. Jane Monroe, Cat Island, Bahama Islands, 1935 (recorded by Alan Lomax and Mary Elizabeth Barnicle; Monroe, LC-AFS 481 B2, 482 A1).

Monroe, BBC 13877.

C14. Gertrude Thurston, New Bight, Cat Island, Bahama Islands, 1935 (recorded by Alan Lomax and Mary Elizabeth Barnicle; Thurston, LC-AFS 388 B3).

Thurston, BBC 13877.

C15. Mary Riddle, Buncombe County, North Carolina, n.d. (reported by Henry, "Ballads and Songs," p. 272.

Henry, *Southern Highlands*, p. 98.

C16. Unidentified informant, Madison County, New York, n.d. (reported by Henry, "Fragments," p. 247; identical with C15).

C17. "Old woman," Pittsylvania County, Virginia, 1917 (reported by Davis, *Virginia*, pp. 364–365).

C18. Mrs. Otey, Montgomery County, Virginia, 1916 (reported by Davis, *Virginia*, pp. 371–372).

C19. Norma Grindstaff, Beaver Creek, North Carolina, n.d. (reported as having been learned from mother whose name was McClellan [cf. C25]; Sheppard, *Cabins*, p. 282).

C20. John Henry King, Woolsey, Virginia, 1941, reported as learned from "an old colored man" (reported by Susan R. Morton; UVL-M).

C21. Mrs. J. D. Blanton, Florida, n.d. (reported as learned from Bob Miller [cf. B92, also reported as having been learned from Miller]; Morris, *Florida*, pp. 295–296).

C22. Roy Crimes, De Valls Bluff, Arkansas, 1953 (recorded by Mary C. Parler; Crimes, LC-AFS 11,891 A21).

C23. Belvia Hampton, Clay County, North Carolina, 1915 (cf. B34, B75, from same informant; reported by Belden and Hudson, *North Carolina*, II, 143).

Bronson, *Traditional Tunes*, II, 456.

C24. Myrtle Love Hester, Alabama, n.d. (reported by Arnold, *Alabama*, pp. 68–69).

C25. Ellen Crowder, Gouges Creek, North Carolina, n.d. (reported as having been learned from mother, whose name was McClellan [cf. C19]; Kittredge, "Ballads and Songs," p. 321).

Sheppard, *Cabins*, pp. 281–282.

C26. Mrs. H. L. (Laura) McDonald, Farmington, Arkansas, 1942 (reported by Randolph, *Ozark Folksongs,* I, 147–148).
  Bronson, *Traditional Tunes,* II, 468.
  McDonald, LC-AFS 5418 B1.
  McDonald, LC-AFS 11,904 A9 (new but identical recording by Max Hunter, 1958).

C27. Sadie Spencer, Dumas, Arkansas, 1962 (recorded by Libby Hellums; Spencer, LC-AFS 13,138 A12).

C28. Morley Roberts, Barnstaple, Devonshire, 1895 (reported as having also been known in this form to Norman Gale in the Midlands; Roberts, "Folk Song," p. 16.

C29. Mrs. Calvin S. Brown, reported as learned "in the canebrakes of Alabama," n.d. (reported by Hudson, "Ballads and Songs," p. 105).
  Hudson, *Mississippi,* p. 112.
  Hudson, *Folk Tunes,* p. 19.
  Bronson, *Traditional Tunes,* II, 468.

C30. Aldah Louise Womble, Water Valley, Mississippi, n.d. (reported by Hudson, "Ballads and Songs," p. 106).

C31. Wilma Clark, Louisville, Mississippi, n.d. (reported by Hudson, *Mississippi,* p. 113).

C32. W. S. Harrison, Fayette, Mississippi (reported as having been learned from T. D. Clark, father of informant for C31, who learned it from Allie May Estes; reported by Hudson, *Mississippi,* pp. 113–114).

C33. Mrs. M. E. Whisenhunt, Slick, Oklahoma, n.d. (reported as learned from grandfather, who learned it in Aberdeenshire, Scotland; Moore and Moore, *Southwest,* p. 76).

C34. Earl Humphries, Kansas, n.d. (reported by Coleman and Bregman, *American Folks,* pp. 116–118).

C35. William F. Burroughs, Washington, D.C., 1925 (reported by R. W. Gordon; LC-AFS, Gordon MS 1033).

C36. "W. F. B.," Livingston, Montana (hobo jungle), n.d. (reported by R. W. Gordon, *Adventure Magazine,* December 20, 1925, p. 191).
  Reed Smith, *South Carolina,* pp. 48–49.

C37. Della Causey, Florida, n.d. (reported by Morris, *Florida,* pp. 298–299).

C38. Hetty Twiggs, North Carolina, 1931 (reported by Henry, *Southern Highlands,* p. 99).

C39. Luther Wright, Amherst County, Virginia, 1936 (reported by Davis, *More Virginia,* pp 227–228).

C40. Charlie Poole and his North Carolina Ramblers, "The Highwayman," 1926 (Columbia Records 15160-D [142659]).
  UVL-M.

C41. Eunice Yeatts, Virginia, 1932 (reported in *Grapurchat,* August 25, 1932, p. 3).

C42. Unidentified informant (John Burch Blaylock, collector), North Carolina, n.d. (reported by Belden and Hudson, *North Carolina,* II, 148–149).

  Friedman, *Viking Book of Folk Ballads,* pp. 136–137.

C43. "Lester the Highwayman" [Lester "Pete" Bivins], "The Highwayman," ca. 1937 (Decca Records 5559 [64112-A]).

C44. Pearle Webb, Avery County, North Carolina, 1939 (reported by Schinhan, *Music,* p. 80).

C45. "Blue Sky Boys" [Bill and Earl Bolick], "Poor Boy," 1965 (Capitol Records T/ST 2483 [12-inch LP]).

C46. Lola Mae Cole, Durham County, North Carolina, 1921 (reported by Mary A. Hicks; LC-AFS, WPA MSS, North Carolina Songs and Rhymes, W 8471).

C47. "Leadbelly" [Huddie Ledbetter], "The Gallis Pole" / "Mama, Did You Bring Me Any Silver?" 1938 (LC-AFS 2501 A).
   Lomax and Lomax, *Leadbelly*, p. 60.
   Asch and Lomax, *Leadbelly Songbook*, p. 52.
   Ames, "Negro Folklore," p. 242 (partial text).
   Johnny Bond Compositions (for professional use only), p. 50; copyright by Harlan Howard, 1964 (Vidor Publications, Inc., Burbank, California slightly modified).
   Leadbelly, Elektra Records EKL-301/1.
   Leadbelly, LC-AFS 139 A2 (recorded by John A. Lomax, 1935).
   Leadbelly, LC-AFS 4473 B2 (recorded by Alan Lomax, 1940).
   Numerous recordings and reprints.

C48. Unidentified informant, Jamaica, n.d. (reported by Jekyll, *Jamaican Song*, pp. 58–59).
   Reed Smith, *South Carolina*, pp. 89–90.
   Bronson, *Traditional Tunes*, II, 473.
   Numerous other reprints.

C49. Mrs. J. E. Schell, North Carolina, 1933 (reported by Henry and Matteson, *Beech Mountain*, p. 18).
   Bronson, *Traditional Tunes*, II, 467.

C50. Laura Ferrara, Jersey City, New Jersey, n.d. (reported as learned from Edith Williams in Oklahoma; Henry, "Fragments," p. 247).
   Henry, *Southern Highlands*, p. 98.

C51. Unidentified Negro nurse, Newberry, South Carolina, n.d. (reported by Belden and Hudson, *North Carolina*, II, 146).

C52. Fred Gerlach, "Gallows Pole," 1962 (Folkways Records FG 3529 [12-inch LP]).
   Gerlach, LC-AV 102.

GROUP D

The variants of group D show a more regular pattern than has been discernible in groups A, B, and C. All but nine (D2, D4, D6, D35–39, D44) begin with "hangman, hold the rope"; D2 alternates "hold the rope" with "throw me a rope," D4 calls the executioner "Mr. Brakeman," D6 has "loosen the rope," D35 has "spare the lines," D36 has "stop the rope," and D44 has "hold your horses." D37 is included here only because it shares the unusual "I see my father's face" (Ea1a) with D36. D36, together with D38 and D39, demonstrates that the "ropeman" tradition (eight variants in all) did originate in this context and not with "slack the rope." All but ten variants in group D (D1 and D12 with "walking," D3, D7, D13, D14, D33, D36, D39, D43 with "riding") have "I see my father coming" with no qualifying participle. Only the defective texts (D4, D5, D6, D16, D17, D26, D41, D42) fail to rhyme "while" with "mile" in Stanza I; the six featuring "gold to pay my fee" (D1–6) include three of these and one other lacking material in the second stanza. In the dominant "gold to set me free" group, all but D41 and D42, with "for I am going to be hung" (Ge), and D17 and D29, with "or did you come to see me hang [hung]" (Gg), have the alternative query "or have you come," usually with the quasi-rhyme "to see me hung" (Gf1b). The texts are almost evenly divided between "gallows tree" and "willow tree" (Ha1, Ha3); "beneath" (Ha5) occurs with both.

"Beneath" was present in one group A text (A6, "hangman, hold your hand—gold to pay my fee"), five in group B (B10, with "gold to pay my fee" and "willow tree," and B78, B79, B81, and B82. Two texts in group B are "ropeman" variants; the fourth and fifth use "spare" in the injunction, as does D35 in this group)[54] and two in group C (C26 and C50, the former with "maple" and the latter with "willow" tree). Since "willow tree" occurs independently only in closely associated texts (B8 and B9, B77 and B78, and C24, C29, and C30), it is certain that "willow tree," like "ropeman," originated in this textual complex. (That "beneath" is a secondary development of "yonder" in conjunction with "tree" is strongly suggested by the appearance in B16 of "*under* the *gallent* tree.")

It is scarcely possible to doubt that "hangman, hold the rope" is derived from "hangman, hold your hand" (A6, A31–36), and that the latter in turn is a revision of "hold your hand, Lord Judge" (A10, A14, A15, and derivatives A2–5, A8–9, A13, C1–11). The "gold to set me free" of this group, like the "gold to set me free" of A31–34, is similarly traceable to the "gold and silver—money to set me free" of A14–15. The independent tradition associating "gold and silver—money" (with or without "set me free") with "stay your hand" (A20, A22) and "wait" (A26, B79, group C) shows that "gold and silver to set me free" probably did not originate in a "hold thy hand" context. "Hold thy hand—gold and fee" and "slack the rope—pay my fee" appear from surrounding evidence in the Child corpus to be secondary Scottish developments, as do "stand" and "wait." The variants in this group attest a shift in the text from "hangman, hold your hand" to "hangman, hold the rope" in English tradition, with "Have you any gold . . . to set me free" the only remaining trace of the parent version.

The homogeneity of these variants once more invites speculation regarding the intervention of mass media dissemination; but I have not found a single instance in which such intervention has succeeded in imposing conformity to the extent manifested here. The closest parallel is with relatively small subgroups in A and B characterized by a high degree of economy (A32–37, B2–27). Twenty of the texts were collected in Virginia; what the group represents, then, is first of all a regional oikotype. But it also represents the ballad as an end product, an "achieved form" like that of Rooth's European Cinderella tale, or Walter Anderson's *Normalform,* in which all that is nonessential or archaic has been abandoned. Attempts that have been made to deal with this phenomenon in balladry have generally focused upon the dramatic or lyrical qualities involved, which perhaps is as it should be.[55] But my concern is with verbal formulas: "The Gallows Tree" as it is sung by these informants is a remarkable version of an otherwise complex tradition. It is simple yet distinctive (its only excrescence being "beneath the willow tree"); and it has been altered almost beyond recognition, yet remains fundamentally conservative.

SOURCES OF VARIANTS (TABLE 4)
(FOR FULL CITATIONS, SEE BIBLIOGRAPHY)

D1. Mary Drain, Farmington, Arkansas, 1942 (reported by Randolph, *Ozark Folksongs,* I, 146–147).

D2. Mrs. W. L. Martin, Hillsville, Virginia, 1939 (recorded by Herbert Halpert; Martin, **LC-AFS** 2757 B4).

D3. Texas Gladden, Roanoke County, Virginia, 1917 (reported by Davis, *Virginia,* p. 373).

D4. Bascom Lamar Lunsford, as learned from Mrs. Deal [Dill?], Henderson County, North Carolina, 1935 (recorded by George W. Hibbett and William Cabell Greet, Lunsford, **LC-AFS 1782** B1).
BBC 12795.
LC-AFS 9474 A3

D5. Nancy Crow, Oklahoma, n.d. (reported by Moore and Moore, *Southwest,* pp. 75–76).

D6. "Lucy," Virginia, n.d. (reported by Scarborough, *Negro Folk-Song,* pp. 35–37).

D7. S. E. Lowden, Gilmer County, West Virginia, 1924 (reported by Carey Woofter; UCLA-WKF, Josiah Combs Collections of Songs and Rhymes).

D8. Mrs. J. F. Dowsett, Virginia, 1937 (reported by Bronson, *Traditional Tunes,* II, 466).

D9. Grace Grinstead, Barren County, Kentucky, 1952 (UCLA-WKF).

D10. Martha E. Gibson, Albemarle County, Virginia, 1931 (reported by Davis, *More Virginia,* p. 227).

D11. Mary Biggs, Knoxville, Tennessee, n.d. (reported by Kirkland and Neal, "Knoxville, Tennessee," p. 71).
Bronson, *Traditional Tunes,* II, 466.

D12. Mrs. Hester Fields, Esserville, Virginia, 1940 (reported by Emory L. Hamilton; UVL-M).

D13. C. J. Cagle, Wesley, Arkansas, 1954 (recorded by Mary C. Parler; Cagle, LC-AFS 11,893 A2).

D14. Helene Bellaty, Ellsworth, Maine, n.d. (reported as learned from father, Captain W. C. Bellaty; Barry, Eckstorm, and Smyth, *Maine,* pp. 206–207).

D15. Morrow Davis, Elizabeth City County, Virginia, 1913 (reported as learned from cousin; Davis, *Virginia,* p. 376).

D16. Mich Whitey, 1923 (attributed to Negro tradition; reported by R. W. Gordon; LC-AFS, Gordon MS 1033).

D17. Emma Chandliss, Anderson County, Missouri, 1929 (reported by Randolph, *Ozark Folksongs,* I, 144).

D18. Jennie Mason, Cannon County, Tennessee, n.d. (reported by Robert Mason, "Cannon County," pp. 20–21).
Mason, "Middle Tennessee," pp. 129–130.

D19. Robert Lassiter, Tennessee, n.d. (reported by McDowell and Lassiter, *Memory Melodies,* pp 21–22).

D20. Robert Shiflett, Brown's Cove, Virginia, 1961 (recorded by George Foss; Shiflett, LC-AFS 12,004 A5).
Abrahams and Foss, *Folksong Style,* pp. 41–42.

D21. Mary Nash, Stafford County, Virginia, 1922 (reported by Davis, *Virginia,* p. 370).

TABLE 4
Texts, Group D

Text no.	Sex of protagonist	Initial address	Injunction (lines 1–2) Verb	Injunction Object	Injunction Precedes	Qualification (line 3) Verb	Qualification Participle	Rhyme (line 4)	"Yonder" (line 4)	Appeal Initial	Appeal Final	Appeal Not granted	Injunction (lines 5–6) Verb	Injunction Object	"Yonder" (line 7)	Alternative qualification (line 7)	"Yonder" (line 7)	Final words (line 8)	"Yonder" (line 8)	Borrowed materials	Refrain	Game
1	Za	Ad	Ba1	b3		Ca1	b1,3	Da1a		Ea2	b1		Fa2b	b1,10a		Gf1b		Ha1				
2	Za	Ad	Ba9,1	b1		Ca1	b1	Da1a		Ea1	b1		Fa2b	b1,4,10a		Gf1b		Ha1				
3	X	Ad	Ba1	b3		Ca1	b1,2	Da1a		Ea2	b1		Fa2c	b10a				Ha1				
4	X	Ai	Ba1	b3		Co1		Dc		Ea1	b3		Fa2b	b1,10a		Gf1b		Ha1				
5	X	Ad	Ba1	b3		Ca1		Dc		Ea1	b3		Fa3	b1,10a		Gf1b		Ha1				
6	Z	Ad	Ba9	b3		Ca1	b1	Dc		Ea1	b2		Fa2b,c	b1,10a		Gh		Ha3		Ic		K
7	Ya	Ad	Ba1	b3		Ca1	b1,2	Da1a		Ea1	b1		Fa2a	b1,3,11a		Gf1b		Ha1	o			
8	X	Ad	Ba1	b3		Ca1		Da1a		Ea1			Fa2a	b1,11a		Gf1b		Ha1				
9	X	Ad	Ba1	b3		Ca1	b1	Da1a		Ea1	b1		Fa2a	b1,11a		Gf1a		Ha1				
10	Z	Ad	Ba1	b3		Ca1	b1	Da1a		Ea1	b2		Fa2a	b1,11a		Gf1b		Hf		Ic		
11	Z	Ad	Ba1	b3		Ca1	b1	Da1a		Ea1	b1		Fa2a	b1,11a		Gf1b		Ha1		Ic		
12	Z					Ca1	b3	Da1a		Ea2	b3		Fa2b	b1,11c		Gf1b		Ha1		Ic		
13	Z	Ad	Ba1	b3		Ca1	b1,2	Da1a		Ea1	b3		Fa2b	b1,11c; b3,1		Gf1b		Ha1				
14	Ya	Ad	Ba1	b3		Ca1	b2	Da1a		Ea1	b1		Fa2a	b1,11a		Gf1a		Ha1				
15	X	Ad	Ba1	b3		Ca1	b1	Da1a		Ea1	b3		Fa3	b1,11a		Gf1a		Ha1				
16	Z	Ad		b3		Ca1				Ea1	b3		Fa2b	b1,11a		Gf1a		Ha1				
17	X	Ad		b3		Ca1				Ea1			Fa2b	b1,11a		Gg1b		Ha1				
18	X	Ad	Ba1	b3		Ca1	b1	Da1a		Ea2	b3		Fa2b	b1,11a		Gf1a		Ha1		Ic		
19	Za	Ad	Ba1	b3		Ca1	b1	Da1a		Ea1	b1		Fa3	b1,11a		Gf1b		Ha1				
20	Za	Ad	Ba1	b3		Ca1	b1	Da1a		Ea1	b3		Fa2a	b1,11a		Gf1b		Ha1				
21	Za	Ad	Ba1	b3		Ca1	b1	Da1a		Ea1	b1		Fa2a	b1,11a		Gf1b		Ha5,1				
22	Za	Ad	Ba1	b3		Ca1	b1	Da1a		Ea1	b3		Fa2a	b1,11a		Gf1b		Ha5,1				

№													K	
													o	Ic
…	X	Ad	Bal	b3	Cal	b1	Dala	Eal	b1	Fa2a	b1,11a	Gflb		Ha5,1
25…	X	Ad	Bal	b3	Cal	b1	Dala	Eal	b3	Fa2a	b1,11a	Gflb		Ha5,1
26…	X	Ad	Bal	b3	Cal	b1	Dala	Eal	b1	Fa2a	b1,11a	Gflb		Ha5,2
27…	X	Ad	Bal	b3	Cal	b1	Dala	Eal	b1	Fa2a	b1,11a	Gflb		Ha3
28…	X	Ad	Bal	b3	Cal	b1	Dala	Ea2	b3	Fa3	b1,11a	Gg1a		Ha3
29…	Ya	Ad	Bal	b3	Cal	b1	Dala	Ea2	b1	Fa2a	b1,11a	Gflb		Ha3
30…	X	Ad	Bal	b3	Cal	b1	Dala	Eal		Fa2a	b1,11a	Gflb		Ha5,3
31…	X	Ad	Bal	b3	Cal	b1	Dala	Ea3	b2	Fa2a	b1,11a	Gflb		Ha5,3
32…	X	Ad	Bal	b3	Cal	b1,2	Dala	Eal	b2	Fa2b	b1,11d	Gflb		Ha5,3
33…	X	Ad	Bal	b3	Cal	b1	Dala	Eal	b1	Fa2a	b1,11a	Gflb		Ha5,3
34…	X	Ad	Ba4	b4	Ca2	b1	Dal	Eala	b1	Fa2a	b1,11a	Gflb		Ha5,3
35…	Ya	Ae	Ba8	b3	Ca2	b1,2	Dala	Eala	b3	Fa2a	b1,11a	Gflb		Ha5,3
36…	Ya	Ae	Ba3	b3	Cal	b1	Dala	Eal	b3					
37…	X	Ad	Bal	b3	Cal	b1	Dala	Eal	b3	Fa2a	b1,11a	Gflb		Ha5,3
38…	X	Ae	Bal	b3	Cal	b1	Dala	Eal	b7	Fa2b	b1,11b	Gfla		Ha4
39…	Ya	Ae	Bal	b3	Col	b2	Dala	Eal	b2	Fa3	b1,11a	Gflb	o	Ha4
40…	Za	Ad	Bal	b3	Col		Dbla	Eal		Fala	b1,11a	Gflb		Ha3
41…	Zb							Ea2	b3	Fala	b1,11a	Ge		Ha3
42…	Zb							Ea2	b3	Fala	b1,11a	Ge		Ha3
43…	X	Ad	Bal	b3	Cal	b1,2	Dala	Eal	b1,2	Fa2c	b11a	Gflc		Ha3
44…	X	Ad	Bal	b7	Cal	b1	Dala	Eal	b1					

D22. N. B. Chisholm, Albemarle County, Virginia, 1916 (reported by Sharp and Karpeles, *Southern Appalachians,* I, 210).
     Davis, *Virginia,* p. 369.
     Bronson, *Traditional Tunes,* II, 465.

D23. Mae Cosnor, West Virginia, 1915 (reported by Cox, *South,* p. 115).

D24. Margaret A. Pound, Westmoreland County, Virginia, 1915 (reported by Davis, *Virginia,* p. 379).

D25. Mary Bird McAllister, Brown's Cove, Virginia, 1956 (Putative; recorded by Paul Clayton; reported as having been learned in Los Angeles in 1951; McAllister, LC-AFS 11,305 A18).
     McAllister, BBC 16206.

D26. Ed Davis, Nelson County, Virginia, 1915 (reported by Davis, *Virginia,* p. 374).
     Bronson, *Traditional Tunes,* II, 466.

D27. Mrs. J. D. Carpenter, Madison County, Virginia, 1920 (reported by Davis, *Virginia,* pp. 374–375).
     Bronson, *Traditional Tunes,* II, 464.

D28. Mrs. H. S. Paugh, West Virginia, 1915 (reported by Cox, *South,* p. 117).

D29. Unidentified informant, Rensselaer County, New York, n.d. (reported by Harold Thompson, *Body, Boots, and Britches,* p. 397).

D30. Cecil R. Knight, Virginia, n.d. (reported by Scarborough, *Song Catcher,* pp. 199–200).
     Bronson, *Traditional Tunes,* II, 463.

D31. Addie Gibson, Virginia, n.d. (reported by Scarborough, *Song Catcher,* p. 200).

D32. "Mountain woman," Rockingham County, Virginia, 1914 (reported by Davis, *Virginia,* pp. 362–363).

D33. Alice Sloan, Kentucky, 1917 (first stanza only; Sharp and Karpeles, *Southern Appalachians,* I, 212 [Tune D33b]).
     Bronson, *Traditional Tunes,* II, 458.
     Full text, Bronson, *Traditional Tunes,* II, 469 (Tune D33a).

D34. Z. B. Lam, Virginia, 1935 (reported by Bronson, *Traditional Tunes,* II, 465–466).

D35. Orilla Keaton, Albemarle County, Virginia, 1916 (reported by Sharp and Karpeles, *Southern Appalachians,* I, 209).
     Davis, *Virginia,* pp. 363–364.

D36. Unidentified informant, Kentucky, n.d. (reported by Josiah H. Combs; UCLA-WKF, Josiah H. Combs Collections of Songs and Rhymes).

D37. David Webb, North Carolina, 1918 (reported by Bronson, *Traditional Tunes,* II, 450).

D38. Cleona Farnsworth, Harrisville, Ohio, n.d. (reported by Eddy, *Ohio,* pp. 63–64).

D39. Vernon Allen, Shafter, California, 1941 (recorded by Charles Todd and Robert Tonkin; Allen, LC-AFS 5100 A).

D40. Oscar Thomason, Crum Lynne, Pennsylvania, 1969 (see B57, reported as learned from him in 1913; reported by Arthur G. Brodeur, Berkeley, California).

D41. Robert P. Tristram Coffin, Brunswick, Maine, 1943 (reported as having been learned from a Negro in Indianapolis; Flanders, *New England,* III, 21–23).

D42. Peggy Coffin Halvosa, Barre, Vermont (reported as learned from father, informant for D41; Flanders, *New England,* III, 23–27).

D43. Leah Arnold, Baltimore, Maryland, n.d. (reported by Davis, *Virginia,* p. 374).

D44. Louis J. Hebel, Louisville, Kentucky, 1957 (reported as learned from [white] maid sixty years earlier; Trout, "Greetings," December 19, 1957).

GROUP E

The final group of texts is composed of those which, as was shown in chapter i, have perhaps received the greatest amount of scholarly attention. Like A25, C12, C13, and C48, a number of these variants (E1, E2, E7, E14, E19, E20) are embedded in prose narratives; five more (E3–5, E12, E13) offer brief prose explanations of the narrative situation, as did A5, A12, A18, A21, A30, B26, B28, B80, C25, C47, C52, D6, D10, D11, D12, D16, and D40 (some of these in the form of innovative narrative stanzas rather than prose). Three (E6, E8, E12) were reported as games, as were B93, C51, D6, D23, and D26.[56]

Analysis of the ballad's textual tradition has shown that significant major alterations have taken place in the title of the executioner (from "Judge" to "hangman"), the nature of the injunction (from "stay your hand" to "hold your hand," from "hold your hand," to "hold the rope," and from "hold the rope" to "slack the rope," with "stand" and "wait" occurring as corruptions arising from the abandonment of "stay your hand"), and the wording of the appeal for ransom (from "gold and silver to set me free" to "gold and fee," "gold to pay my fee," "gold and silver," "silver and gold," and "gold to set me free"). The assumption of those who sought to establish the ballad's origin in the narrative situation of a girl punished by death for losing her virginity was that such alterations could be traced to this group of variants. This possibility must be carefully considered, for a narrative situation thus defined does have traditional analogues. In the Germanic "Lady Maisry"—"König von Mailand" ballad cycle (Child 75, Erk-Böhme 97, *DVM* 67),[57] a girl's parents sentence her to be executed for having become pregnant by a stranger; she sends word to him, and he arrives just as the execution is being carried out. A corresponding Lithuanian tradition involves the loss of a wreath that is clearly symbolic of the girl's chastity.[58]

The *cante-fables* of group E seek the restoration of a lost golden ball (Fb5), a comb (Fb6), a key (Fb8), or a silken cloak (Fb9). The *cante-fables* encountered in groups A and C requested "gold and silver" or "silver and gold," sometimes but not always in restitution for putative theft of a watch or a thimble. The injunction here is to "hangman" (Ad) or "captain" (Af), except for three variants of Irish origin (E21–23) addressing "Lord James" (Aa5), "grand jury" (Aa3), and "Lord Judge" (Aa1). None of the Irish texts is furnished with a narrative, and only one of them, collected in the United States, features a golden ball (E21). As we have seen, "hangman" is the statistical norm for the ballad, but such variations upon "Judge" as "Lord James" and "grand jury" have been noted in group A (with "hold up your head," "hold your hand," "stand," "pass your hands"), group B (with "slack the rope," "hold your keys," "lengthen the rope"), group C (with "hold your hand and wait"), and group D, whose variants 41 and 42, collected within the same family, name the victim respectively "George" and "John," clearly establishing the phonological development. The informant for E4 had forgotten most of the story, but was sure that it had included "a trial scene, with judge and jury" (Gilchrist and Broadwood, "Children's Game-Songs," p. 233).

All three of the Irish variants (E21–23) combine a form of "Judge" with "stop your hand" (Ba8b1); two texts with prose summaries of the dramatic situation have "stop the rope" (Ba8b3), and three others simply "stop" (E4–9). "Stop the rope" was also found in B64 (with "money to pay my fee," resembling E22 with its "money and fee"), C29 (where it is intrusive upon a "daughter-wait-yonder-traveling-gold" pattern), and D36 (with "ropeman" and "gold to set me free"). Only one "stop" text in this group (E21) is not defective in its first stanza (Dc). "Stop," then, is a secondary and sporadic development, which might have originated either with an Irish ballad text featuring "money and fee" and "Judge" or with an English *cante-fable* text featuring "golden ball" and "hangman."

Three texts (E1–3) have "wait" (Ba6); one of them, collected in Illinois, combines it with "slack the rope" and features the male victim usually associated with that tradition. "Wait" is found elsewhere with "silver and gold" (A26, C17, C31–43, C46, C50), "gold and silver" (C1–7, C11), "money" (B72, C17), "to buy me free" (A26, A31, B74, C11, C19, C20), "to pay my fee" (B3, B72, C1–7, C17), "to pay me free" (C26, C27), "to bring me free" (B32, C23, C25). In only two other exemplars (C21, with a male victim and "hangman, hold the rope," and C22, with "daughter") is this verb associated with "set me free" as it is here. Like "stop," "wait" is consistently associated with secondary verbal manifestations.

Where present at all, the third line of Stanza I is the simplistic one (Ca1a) characteristic of "hold your hand / hold the rope—gold to set me free" texts in group A and group D; only three variants in this group (E10–12), all collected in the United States, have such a pattern. Eleven variants have an appropriate "have you found" (Fa2d), one the command "find" (Fa1c); seven have a conventional "have you brought" (Fa2b), and two "did you bring" (Fa3). "Have you any" (Fa2a) and "some of" are, of course, precluded by the nature of the ransom. But there is no such logical explanation for the absence of "to keep me" or "to save me," which were featured in the texts with narrative settings A25 and C47; the presence in E18 and E20 of "to take me off" (Gc), found previously in A2, C12, C13, and C39 and proposed as a survival of such a trait, and the fact that E18 was collected in Maine, E20 on the Isle of Wight, render the hiatus more puzzling if these texts are to be considered "original."

Finally, it is to be observed that every American text in this group (E3, E10, E11, E12, E13, E15, E16, E17, E18, E21), except for the *cante-fable* E19, to be discussed presently, accompanies the introduction of a golden ball as ransom with an innovation in the final line of Stanza II.

More than thirty years ago, Erik Pohl summarized (*"Losgekaufte,"* pp. 59–61) the logical case against accepting the "golden ball" version as the original form of "The Gallows Tree":

1. There is no apparent reason for the introduction's being in prose.[59]

2. There is no reason to assume that a ballad lacking motivation in its text must originally have had an introduction.

3. Popular balladry offers analogous cases that can always be demonstrated to be secondary.

4. The lost golden ball does not satisfactorily motivate the situation.

The textual evidence corroborates Pohl's argument. What is manifested in these "golden ball" texts is neither an *Urform* (original version), ascertainable from the presence of significant archaic traits, nor a *Normalform* (achieved version), although there is evidence in C, F, and G features that the *Normalform* of groups A and D underlies the tradition. The majority of the ballad texts are fragmentary; the injunctions to the hangman are those already demonstrated to be secondary; American variants tend to reverse the sex to the one that is normative in the tradition and to elaborate upon the adjective qualifying "tree" (E3, E10, E11, E12, E13, E15–18, E21). The symbolic values of the golden ball and the key are discussed in chapter v, when the narrative portions of these texts are examined more closely. But that the narratives in question were attached to a ballad tradition that already was possessed of several distinct versions, each with its own characteristics in terms of the injunction to the executioner and the formulation of the ransom, is abundantly clear.

E19, an elaborate tale reportedly collected from a plantation Negro, deserves the same special attention afforded in chapter i to E7, the text composed by the Reverend Sabine Baring-Gould. In the tale, a black couple are rewarded for their kindness to a stranger by the gift to their infant daughter of a golden ball pendant that turns her skin white and her hair long, straight, and yellow. Her mother dies and her father remarries; the new stepmother cuts the pendant from its chain, and the girl becomes black again. She is accused of being a stranger who has murdered the fair child;[60] at the gallows, she begs her father, stepmother, and "beau" to "fin' dat golden ball," but to no avail. At last the beggar whom her parents had befriended appears with the ball, turns into a handsome young man, and rides off with her into the side of a hill.

The major narrative motif in this tale is that of AaT 412 "The Maiden with a Separable Soul in a Necklace," which has been reported from oral tradition only in India. Other themes employed are those of AaT 750 (protagonists rewarded for showing kindness to an unprepossessing stranger), AaT 463B (enchantment causes change in skin color), and AaT 403 (a cruel stepmother tries to bring about the death of a favored daughter, also utilized by the narrator of C48). As Phillips Barry pointed out (Barry, Ekstorm, and Smyth, *Maine*, pp. 210–211), the fairy hill in the conclusion is borrowed from Irish mythology.[61] Such complexity in narrative structure has been manifested in no other *cante-fable* in the "Gallows Tree" tradition except the one composed by Baring-Gould in support of his solar myth hypothesis. Moreover, three of the elements involved are oikotypal ones (an Indian separable soul residing in a necklace, a predominately Mediterranean change of skin color by means of enchantment,[62] and an Irish other world). This tale is more likely to have emanated from a library than from an illiterate informant.

SOURCES OF VARIANT BIBLIOGRAPHY: GROUP E (TABLE 5)
(For full citations, see Bibliography)

E1. Unidentified informant, unidentified location, n.d. (reported by Addy, "Folk Song," pp. 148–149).

E2. Ellen M. Hill, Shrewsbury, 1895 (reported as learned thirty-five years earlier; Hill, "Folk Song," p. 119).

E3. Mrs. Lessie Parrish, Carbondale, Illinois, 1945 (reported by McIntosh, "Golden Ball," pp. 98–100).

TABLE 5
Texts, Group E

Text no.	Sex of protagonist	Initial address	Injunction (lines 1–2) Verb	Object	Precedes	Qualification (line 3) Verb	Participle	Rhyme (line 4)	"Yonder" (line 4)	Appeal for ransom Initial	Final	Not granted	Injunction (lines 5–6) Verb	Object	Alternative qualification (line 7)	"Yonder" (line 7)	Final words (line 8)	"Yonder" (line 8)	Borrowed materials	Refrain	Game
1	Y	Ad	Ba6			Ca1	b1	Da2a		Ea1	b3		Fa2b	b5,11a	Gf1a		Ha1		Ib		
2	Y	Ad	Ba6			Ca1	b1	Da2a	o	Ea2	b2		Fa2d	b5,11a	Gf1a		Ha1		Ib		
3	Z		Ba3,6	b3		Ca1	b1	Dc		Ea1	b1		Fa2d	b5,11a	Gf1b		Ha4		Ic		
4	Y	Ad	Ba8	b3		Ca1	b1	Dc		Ea2	b3		Fa2b	b5	Gf1a		Ha1		Ic		
5	Y		Ba8	b3		Ca1	b1	Dc		Ea2			Fa2b	b5,11a	Gf1c		Ha1		Ic		
6	X		Ba8			Ca1	b1	Dc		Ea1			Fa2b	b9,8	Gf1a		Ha1]*		Ib		K
7	Ya		Ba8			Ca1	b1	Dc		Ea2	b3		Fa2b	b5,11a	[Gf1b]		Ha1				
8	X	Ad	Ba8			Ca1	b1	Dc		Ea4	b3		Fa2d	b5,8	Gf1b		Ha1				K
9	X	Ad	Ba8	b1		Ca1	b1	Dc		Ea1	b3		Fa2d	b8,11a	Gf1a		Ha4				
10	X	Ad	Ba1	b3		Ca1	b1	Dc		Ea1	b3		Fa2b	b5,11a	Gf1b		Ha5,1				
11	Z	Ad	Ba1	b3		Ca1		Da1a		Ea1a	b3		Fa2b	b5,11a	Gf1c		Hf	o	Ic		
12	Z	Af	Ba1	b3		Ca2		Dc		Ea2a	b10		Fa2c	b5,11a	Gf1a		Ha4		Ic		K
13	Y									Ea2	b3		Fa2d	b5,11a	Gf1b		Ha1]*		Ib		
14	Y									Ea1	b2		Fa2d	b5,11a	[Gf1a]		Ha4				
15	Y									Ea1	b9		Fa2d	b5,11a	Gf1a		Ha4				
16	X									Ea5		c	Fa2d	b6,11a	Gf1b		Ha2				
17		Ad	Ba1	b7		Ca1	b1	Dc		Ea5	b1		Fa2d	b5	Gf1a		Ha3				
18	Y									E	b2		Fa1c	b5	Gc		Ha1		Ib		
19	Y									Ea1	b12		Fa2d	b5,10a	Gc		Ha1		Ib		
20	X									Ea1	b7		Fa3	b5,12	Gg1b		Ha3				
21	X	Aa5	Ba8	b1		Ca1	b1	Da2a		Ea2	b1		Fa3	b4,2,12							
22	X	Aa3	Ba8	b1	c	Ca1	b1	Dc		E	b3		F	b5							
23	X	Aa1	Ba8	b1	c																

* Occurs in relative's reply; stanza 2 truncated.

E4. Mrs. Thompson, Southport, Lancashire, n.d. (reported by Gilchrist and Broadwood, "Children's Game-Songs," p. 233).

E5. Kate Thompson, Lancashire, 1884 (reported as learned from two servants from Northumbria; Thompson, "Lancashire Ballad," p. 354; Child Hb-text).

E6. "W. F.," Lancashire, 1882 (reported as a game played by children in Forfarshire, Scotland; "W. F.," "Lancashire Ballad," p. 476; Child F-text).

E7. "Two Yorkshire lasses," n.d. (reported by Baring-Gould, "Golden Ball," pp. 334–335; Child Ha-text).
Jacobs, *More Tales*, pp. 12–15.

E8. A. Knight, Oxford, 1895 (reported as children's game played thirty years earlier; Knight, in *Athenaeum*, 3508 [January 19, 1895], 86).

E9. H. Fishwick, Lancashire, 1882 (Fishwick, in *NQ* [ser. 6], VI [1882], 415; Child G-text).

E10. W. R. Dehon, Summerville, South Carolina, 1913 (reported as learned from Negro nurse named Margaret, 1856–1857; Reed Smith, *Survivals*, p. 121).
Reed Smith, *South Carolina*, pp. 145–146.

E11. Miss Grauman, Michigan, n.d. (reported as learned from an Irish nursegirl in Kentucky, 1883; Gardner and Chickering, *Southern Michigan*, pp. 146–148).

E12. "Slum children in New York City," 1916 (reported by George Lyman Kittredge as received from Mary F. Anderson; Kittredge, "Ballads and Songs," pp. 319–320).
Reed Smith, *Survivals*, pp. 62–63.
Reed Smith, *South Carolina*, p. 93.
Mary F. Anderson, UO-RG.

E13. Nancy Pearson, Pulaski County, Virginia, 1916 (reported by Davis, *Virginia*, p. 371).

E14. Mrs. Bacheller, Jacobstown, North Cornwall, n.d. (reported by Sabine Baring-Gould; Child Hc-text, Child, V, 233).

E15. Phebe [Gilley] Stanley, Baker Island, Maine, n.d. (reported by Barry, Eckstorm, and Smyth, *Maine*, pp. 208–209).

E16. Nancy [Gilley] Stanley, Big Cranberry Island, Maine, 1926 (reported by Barry, Eckstorm, and Smyth, *Maine*, pp. 207–208).

E17. "Colored girl," Gloucester County, Virginia, 1913 (reported by C. Alfonso Smith, "Ballads Surviving," pp. 118–119).
Scarborough, *Negro Folk-Song*, p. 42.
Reed Smith, *Survivals*, p. 55 (first stanza only).
Davis, *Virginia*, p. 372.

E18. Mrs. Frank Matthews, Eastport, Maine, 1927 (reported by Barry, Eckstorm, and Smyth, pp. 209–210).

E19. Unidentified informant, unidentified location, n.d. (reported by Owen, *Old Rabbit the Voodoo*, pp. 185–189).
Barry, Eckstorm, and Smyth, *Maine*, pp. 210–212.
Numerous other reprints.

E20. M. Damant, Lammas, Cowes, Isle of Wight, 1895 (reported as learned from a "young woman of Romsey"; Damant, "Golden Balls," pp. 306–308).

E21. Ellen M. Sullivan, Springfield, Vermont, 1932 (reported as having been learned in County Cork, Ireland; Flanders, *New England*, III, 18–20).

E22. Irish nursemaid, New York (?), 1909 (reported by Kittredge, "Various Ballads," p. 175).

E23. Anonymous and untitled report in *JIFSS*, XIII (1913), 14.

E24. Mrs. Fred Morse, Islesford, Maine, n.d. (reported as learned from an "old wandering beggar man" in Ireland; Barry, Eckstorm, and Smyth, *Maine*, p. 210).

CONCLUSIONS

In regard to the sex of the victim in the "Gallows Tree" tradition, eighteen of group A's thirty-seven ballad texts, forty of group B's ninety-three, and twenty-three of group D's forty-four make no specification, while only eight of group C's fifty-two variants and eight of group E's twenty-three fail to do so. Group C and group E are dominated by extratextual traditions (the theft of a cup, watch, thimble, or key, the murder of a rival, the loss of a golden ball); the ballad situation itself, then, focusing as it does upon release from execution by payment of ransom, is bound to no sexual preference. The appearance of the word "daughter" in five variants in group A, two in group B, thirteen in group C, six in group D, and one in group E is traceable to Scottish tradition; "son," in one text in group A, thirty-seven in group B, twelve in group C, and seven in group D is undoubtedly a re-modeling of that tradition. "Daughter" tends to be associated with the verb "hold," "son" with "slack"; but both are found with "wait."

When the text is dissociated from this kind of sexual attribution, we find a female victim associated with "crossing" narrative materials in three variants in group A, three in group C, and six in group E, a male in only one in group A and four in group C. Males preponderate when the sex is attributed without benefit of such materials: there are only three female attributions in group B, four in group C, and two in group E, but male attributions occur in four of group A's texts, seven of group B's, two of group C's, six of group D's, and three of group E's. Both the chronological antecedence of the male victim and the fundamental irrelevance of the victim's sex and offense to the ballad's tradition are illustrated by the following conversation between a mother and daughter, recorded by Peter Kennedy in Dorset in 1952:

Mother: A man was gonna—wan't it?—hang 'imself, drown 'imself?
Daughter: No, 'twas a girl, wan't it?
Mother: Eh?
Daughter: Must 'ave been a woman, because she said, "'Ave you brought me gold, or can you set me free?"—'Twas a woman.
Mother: The prickly prickly bush—that's—I don't know what's the beginning on 't.
Daughter: The prickly prickly bush, that pricks my heart so sore; if I once get out of this prickly bush I won't go there any more. Well—you don't remember—I don't think Mother remembers what it's about, she only knows part of it.
Mother: Well, I know a lot of the verses of it, you see, mother, father, sisters and brothers—and the young lady, I know all that—see? But—I don't really know—
Daughter: Oh, 'twas a man, was it? I thought it was a woman.
Mother: Well, man, 'twas a man.
Daughter: Was goin' to be hung?
Mother: Ay.
Daughter: Oh, I see.[63]

Four conclusions can be drawn:

1. As Walter Anderson, D. K. Wilgus, and Bertrand Bronson[64] have noted, the tendency of the ballad is to maintain or revert to its simplest, most primitive narrative form, to which in the present instance it is obvious that neither the sex of the victim nor the crime imputed is strictly relevant. It follows that no interpretation of the ballad situation which depends upon one or both can be valid.

2. A predilection for female victims is characteristic of Scottish and Border tradition, and is perhaps comparable to the predilection for supernatural trappings in Scottish and Scandinavian balladry that has been documented by Marta Pohl, Holger Nygard, and Lajos Vargyas.

3. There is also a strong tendency for female protagonists to be introduced together with "stories" explaining, although seldom very logically, the ballad situation. Willa Muir has attempted to relate the "golden ball" story to nineteenth-century concepts of romantic love and family authority.[65] Although her thesis lends itself to overinterpretation, the regular association of narrative materials of this kind with secondary textual features and fragmentation of the ballad texts bears it out so far as the dating is concerned. It must be remembered, however, that the "story," the sex of the victim, and the order of the relatives' appearance in any given text is the manifestation of the psychology of an individual, not of an entire social group or of a period;[66] only when regular and consistent patterns are present can legitimate inferences be drawn about the tradition of an isolable "folk."

4. This being true, the substitution of "son" for "daughter" in "slack the rope" and "silver and gold" texts, both of Scottish derivation, male victims for female ones in "golden ball" variants collected in the United States, and "George" and "John" for "Judge" in the United States, Australia, and England, corroborates the testimony of nonnarrative attributions in variants from all five textual groups: insofar as the sex of the victim *is* relevant to the ballad proper, it is traditionally male.

The *Normalform* of the ballad has three manifestations, which may be regarded as English, Scots-American, and Anglo-American oikotypes:

I Hangman, hold your hand,
  Hold it for a while,
  I think I see my father coming
  Over yonder stile.

  Have you brought my gold,
  And will you set me free?
  Or have you come to see me hung
  Upon the gallows tree?

II Hangman, hangman, slack the rope,
  Slack it for a while,
  Yonder comes my father,
  He's traveled [walked for] many a mile.

  Have you brought my gold,
  And have you paid my fee?
  Or have you come to see me hung
  Upon the gallows tree?

III Hangman, hangman, hold the rope,
   Hold it for a while,
   I think I see my father coming,
   He's come for many a mile.

   Have you any gold?
   For gold will set me free.
   Or have you come to see me hung
   Beneath the willow tree

Parallel to these versions, however, are the traces of two others:

IV Hangman, hangman, wait a while,
   Just wait a little while,
   I think I see my father coming,
   He's come for many a mile.

   Have you brought me silver,
   And have you brought me gold?
   And have you walked this long, long way
   To take me from the gallows pole?

V Hold your hand, Lord Judge,
   And wait a while for me,
   I think I hear my father coming,
   Rambling o'er the sea.

   Have you any gold
   And silver to pay my fee?
   For I am going to be hanged
   Upon the gallows tree.

And behind all these traditions lies the one responsible for other corrupt forms of "Judge," "stay your hand," "stop your hand," and "stand," "riding," "to keep my body from the grave," and "to save me," and "yonder gallows tree," which can be reconstructed only as follows:

VI Stay thy hand, Lord Judge,
   Stay it for a while,
   I think I see my father coming,
   Riding many a mile.

   Have you any gold
   And silver to set me free?
   To keep my body from yonder grave
   And my neck from the gallows tree?

Neither "slack the rope" nor "hold the rope" could well have become part of the tradition before "Judge" was replaced by "hangman." Since both *Normalformen* featuring "hold" are characterized by "gold to set me free," it is probable that "fee" entered as "to pay my fee" with "slack the rope," and that its association with "hold" in some variants represents an archaization of that tradition facilitated by the existence of "gold and fee" as a commonplace formula in northern balladry. "Hold," in turn, is derived from the commonplace "hold your tongue." But the variant record is one of continual interpenetration of one version by another. Although each innovation must have originated in some such fairly massive re-creation of the text as those proposed above, the tradition *qua* tradition shows minimal, not maximal change from variant to variant. The majority of the singers of this ballad are conservative, and will change few textual components at one time.

Innovations supported by mass media dissemination seem to have no greater effect upon the course of the tradition in this respect than do those originating and circulating without such support. Perhaps the most far-reaching change is that from "Judge" to "hangman," which took place entirely within the oral tradition. The "briery bush" refrain in England, the "stolen cup" and "beneath the willow tree" versions in the United States, and the "wait a while," "hangman, slack the rope," and "silver and gold" developments emanating from Scotland have exerted influence comparable to, if not greater than, that of the "prickly bush," "you won't love and it's hard to be beloved," "slack the rope, hangman," and "wait, Mr. Judge," versions promulgated by mass media.

There remains the question of the immediate provenance of "The Gallows Tree." Reed Smith's assertion that it orginated "before Chaucer's pilgrimage"[67] has long been discredited; Erik Pohl thought that it could not be dated before 1550 (*"Losgekaufte,"* p. 63). Patrice Coirault and Holger Nygard have shown that "simple situation" ballads, structured by incremental repetition, did not appear in European tradition before the seventeenth century;[68] Louise Pound, E. Joan Miller, and David C. Fowler concur with regard to Anglo-Scots balladry *in toto*, Miller and Fowler proposing the eighteenth century as even more probable than the seventeenth for the real development of the genre.[69]

The wide distribution of variant forms in the Western Hemisphere showing trait relationships with British traditions demonstrates that "The Gallows Tree" emigrated not once but many times since its inception. Scottish traits predominate to a marked degree, however, and traces of the reconstructed *Urform* can be found only in variants demonstrably based upon secondary developments (e.g., "Judge" with "gold and fee," "gold and silver" with "hangman"). Assuming that the perpetuation of an oral tradition is dependent upon the continuous association of a relatively large number of persons who share it,[70] it seems evident that the massive Scottish emigrations that did not begin until the eighteenth century are responsible for the bulk of the American tradition.[71]

The third and fourth decades of the seventeenth century, however, saw an influx of English bondsmen into the southern colonies,[72] and it is reasonable to suppose that the community thus formed would have brought its ballads with it if they existed; from 1640 until the turn of the eighteenth century, however, the exportation of such persons was negligible.

Taking into account its style, its language, and the condition of its texts in America, then, the period 1650–1700 seems the most propitious for the introduction of "The Gallows Tree" into English tradition.

IV

THE TUNES

Scholars who have investigated the melodic traditions associated with the Anglo-American ballad have long attested to the fluidity of the relationship between text and tune. A dearth of evidence for text-tune affiliations before the end of the eighteenth century (and in most cases considerably later than that)[1] has necessitated approaches based primarily upon current materials, and the focusing of the investigator's attention upon tunes *qua* tunes rather than upon text-tune complexes, variation in melodic tradition rather than upon stability. Circumstances in which tune and text are organically united are rare.[2] As Bronson, Bayard, and Philip Gordon have observed, neither can the singing of a given text to a particular tune be very often justified in terms of "sense and spirit," nor can truly stable text-tune associations often be found.[3] J. W. Hendren, writing in 1936, found relative stability only in regional traditions and in ballads enjoying unusual popularity; he noted that very seldom could identical melodies be found in American and in British repertories (*Ballad Rhythm,* pp. 57–58).

Melodic variation has been attributed to several operative factors. Individual idiosyncrasies are felt to play a large role; Cecil Sharp, Phillips Barry, Bertrand Bronson, and Sirvart Poladian have all called attention to the creative innovations of folk singers (embellishment and ornamentation, the preference for one mode as opposed to another) as well as to changes induced by loss of memory.[4] Ethnic and national characteristics of style have been cited by Sharp, Barry, Bronson, Bayard, Gilchrist, W. B. Reynolds, George Boswell, and Victor A. Grauer.[5] English folk songs have been found to favor the Ionian mode and triple rhythm, Scottish and Irish songs "gapped" (pentatonic or hexatonic) scales filling out to the Mixolydian and Dorian modes and ornamented rhythms, a characteristic device being the "Scotch snap" (extension of the time value of a normally unaccented syllable). Gaelic music thus corresponds to some degree with the free rhythms and embellished style characteristic of the Near East, as opposed to a Western preference for strong rhythmical patterns and rounded melodies.

More intrinsic influences upon the character of a tune are those of "crossing" tunes or texts (see Hendren, *Ballad Rhythm,* p. 55, n. 8, and Bronson, "Interdependence," pp. 195–199) and plagally related modes. For instance, the plagal range of the Ionian mode, with its tonic on C, extends to the lower fifth, or G, so that the authentic range of the Mixolydian mode, whose tonic is on G, is encompassed by it. It is therefore possible for a tune in such a mode to shift its tonic in either direction (see Bronson, "Modes," p. 39, and commentary below on tunes A26, C8, C12, D2, and E11).

One obvious inference from the data supporting such statements is that the older the ballad tradition, the wider the divergences in its tune variants may be expected to be. As Bronson has tirelessly pointed out, however, no discussion of variation is able to free itself of the assumption that there must at some time have been something to vary from—what Bronson called "some inner, essential core of identity," Bayard "a memorable air."[6] My task, therefore, has been to determine whether such a "memorable air" can be extrapolated from the one hundred and eight tunes that have been collected with the ballad texts, and if so, to establish if possible its relationships to its own variants and to the surrounding tradition.

The first question that must be asked is one Bronson called "metaphysical" ("Words and Music," p. 238): exactly what constitutes a ballad tune? In 1937 George Herzog criticized the practice of Cecil Sharp in differentiating melodies according to their modes, and also commented that the musical content of a tune's first phrase is a poor indication of the total structure.[7] Twelve years later Bronson published his own criteria: range (authentic [eight-tone] or plagal [twelve-tone]); mode (Ionian with tonic on C, Dorian with tonic on D, Phrygian with tonic on E, Lydian with tonic on F, Mixolydian with tonic on G, Aeolian with tonic on A); prevailing time-signature (duple [2/4 or 4/4] or triple [3/4 or 6/8]); number of phrases (segments of tune corresponding to lines of stanza); refrain pattern (internal [alternating with lines of text-related melody] or external [attached to the end of the ballad stanza], simple or complex); phrasal scheme (pattern of phrase repetition or lack of it); initial interval (distance between the first tone and the second); and cadences (tones on which each phrase ends).[8] In his own collection of Child ballad tunes, however, he chose mode and melodic contour as the most reliable indices of tune relationships (Bronson, *Traditional Tunes,* I, xxv–xxvi). Jan P. Schinhan annotated the tunes accompanying the ballad texts in the Frank C. Brown Collection of North Carolina Folklore in terms of scale, mode, range, melodic line, meter, over-all rhythmic structure, and rendition.[9] In 1960 Donald Winkelman called for greater attention to be paid to tempo and rhythm, and in 1963 George List proposed to index tunes according to pitch sequence (melodic contour), rhythm, and meter, although he acknowledged the possible value of utilizing mode, range, number of phrases, and phrasal cadences.[10]

For purposes of classification and analysis, however, the effects of individual preferences, ethnic tendencies, and erosion through forgetting and intrusion can render most of these aspects of a given tune variant as obfuscatory as the mode and first phrase objected to by Herzog. What is consistent in Anglo-American ballad tunes was identified in 1925 by George R. Stewart as consistent in ballad texts: the pattern of stressed syllables.[11] Stewart showed that the typical ballad septenar is dependent upon Germanic prosody for its metrical style; each line has four stressed syllables or three with a final stressed pause, with unaccented syllables distributed at random. So, too, can the melodic phrases of the ballad tune be distinguished in terms of their accented tones, corresponding to the stressed syllables of the text.[12]

Identification of a tune, therefore, seems most likely to be arrived at through a melodic contour established on the basis of the stressed tones. Two further questions remain: how may that contour best be transcribed, and which aspects of the contour should be used for classification purposes?

Various systems for transcription have been proposed. Sigurd Hustvedt has prepared a formula based on half tones, using arabic numerals for each ascending half tone, capital letters for each descending one. (No allowance is made for relative stress or rhythm.) According to this method, "Mary Had a Little Lamb" would be set down BB22B23 CBB22BB4BB.[13] The technique has been endorsed by William J. Entwistle and Samuel Bayard as a transcribing tool, although Bayard expressed some doubt as to its utility for indexing materials because of its reliance upon the initial phrase.[14] For my purposes the system seems needlessly abstract, and less useful than it might be if the patterns of stressed syllables were indicated more precisely.

Sirvart Poladian recommended a more simplified technique, representing the melodic contour by a curved line and indicating phrase finals by arabic numerals ("Melodic Variation," p. 209). His "Mary Had a Little Lamb" would be depicted

Figure 1. "Mary Had a Little Lamb," according to Poladian

as in Figure 1, followed by 3 5 3 1. The inclusion of phrase finals (3 5 3 1) is helpful, but the curved line so drawn, in contrast to the scrupulosity of Hustvedt's method, is too vague to permit easy differentiation of one melodic variant from another. A more graphic scheme is that offered by Mieczyslaw Kolinski, who followed the stressed-tone principle and set his tunes within a scaled box, each scale representing a full tone.[15] Here "Mary Had a Little Lamb" is more recognizable (see Fig. 2).

Figure 2. "Mary Had a Little Lamb," according to Kolinski

More efficient than any of these seems to be the system first introduced by Oswald Koller[16] and adopted by Bronson for such studies as his "Melodic Stability in Oral Transmission." Only the stressed tones are given value, and all keys are reduced to a common tonic;[17] the authentic scale is represented by roman numerals I, II, III, IV, V, VI, VII, the upper octave by arabic numerals 1, 2, 3, 4, 5, 6, 7, and the lower octave by bold face roman numerals **VII, VI, V, IV, III, II, I**. Rhythm can be inferred at least in part from the arrangement of these stressed tones into phrases; "Mary Had a Little Lamb" would be transcribed III I III III; II II III V; III I III III; II III I. Phrase endings are indicated by a semicolon (;), the end of the tune by a period (.). The technique also obviates the necessity for excessive concern with the tune's phrasal structure, a concern that has lead to such contradictory assertions as those of Bronson ("Morphology," pp. 1–13) and Boswell ("Middle Tennessee, pp. 64–69) that an ABCD structure, with each phrase different from every other one, predominates in Anglo-American balladry, and of Sharp (*Conclusions,* pp. 93–94) and Hendren (*Ballad Rhythm,* p. 8) that ABBA is more common. The contradiction is probably more apparent than real; Sharp and Hendren both comment that the third phrase is usually a free rendition of the second, and an emphasis upon phrase finals on the one hand, general contour on the other, is to be suspected. Nevertheless, Koller's annotating system resolves such difficulties.

Classifying the transcriptions thus obtained requires a somewhat more difficult choice. It has been mentioned that Bronson used both mode and contour in distinguishing variant traditions for the Child ballad tunes. Since the Ionian mode with a final cadence on I clearly dominates the entire Anglo-American tune tradition (see Bronson, "Modes," p. 43), and since an arbitrary change of mode by an individual is likely to entail a change in final cadence that obscures the tune relationships (see Sharp, *Conclusions*, p. 35), neither mode nor final cadence appears to be particularly useful. On the other hand, Bayard ("Hustvedt Indexing Method," pp. 251–252) and Bronson ("Melodic Stability," p. 54) have proposed that the point of greatest stability after the final cadence is the final of phrase 2. This mid-cadence, therefore, offers the most promising ground for differentiating the variants. Further differentiation on the basis of the finals of phrase 4 (the most stable) or phrase 3 (the least so) would be untrustworthy; there remains the phrase 1 cadence, which Bronson attests is next in stability after phrase 2. Arranging "Gallows Tree" tunes accordingly, I find the largest group to be one in which the phrase 2 cadence falls on V,[18] followed in order of frequency by II, III, and IV; there are random occurrences of I, VI, and other anomalous tones. Phrase 1 cadences fall regularly on I, V, and V in most groups; variation tends to occur in groups with mid-cadences on III or outside the II–V range. Other traits that will be noted in relation to the tune tradition have been suggested by Bayard ("Tune Families," pp. 13–33): the ousting of one melodic formula by another that normally occurs at some other point in the tune (displacement), modal change, and lengthening and compression (telescoping) of melodic elements.

GROUP IA

Group IA (table 6) is composed of tunes having a mid-cadence on V and a phrase 1 cadence on I. Five variants in the group (A29, A33, C29, D13, D42) manifest a second strain that varies only slightly from the first; two of them belong to the southern English oikotype associated with a "prickly bush" and have III II I in phrase 1. But B30 also has III II I in phrase 1 with a textual "do up your rope," "yonder," "traveling," and "gold to buy me free." Such a first phrase, therefore, is not peculiar to "prickly bush" variants. Nor is the presence of a second strain attributable to the "prickly bush" refrain; C29, with "hangman, stop your rope and wait," "silver and gold," and "willow pole" in its text, and D13, with "hangman, hold the rope," "riding," and "gold to bring me free," are also two-strain tunes. But D13's hesitation in textual matters as well—after introducing the figure "ten thousand miles" (characteristic of American "blues-ballad" tradition) in describing the sweetheart's approach, the singer changes the ransom from "gold to bring me free" to "silver and gold"—suggests that a second strain of this kind reflects conflict between an original tune and a different one introduced with new textual materials.

TABLE 6
Tunes, Group IA. Group I: Mid-Cadence on V. A: Phrase 1 Cadence on I

Tune	Phrase 1 (Phrase 5, etc.)				Phrase 2 (Phrase 6)			Phrase 3 (Phrase 7)				Phrase 4 (Phrase 8)		
A3	V	V	V	I	VI	1	V	1	V	V(VI)*	I	III	III	I.†
A5		III	V	I	VI	V(1)	V	VI(1)	V	V(VI)	I	III	III	I.
A16		II	**VII**	I	IV	VI	V	V	II	IV	I	III	V	I.
A17	III	I	III	I	IV	VI	V	V	V	IV	III	V	II	I.
A29		III	II	I	1	VII	V	1	V	VI	VI	III	II	I
A29		III	II	I	1	VII	V	1	1	IV	V	V	IV	I.
A31	V	VI	V	I	V(1)	VI(1)	V	1(VI)	1(VI)	V	I	V	IV	III.
A33		III	II	I	1	IV	V	1	IV	V	I	V	II	I.
A33		III	II	1	VI	IV	V	1	IV	V	I	V	II	I.
A39	III	III	VI	I	III	IV	V	III	III	VI	I	II	VII	V
A39	V	1	II	VII	V	IV	I.	III	III	VI	I	II	VII	V
B30		II	I	I	1	1(VI)	V	1	1(VI)	V	I	III	III	I.
C27		V	III	I	(♭)VII	VI	V	1	V	V	I	V	III	I.
C29	I	I	V	I	VI	1	V	1	III	V	III	III	V	I
C29	I	I	V	I	VI	1	V	1	III	V	I	III	III	I.
C33	V	V		III	I	V	V	V	V	V	V	V		I

Key to the following table (tune analyses, reading each tune as a sequence of scale degrees from first note to final). Cells in the same tune that show two stacked values represent alternate readings; the final column (I.) marks the end of a complete tune.

Tune														
D8	V	V	V	I	I	VI	V	VI	I	(♭)III	III	III	IV	I.
D11	V	V	V	I	I	VI	V	V	I	VI	I	III	IV	I.
D13	V / III	V / III	IV / I	VII / I	VI / VI	1 / 1	V / V	1 / 1	V / V	V / V	III / III	V / V	III / III	I / I.
D20	V	V	V	I	I	1(VI)	I	VI	V	V	III	I	IV	I.
D22	V	V	V	I	I	VI	V	1	V	VI	III	III	II	I.
D25	V	V	V	I	I	VI	V	VI	V	V	I	I	V	I.
D26	V	V	V	I	VI	VI	V	V	V	V	I	III	II	I.
D27	V	V	V	I	I	III	V	I	V	III	I	V	II	I.
D33a	I	III	III	I	VI	IV(1)	V	I	V	V	I	V	II	I.
D34	V	V	V	I	I	1(VI)	V	VI	V	V(VI)	I	III	V	I.
D42	V / III	V / III	V / V	III / III	IV / V	V / IV	IV / V	1 / V	VI / VI	VI / 1	IV / IV	V / V	V / V	I / I.

* Notes furnished in parentheses are unstressed passing tones; they are used primarily to indicate the presence of the characteristic leitmotif VI 1 V
† Notes followed by a period indicate the end of a complete tune

The two other tunes with "gold-pole" texts (C33, C47) are both *zersungen,* one of them being a "through-composed" (*durchkomponiertes*) tune embedded in a *cante-fable* and sung in the style characteristic of the singer.[19] Their general relationship to the tune for C29 is nonetheless clear. The tune for C29 also features the VI 1 V in phrase 2 which is characteristic for tunes in this group regardless of their texts. That tune, therefore, can justly be regarded as representing an older stratum in the tune's traditional history than that of the "Prickly bush" variants; C29's second strain seems to result primarily from the singer's desire to vary his melodic material (see Hendren, *Ballad Rhythm,* pp. 39, 53, and List, "Indexing," p. 7).

A39 manifests a different tendency. It is a "prickly bush" refrain sung without a narrative text, and has two additional phrases accompanied by a repetition of the refrain's final line: "Any mo-ore, any mo-ore, I'll never get in any more." As Sharp and Hendren had occasion to note, this is a relatively common phenomenon in ballad singing (Sharp, *Conclusions,* p. 97; Hendren, *Ballad Rhythm,* p. 17). To be observed here, however, is that it does not occur in any "prickly bush" tune attached to the narrative stanzas of "The Gallows Tree."[20] It does not seem likely that the refrain enjoys a stable melodic tradition of its own which might have affected the ballad tune (as it is supposed that the "Broom of Cowdenknowes" refrain did).

The tunes accompanying D8–42 have the remarkable similarity attributed by Hendren to regional oikotyping, and correspond to the oikotypal quality of their texts. Only one, D33a, from Kentucky, varies in its initial phrase; it is in 6/8 rather than 4/4 time, but it retains the "beneath the willow tree' characteristic of the oikotype.

The fact that the contour represented here (mid-cadence on V, phrase 1 cadence on I, ABBA structure in terms of a leitmotif VI 1 V or 1 VI V commonly occurring in phrases 2 and 3) occurs in all four major textual groups, and is associated almost universally with a "free-tree" rhyme (the exceptions, A3 with "gold to pay my fee" and C29, C33, and C47 with "silver and gold" can be seen as modifications of A16's "gold and silver to set me free"), argues that this is the original and basic tune for the ballad, and that the text with which it was first associated had "gold and silver to set me free" in its second stanza. Survivals of our postulated *Urtext* are observable in the "old man" and "yonder gallows tree" of A3, the "George" of A5 and the "Judge" of A16, the "take a while" of A16, "stay thy hand" of A29 and C27, and "wait" of A31, C29, C27, and C33, and the "silver" of A16 and C47. It should be noted that the tune for C27 is Mixolydian, like tunes with quite different textual associations to be considered later.

GROUPS IB, IC

The tunes in group IB (table 7) have a mid-cadence on V and a phrase 1 cadence also on V. All but one of these tunes show the kind of reduplication of strain that was observed in A29, A33, C27, D12, and D42. Since the "correction" invariably occurs in the first phrase, the hesitation appears to be the consequence of shifting the group IA initial cadence from I to V; C24's return to a cadence on I in the second strain regularizes it in that pattern. Repetition of VI 1 V or 1 VI V in phrases 2 and 3 is perpetuated.

These tunes, then, show a very simple modification of the basic tune, either through forgetting (C24, D30) or deliberate manipulation (in addition to B33's introduction of a second strain that, even more than that of C47, appears to be what Alexander Keith called in Scottish tradition "an exotic development,"[21] B33 and C49 both have an unusual heavy accentuation of the stressed tones).

Textually, B33 and C49 can be related to the *Urtext* through "tarry a little while" and an imperfect "gold-pole" rhyme in the former, "Judges, hold your ropes" and "gold and money to set me free" in the latter. C24 has "hang up your ropes and wait a little while" with "gold to set me free," but shares the "willow tree" of group IA's oikotypal subgroup with D30.

In group IC (table 8), with a phrase 1 cadence on plagal V, B10 also features "beneath the willow tree." Its first-phrase pattern is undoubtedly due to its "slack the rope—gold to pay my fee" text, but together with B12 and B69 it furnishes additional evidence for the limitations on the influence of even such widely promulgated and reinforced text-tune complexes as that of B41. The schematic representation of B41 shows that the tune shaping of the Settlement School version was as elaborate as its text shaping; the second stanza is truncated melodically as well as textually, and the refrain stanza changes its rhythm as well as its melody. B36 and B43 adhere closely to the pattern (the first sung by the noted popularizer of ballad tradition, Jean Ritchie).[22] The tune to which two differing texts (B19–20) are sung by the same singer is somewhat less faithful, but retains the repeated V V V in phrase 2 and the characteristic "Scotch snap" of the anacrusis (the opening phrase of B36, B41, and B43 is patterned ♩♪♩♪♫♩♩ ; B19–20 ♩. ♪♩♩♩♩♫♫♩). Both textually and melodically, B10, B12, and B61 show affiliation in only the grossest aspects. When it is remembered that B19–20 and B36, whose tune correspondences with B41 are closer, do not follow the "fine—line" rhyme scheme of the Settlement School version, it becomes very clear that neither formal instruction nor broadside distribution have succeeded in obliterating the pre-existing oral tradition.

Furthermore, a first-phase III II I in group A lacks only the descent to the plagal range and is accompanied by I VI V in phrases 2 and 3. B10, B12, and B69 echo this pattern with VI in one or the other phrase. It can be hypothesized, therefore, that the composer of the Settlement School tune modified one already in traditional circulation in the same way that the text was altered from "yonder comes" and "gold to pay my fee" to "I looked over yonder" and "gold to pay my fine." The remaining tunes in this group suggest that the extension to the plagal range, as well, is borrowed from antecedent tradition.

Variants C6 and C8 belong to the text-tune complex of the "Lord Joshua—stolen cup" tradition. That textual tradition was shown to be a composite one, derived from independent "hold your hand, Lord Judge—gold to pay my fee" and "hangman, wait a while—gold and silver to set me free" versions. The tune may also be expected to show evidence of conflict; and C8 suggests in its second-

TABLE 7

TUNES, GROUP IB. GROUP I: MID-CADENCE ON V. PHRASE 1 CADENCE ON V

Tune	Phrase 1 (Phrase 5, etc.)				Phrase 2 (Phrase 6)			Phrase 3 (Phrase 7)				Phrase 4 (Phrase 8)		
B33	I	III	III	V	VI(1)	VII	V	1	V	1	V	V	IV	I.
	V	III	V	III	VI(1)	VII	V	1	V	1	V	V	IV	I.
C24	III	III	V	V	VI	1	V	1	1(VI)	V			III	I.
	III	III	V	I	VI	1	V	1	1(VI)	V		V	IV	I.
C49	I	I	V	V	VI(1)	VII	V	1	I	V	III	V	IV	I.
D30	III	III	V	V	VI	V	V	VI	III	II	VI	I	II	I.
	I	I	III	V	VI	V	V	VI	V	III	I	III	II	I.

TABLE 8

TUNES, GROUP IC. GROUP I: MID-CADENCE ON V. C: PHRASE 1 CADENCE ON PLAGAL V

Tune	Phrase 1 (Phrase 5, etc.)				Phrase 2 (Phrase 6)			Phrase 3 (Phrase 7)				Phrase 4 (Phrase 8)		
B10	I	I	I	▶	III	IV	V	VI	V	III	▶	I	III	I.
B12	III	II	I	▶	III	VI	V	V	IV	III	▶	III	II	I.
B19–20	III	I	I(VI)	▶	V	V	V					V	III	I
	III	I	I(VI)	▶	V	V	V	V(VI)	V	V	I	V	III	I.
B36	(III)II	I(V)	VI	▶	V	V	V	III	II	III	▶	III	III	I.
B41	(III)II	I(V)	VI	▶	V	V	V	III	II	III	▶	III	IV	I.
	(III)II	I(V)	VI	▶	V	V	V	(III)II	I(V)	VI	▶	V	V	V
	III	II	III	▶	III	IV	V	III	II	III	▶	III	IV	I.
B43	(III)II	I	VI	▶	V	V	V	III	II	III	▶	III	IV	I.
	(III)II	I	VI	▶	V	V	V	(III)II	I(V)	VI	▶	V	V	V
								III	II	III	▶	III	IV	I.
B69	I	I(III)	I(VI)	▶	I	III	V	VI(1)	V	III	▶	I	VI	I.
C6	I	I	I	▶	V	IV	V	V	V	I	I	I	V	I.
	I	VI(V)	I.											
C8	I	(♭)VII		▶	V	(♭)VII	V	II	I	I	▶	II	II	I.
C26	I	I	I(VI)	▶	V	1(VI)	V	1	I			V	II	I.
D19	I	I	I(VI)	▶	V(VI)	1	V	1(VI)	V	II	▶	I	II	I.

TABLE 9

TUNES, GROUP IIA. GROUP II: MID-CADENCE ON II. A: PHRASE 1 CADENCE ON I

Tune	Phrase 1 (Phrase 5, etc.)	Phrase 2 (Phrase 6)	Phrase 3 (Phrase 7)	Phrase 4 (Phrase 8)
A6	III IV V I	III III II	III IV V I	II III II I.
	III IV V I	III III II	III IV V VI	III V IV I.
	III IV VI I	III III II	III IV V VI	III V IV I.
A7	II II I	I V II	V V IV I	II V IV I.
	II II I	I V II	V V IV I	II V IV I.
A24	I II I	III V II	V V IV I	V II V I.
	I II I		V V IV I	V II V I.
A34	I VI II VII	I V II	I III IV VI	III IV II I.
	I VI II VII	I V II	I III IV VI	V IV II I.
A35	III II I	III IV II	III III VI V	II IV II I.
	III II I	III IV II	III III VI V	II IV II I.
A36	(4)III III II I	IV IV II	IV V VI V	III III II I.
	III III II I	IV IV II	IV V VI V	(4)III III II I.
A38	III II VII I	I V II	V IV IV III	III V V I.
A40	III III IV IV	V V II	III IV IV VI	IV V IV I.
B8	V V IV I	I V III	I V V I	III II III I.
D1	I I I I	I III II	I I III I	II III II I.
D41	III II III I	III IV II	II II V V	V V V I.
D43	III I III I	III III II	VII VII II VII	V II V I.
E11	[1 III 1 1	2 2 2 V	1 1 2 1	2 1 V.
	IV VI IV IV	V V V I	IV IV V IV	V IV I.]

phrase resemblance to C26 and D19 (one of which has "wait a while" and the other "hold the rope," but both rhyming "free" with "tree") that one of the conflicting tunes was indeed the one extrapolated from those in group IA. Another *zersungen* tune is evident in C6, which is restricted to a range of eight tones and features the repetition of phrase 4 found elsewhere only in the "prickly bush" A39. Tunes C26 and D19, however, with leading tones on the plagal sixth (**VI**) instead of C8's flattened seventh (**VII**), indicate that we may expect to find another basic tune in which 1 VI V is displaced from the authentic octave to the plagal and from phrase 2 to phrase 1. That basic tune will be the one adapted by the Settlement School composer.

GROUP IIA

Group IIA (table 9) is characterized by a mid-cadence on II and a phrase 1 cadence on I. A7, A34, A35, A36, A38, and A40 accompany a "prickly bush" refrain, A38 and A40, like A39 in group IA, having been collected without a narrative text. If there is a possibility that the refrain influenced the tune, it is here, then, that the influence would have been exerted.

A certain resemblance obtains between these tunes and one of those associated with Child 155 "Little Sir Hugh," to which the "prickly brier" refrain was attached in A41: its contour is (III)II (III)I (**VI**)V (**VI**)I; (III)II (III)I (**VI**)V (**VI**)II. The first-phrase pattern is reminiscent of the Settlement School initial phrase (B41), but it is there associated with the "slack the rope" tradition, not the "hold—set me free" formula that dominates here. Two tunes in group IA (A29, A33), both collected in Langport, Somerset, combined a phrase 1 III II I with an upper register 1 VI V in phrases 2 and 3; one of these hesitated in the text between "hold thy hand" and "stay thy hand." Two in the present group (A35, A36), both from Dorset, combine III II I with a mid-cadence on II and a text agreeing very closely with that of the late nineteenth-century concert hall "prickly bush" version. That version is represented here (A34); but its first-phrase II **VII** is echoed in narrative texts only in A7 and A16, whose formulas "John, stand here—gold and fee" and "Judge, take a while—gold and silver to set me free" owe nothing to A34's "hangman, hold your hand—gold to set me free."

The principles of "multiple transmission," "communal re-creation," and "minimal change" (in that ballad *singers* tend to change very few elements at one time, as opposed to "ballad composers" who introduce massive innovations in text and tune) are thus borne out once more. We have seen "hold—gold to set me free" associated with 1 VI V in phrases 2 and 3 on both sides of the Atlantic in group IA, in the United States with V in phrase 1 and in England with III II I. Had the latter developed only out of conflict with a new tune, belonging to the "prickly brier" refrain and having a mid-cadence on II, it would be difficult to explain the "slack the rope" development of B30 and group IC. It is probable that the concert version of A34 is responsible for lowering the mid-cadence of some English tunes to II; however, the two tunes accepting the unusual first phrase of the concert version are those most conservative in other respects, and those adhering to it most closely in general (textually and melodically) substitute III II I in phrase 1.

TABLE 10
TUNES. GROUP IIB. GROUP II: MID-CADENCE ON II. B: PHRASE 1 CADENCE ON V

Tune	Phrase 1 (Phrase 5, etc.)				Phrase 2 (Phrase 6)			Phrase 3 (Phrase 7)				Phrase 4 (Phrase 8)		
B63......	I	V	1(VI)	V	1(VI)	V	II	I	V	VI	I	III	III	I.
B65......	III	III	V	V	I	III	II	III	II	II	VI	I	VI	I.
D5.......	III	V	III	V	VI	IV	II	II	IV	IV	IV	VI	V	III
	III	III	III	VI		IV	III	IV	VI	VI	V	VI	IV	I
	III	III	III	V		V	IV	IV	VI	VI	V	VI	II	I.
D35......	I	I	1(VI)	V	I	I	II	I	I	I	1	(VI)V	II	I.
D37......		I		V	1(VI)	V	II	III	I		I	V	II	I
		V		V	VI(V)		II	III			I			
		I		V		II	I.							

III II I must therefore have been an alternative opening phrase before the concert innovation was composed.

Variant A24 shows adjustment of tune to correspond with the collapsing of the first two lines of Stanza I: its "hangman, stand 'ere a while" rhymes in the ordinary way, but musical phrase 2, in which the rhyme-word normally occurs, is omitted.

The tunes for A6, D41, and D43 furnish examples of the intrusion of other tune-traditions. As Hendren noted (*Ballad Rhythm*, p. 55, n. 8), the tune for A6 (by the informant's testimony a version that had crossed the Atlantic before the Revolution) is an imperfectly realized rendition of "Oh, Susannah!" Tunes D41 and D43 are equally recognizable as versions of "Goodbye, My Lover, Goodbye." But D41 invites comparison with D42 in group IA, sung by the daughter of the informant for D41. It will be recalled that D41 called the victim "George" and D42 "John," showing the relationship of both to "Judge"; both have "gold to set me free," "for I am going to be hanged," and "creep-o, mellow tree." But the daughter's tune, confused and hesitant as it is, is obviously closer to the traditional tune than that of her father, and D41 is an instance of complete forgetting of the tune combined with fair retention of the text.

Modal shift is exhibited in A36 and E11. Two tunes so far encountered have been entirely in the Mixolydian mode (C8 and C27, with flattened sevenths); A36 begins the first phrase of one stanza of the text with a flattened third, as if to cast the tune in Dorian or Aeolian, but reverts quickly to the base tune. E11 follows a pattern different from either: the tune is hexatonic, lacking a seventh, and, although it begins with a tonic on C, the final tonic is on G. Such tunes were referred to earlier as predictable in the case of plagally related modes.

GROUPS IIB, IIC, III

Group IIB (table 10) has a mid-cadence on II and a first-phrase cadence on V, and its five variants are as anomalous in respect to text as they are to tune. Variant B63 has "slack on the line—money to pay my fine"; B19 also had "slack on the line," but with a tune more closely related to the Settlement School tradition where the second stanza "fine—line" rhyme originated. Variant B65 has "slack the rope—money to pay my fee" and a tune resembling in its initial phrase D30, which had "hold the rope—gold to set me free," and in its phrase 3 both D30 and D43. Variant D5 appears to be the result of conflict between "Old Black Joe" (its rhythmical pattern is ♩♩♩♩♩♩♩♩♩♩♩♩.) and the "willow tree" tune of group IA to which D30 and D43 are also related; it has "hold the rope—gold to pay my fee." "Spare my life—gold to set me free" in variant D35 and "slack the rope—I see my father's face" in the fragment D37 complete the picture of a confused and secondary textual and melodic tradition.

The phenomenon of displacement and telescoping is observable in B63, D35, and D37. In B63, the phrase 1 VI V is iterated in phrases 1 and 2; in D36, in phrase 1 and as a bridge between 3 and 4; in D37 it appears in highly abbreviated form in phrase 2.

These tunes with their texts, then, illustrate both the instability and secondary nature of a phrase 1 cadence on V (already noted in group IB) and the ubiquity of the leitmotif 1 VI V even where texts and tunes are considerably deteriorated.

TABLE 11

Tunes, Group IIC. Group II: Mid-Cadence on II. C: Phrase 1 Cadence on V

Tune	Phrase 1 (Phrase 5, etc.)	Phrase 2 (Phrase 6)	Phrase 3 (Phrase 7)	Phrase 4 (Phrase 8)
A26	I VII V / V IV IV	III I II / III V II	III III V I / III III V I	III II I. / III II I.
B6a	I VII V	I(II) II II	III I V I	III II I.
b	I (♭)VII V	II I III	III I V I	III II I.
B25	III VI V	III VII II	III I VI I	III II I.
B67	I (♭)VII V / II V L.	I (♮)VII II	V IV III II	II VII I / II VII I
B68	I VII V	V VII II	III I VII V	II V I.
B73	I VII V	I I II	III III V I	III II I.
B75	I(VI) V V	III II II	III V V I	I V(VI) I.
B84	I I(VI) V	I VII II	III III V I	III I I.
D39	II V II / I(VI) I(VI) V	V V II / V V II	III III V I / III III V I	III III I. / III III I.
E3	I VII V	I I II	III III V I	III II I.

TABLE 12

TUNES, GROUP III: MID-CADENCE ON IV

Tune	Phrase 1 (Phrase 5, etc.)				Phrase 2 (Phrase 6)			Phrase 3 (Phrase 7)				Phrase 4 (Phrase 8)		
B61	(III)I	(III)	II(VII)	V	V	II	IV	V	I	(♮)III	V	(III)I	V	I.
B90		I	(♮)VII	V	V	III	IV	III	V	III	V	III	IV	I.
C1		I	(♮)VII	V	V	V	IV	V	II	I	V	II	V	I.
C2		I	(♮)VII	V	V	III	IV	V	III	I	V	IV	V	I.
C4	I(♮VII)	V	I(♮VII)	I	(♮)VII	I	IV	III	V	IV	V	III	I	I.
C9	V	I	I(VI)	V	V	I	IV	V	V	I		V	II	I.
C11		I	(♮)VII	V	V	IV	IV	III	V	I	V	III	I	I.
C12	V	IV	V	V/III	V	V/VII	IV/VI	VI/1	V/IV	V/VI	IV/III	IV/VI	IV/III	III/I.
C13	V	VI/V	VI	V/III	V	1(VI)/(♮)VII	V/VI	VI	1/V	(♭)3/(4)	1/III	V/V	IV/II	V/I.
C14			1	V/III	V/1	IV/1	V/VI	VI	1	V	1/I	V/III	IV/III	V/I.

Of the ten tunes in group IIC (table 11), four (B25, B75, B84, D39) resemble the plagal tunes of group IC in their retention of **VI** as a leading-tone in phrase 1. Six (A26, B6, B67, B68, B73, E3) substitute **VII**, in two instances flattening the seventh in the initial phrase (B6b, B67). Since **VI** appears with a mid-cadence on V, which is in the dominant tradition for "The Gallows Tree," and belongs to the pentatonic scale, it might be presumed to be antecedent (see Sharp, *Conclusions,* p. 67). However, the tunes in group III (table 12), with mid-cadence on IV and phrase 1 cadence on **V**, give some pause to the presumption. All but B61 and B90 belong to the "Lord Joshua" textual tradition; C8, with a mid-cadence on V and a consistently Mixolydian tune, also forms part of that tradition. The tunes here show the same reflection of amalgamation as their texts. Although they begin with a Mixolydian flattened seventh and drop in phrase 2 from C8's V (♭)VII V to V V IV, the sevenths occurring in phrases 3 and 4 (not shown in the schema) are sharpened in the regular Ionian way. Two explanations are conceivable. Either the normative "Lord Joshua" tunes stem from an Ionian **I VII V** pattern and exhibit the same whimsical phrase 1 flattening of the seventh or the third already seen in A36 and B67 (B67, indeed, shows precisely this configuration), in which case the "Lord Joshua" text is somehow derived from the "hangman" of A36 and B67; or C8 represents the tune on which the "Lord Joshua" tune was based, a Mixolydian version of I (III) V (IV II) I; VI 1 V, (see musical examples 1 and 2), translatable to the Ionian scale as V IV II; 2 4 2.

Both textual and melodic considerations urge acceptance of the latter conclusion. B10 and B12 have "slack the rope—pay my fee," but both are constructed on a hexatonic scale lacking VII; they properly belong to the text-tune complex from which the Settlement School version was derived. C26 and D19 suggest that this complex in turn resulted from a displacement of phrase 2's 1 VI V to phrase 1 and the plagal range. The "slack the rope" tunes utilizing **VII** in a plagal first phrase, however, have been collected with a "pay my fee" text in only one instance. Variant A26 has "slacken your rope and wait—silver and gold and money to buy me free," and its second strain is similar to A31's, with "gold to buy me free." Variants B67 and B68 are fragments lacking a second stanza. Variant B73 is also a fragment but has "money" in Stanza I. Variant B75 has "wait" and no second stanza. Variant E3 has "slack the rope and wait—golden ball to set me free." Variant B61 has "let the rope slide—gold to pay my fine." And variant B90 has "jailer, slack the rope." B6, sung by a husband and wife in unison, does combine "slack the rope—pay my fee" with a plagal seventh; B6a (the husband's version) corresponds melodically to A26, B68, B73, and E3. But B6b (sung by the wife) combines a flattened seventh and "I think I hear" in the text (both characteristic of the "Lord Joshua" tradition) with a mid-cadence on III, a phenomenon to be discussed in connection with groups IV and V. B6a, therefore, is evidently a successful attempt to "correct" and regularize the presumed text-tune vagaries of B6b, and may be taken as representative of the subsuming of one traditional version by another.

When this fragmentary evidence is combined with that of the amalgamated "Lord Joshua" tunes and texts, it seems clear that a "wait a while—I think I hear— gold and silver to set me free" text was set in Scotland to a Mixolydian tune closely resembling, if not identical with, that of C8, which was in turn a modal remodeling of the basic tune. Further melodic attestation is to be found in the second strain of A26 and in the lovely "through-composed" *cante-fable* tunes of C12, C13, and C14; all four convert Mixolydian 1 (♭)VII to Ionian V IV, the last three (all collected in the Bahamas) developing their own idiosyncratic but well-integrated variations on the complex.

GROUPS IV, V

The tunes in group IV (table 13) shed interesting light on the process of oral transmission. All have a mid-cadence on III, and all are demonstrably derivative.

B37 and B50 are versions of a tune normally associated with Child 68 "Young Hunting," Child 110 "The Knight and the Shepherd's Daughter," and Child 209 "Geordie" (Bronson, *Traditional Tunes*, II, 62–63, 539–540; III, 18–28). The tune is Aeolian and of Scottish provenance; in these two identical variants with Settlement School texts, however, it has lost the melodic freedom ordinarily characteristic of its second and third phrases and acquired the rhythm and tone of the Settlement School refrain. Variant B50 was published in a song collection in 1931, and B37 was collected in Missouri six years later. Because of the nontraditional quality of the tune and the literal adherence of one version to the other, it can be inferred that the tune was artificially imposed upon the Settlement School text and transmitted only in print.

B52 is also related to the Settlement School tradition, both rhythmically and textually. It retains the initial rhythmic pattern ♩♪♩♪♩♪♪♩♪ and the refrain lines "You've broke the heart of many a true love, true love, but you won't break mine." The only vestige of the tune which remains is the original first-phrase **V VI V**, here displaced to phrase 3.

Variants B35 and B53 show in their initial phrases affiliations with A31, whose final cadence was on III. The text accompanying A31 included "daughter," "hold your hand and wait," "gold to buy me free," and "yonder tree." B35 has "son," "slack the rope," "I looked over yonder," and "gold to pay my fee"; B53 has "slack the rope" and "gold to pay my fine." The displacement in B53 of 1 VI V to phrase 1 and phrase 3 suggests that such a displacement is responsible for the phrase V VI V I; the texts, however, show no organic relationship except in their manifestly Scottish traits.

The tunes for B72 and C48 are derived from the tune that dominated group IC. Unlike the "slack the rope" texts of that group, which uniformly had "gold to pay my fee" or "gold to pay my fine," these two have "money to pay my fee" and "silver and gold," respectively (B72 also has "wait"). C48 is another "through-composed" *cante-fable* tune. The combination of III II I and **VI V** in phrase 1 is characteristic of the Settlement School version, so that we have in C48 what appears to be the adaptation to a relatively modern tune of a "silver and gold" text like those heretofore found only in group IA, but present as well in C34 and C44 of group V. Its second strain, however, is a modification of that of group IIC, to which C48 is more closely related in textual features; and tune no. 2 in group V, collected without words but entitled "Dan Reade's Gallows Song, or Protection from the Gallows" and bearing a note referring to a text commencing "stop your hand, Lord Judge,"[23] shows that the tune earlier sought as a basis for the Settlement School's pattern was extant in Ireland in the nineteenth century, complete with a second strain. Both C48 and the Settlement School version, therefore (with III II I **VI V** in the dominant strain and a second strain that is not merely a restatement of the first), can be related at least melodically to this Irish tradition.[24]

Modal shift and borrowing are both apparent in tune D2, the first undoubtedly being attributable to the second. The influential tune is that usually associated with Laws L12 "The Boston Burglar." But a stanza belonging to that text-tune tradition ("She took me in her parlor, / And cooled me with her fan"), frequently appearing in group C texts set to a different tune, does not follow its tune into this text.

Tune B89 shares its initial phrase with D1; creative ingenuity is evident not only in its shift of mid-cadence from II to III, but in its addition of a second strain. Finally, D33b stems from C26 and D19, tunes proposed as antecedent to the amalgamation of III II I and I VI V in phrase 1 and the addition of a second strain.

A mid-cadence on III, therefore, is invariably indicative either of deterioration or of individual creativity in this tune tradition.

Of the tunes in group V (table 14), B4, B44, B66, B71, C34 and C44 are under varying degrees of influence from the tune regularly associated with "The Coon-Can Game" (see Bokleman, "Coon-Can Game."[25] Structurally it is very close to group IA's tune, the difference consisting in an ascending first phrase I II III and a shift of phrase 2's VI 1 V to the plagal range. Variants C34 and C44 are the product of "crossing" with that ballad (the same ballad text appeared in C29, C33, and C47 in group IA). The tune for B4 has the "crossing" tune's phrase 1 pattern; those of B44, B66, and B71 have the waltz rhythm (♩♩♩♩♩.♪♩♩.) and minor key associated with it. None of these, however, shows any textual affiliations.

Variant B82 is sung to the tune of "Pop Goes the Weasel"; C5, a "Lord Joshua" text, shows traces of the tune normally associated with it, but is more recited than sung in a style reminiscent of C47. Like D2, C22 is modeled on Laws L12 "The Boston Burglar," without phrase 1 conflict and also without borrowed stanzas. Both texts, however, depart from "Gallows Tree" norms in their initial address, D2 substituting "throw me a rope" and C22 "Mr. Brakeman."

Tune E21 is badly *zersungen*. Its text is the characteristically Irish "stop your hand, Lord [James]," but it shows little resemblance to the two Irish tunes represented here as no. 1 and no. 2, both reported with an initial "stop your hand, Lord Judge" but without complete texts. It has already been indicated that no. 2 shows an Irish antecedent for certain American melodic patterns; no. 1 is unmistakably derived from such IA tunes as A5, C27, and C29, with a mid-cadence on the flattened seventh rather than the dominant. It is barely possible that E21 represents an attempt to approximate the two-strain no. 2.

Tune no. 3 was also reported without a text, with the suggestion that words furnished elsewhere by the same informant (B34, B75) would fit the tune. Like B37 and B50, D2 and C22, however, it is borrowed from the traditional repertory for other ballads, this time Child 85 "Giles Collins" (Bronson, *Traditional Tunes*, II, 391–397). It appears once in the Child 155 "Little Sir Hugh" tune tradition as well (Bronson, *Traditional Tunes*, III, 85).

TABLE 13
TUNES, GROUP IV: MID-CADENCE ON III

Tune	Phrase 1 (Phrase 5, etc.)				Phrase 2 (Phrase 6)			Phrase 3 (Phrase 7)				Phrase 4 (Phrase 8)			
B35	V	VI	V	I	V	IV	III	V	VI	V	I	I	V	IV	I.
B37	I	VII	VI	III	VI	I	III	V	III	I	VI	VI	VI	VI	VI.
B50	I	VII	VI	III	VI	I	III	V	III	I	VI	I	VI	VI	VI.
B52	V	III	III	III	V	III	III	VI(V)	VI(V)	I	III	III	V	I	I.
B53	I	VI	V	I	I	II	III	1	VI	V	I	I	III	II	I.
B72	III	II	I(VI)	**V**	I	II	III	III	II	I(VI)	**V**	V	I	II	I.
B89	I	I	I	I	I	II	III	I	II	III	I	I	**VII**	**VII**	I.
	VI	IV	V	III	IV	II	**V**	I	II	III	**V**	**V**	IV	V	I.
C48	III	II	I	II	I(VI)	V	III	IV	IV	VI	II	II	VII	VI	I.
	I	I	**VII**	I	II	I(VI)	**V**	(III)IV	IV	IV	II	II	VII	VI	I.
D2	I	I	VI	IV	**V**	VI	III	III	I	**VI**	III	III	**V**	**VI**	I.
	IV	V	III	I	II	III	VII	VII	**V**	III	I	I	II	III	V.]
D33b	I	I	I(VI)	**V**	I	III	III	V	III	III	I	I	I	VI(V)	I.

TABLE 14

Tunes, Group V: Anomalous and "Borrowed" Tunes

Tune	Phrase 1 (Phrase 5, etc.)	Phrase 2 (Phrase 6)	Phrase 3 (Phrase 7)	Phrase 4 (Phrase 8)
B4....	I II III I	II III VI	1 1(VI) V I	III V II.
B44....	I V IV III	V II I	I I V IV	V II I.
B66....	VI VII$_1$ VII VI./VI.	III (#)V VI	VII 1 VI III	(#)V VI VI
B71....	VI$_4$ VII$_3$ VII$_3$	1/4 (#)V/2 VI/3 VI$_3$	VI/VII VII 1 VII	(#)V/1 1 1 VI/VI.
B82....	I II II I	I III I I	II II III I	V I L
C5......	I I(VII) I V	III I I III	I(♭VII) V : *	V V
C22....	V V I I	III II III V	III I VI V	VI VI L
C34....	III II III I	VI I V V	VI II VII V	II III L
C44....	I I III I	VI I V V	VI II VII V	II III L
C52....	1 1 1 1	1 1 1 V	1 V (♭)VII V	(♭)III III L
E21....	III VI/VI/I III/V/L	V/III/III I/I I/I	III/V I/I III V/II	I/III I/I V/II
Tune no. 1..	III V I	V 2 (♭)VII	V (♭)VII (♭)VII	V II I.
Tune no. 2..	III/IV I/III V/V	II/II I/I II/III	V/VI III/I V/VI	II/V II/V V/I.
Tune no. 3..	I V I	V II	I III III	V III I.

* Melody trails off at this point and becomes unintelligible

GROUP VI

Group VI (table 15) is made up primarily of the tunes associated with texts beginning "slack the rope, hangman." There are two exceptions, variants B9 and D4.

Variant B9 has the "willow tree" and characteristic 2/4 rhythm of the regional oikotype of group IA; its mid-cadence on III suggests, as we have seen, some modification of a pre-existing tune, and its contour argues that the change is modal, from Ionian to Aeolian. Converted to Aeolian values, the tune can be transcribed III(I) III(I) III V; I III V; 1 V IV I; III III I. This conforms to the pattern of group IB, most of which also has "willow tree." Its second strain, however, is different from any other thus far encountered in that its structure is not ABCD (as in B89, C48, and tune no. 2) or ABAB (as in the Settlement School tune), but AABC.

D4 addresses the executioner as "handsel" (an archaic Scots word meaningless in this context)[30] and has "hold the rope" and "yonder" in its truncated first stanza, "gold to pay my fee" in the second. It was recorded in 1935 and again in 1949, with no change, a rarity in such multiple collections (see, for example, B19 and B20, B34 and and B75, B37 and B71). The truncated strain 1 resembles not only that of B9, but also those of B75 and D39 in group IIC; the first of these, a fragment, has "hangman, slack your rope and wait," the second, "Ropesiman, Ropesiman, hold your rope." Its second strain, corresponding textually to the present group, has an ABCD structure, but manifests their characteristic rhythmic structure ♩♩♩♩♩ ♩.♩♩♩♩♩. Its first-strain mid-cadence is on III, which has been shown to be typical of hesitation and innovation.

Except for the fragmentary B23, whose first and third phrases are identical with those of B21, all the remaining tunes have second strains, and except for B26 (whose text contained the references to the bishop's golden ball and silver key) and D4, all those second strains have mid-cadences on III. Their structures are invariably AABC or AAAB.

It has been mentioned that the text-tune complex of B21 has been very widely reprinted, the difference between its dissemination and that of B41 consisting in the latter's having circulated in mass culture media (primary school instruction, songbooks, phonograph recordings), the former in learned publications and hardbound books. It is easy, therefore, to account for B24, B26, and B27, all of which are clearly sophisticated reworkings of B21. It is less easy to account for B23, but the precedent of B37 and B50 suggests that this singer, too, must have been exposed to a printed version. Variant B21 was first published together with its tune in 1925, although its text had appeared in the *Journal of American Folklore* eighteen years earlier, and B23 was not collected until 1937.

The tune for B9, however, was recorded on cylinder in 1922, and remained unpublished and unavailable to the general public until 1957. The parallels between the second-strain patterns in this tune and those of B21 and its imitators, since the pattern is a unique one in the "Gallows Tree" tradition, argue that direct and conscious borrowing has been at work; the melodic and textual relationships of B9 with the "beneath the willow tree" oikotype indicates that B21 is the version that borrowed, remodeling the tune as it remodels the text to "slack the rope, hang-

TABLE 15

TUNES, GROUP VI: "SLACK THE ROPE, HANGMAN"

Tune	Phrase 1 (Phrase 5, etc.)			Phrase 2 (Phrase 6)			Phrase 3 (Phrase 7)				Phrase 4 (Phrase 8)		
B9......	I(VI)	I(VI)	III	VI	I	III	VI	III	II	VI	I	I	VI
	(VI)	I(VI)	III	(VI)I(VI)	I	III	VI	III	II	VI	I	VII	VI.
B21.....	VI	III	I	VI	I	I	V	V(VI)	II	V	(III)V(VI)	V	V
	VI(1)	VI(V)	III	VI(1)	VI(V)	III	VI(1)	VI(V)	III	I	I	I	L.
B23.....	VI	III	I	II	I	II	V	V(VI)	1(VI)	V	(III)V(VI)	V	V.
B24.....		V	I	I	I	VI	II	II	II	II	III	I	V
	V	VI	III	V	VI	III	V	VI	III	V	V	VI	III
		III	V		VI	III	III	I	I	V	VI	VI	L.
B26.....	III	V	I	III	V	II	IV	V(VI)	V	I	IV	II	I
	VI	III	I	VI	VI(III)	II	VI	VI	V	I	III	II	I.
B27.....	III	V	I	VI	I	I	V	V(VI)	1(VI)	V	(III)V	V	V
	VI(VII)	VI(V)	III	VI(VII)	VI(V)	III	VI(VII)	VI(V)	III	I	I	I	I.
D4......	I	V	IV	III	II	III	I	III	V	I	V	I	I
	VI	I(VI)	V	II	III	II							

man." This, of course, could only have been done by someone with access to the archives at Duke University.

I have touched upon the nontraditional aspects of two *cante-fable* versions of "The Gallows Tree." In a case very similar to this one, John Meier and Erich Seemann traced a particularly dramatic and appealing version of one of its German analogues to the conscious composition of poetess Annette von Droste-Hülshoff.[27] Such a genesis is evident here.[28]

CONCLUSIONS

A history of the "Gallows Tree" tunes can be traced with some assurance. A large percentage of the tunes follow the pattern of IA (mid-cadence on V, phrase 1 cadence on I, ABBA structure with the phrase VI 1 V or 1 VI V characterizing phrases 2 and 3). Other tunes manifest regular and recognizable alterations in that pattern (substitution of III II I for I V I in phrase 1; shift of mid-cadence from V to II, IV, or III; extension to the plagal range; displacement, compression, and lengthening of the VI 1 V leitmotif; and change of mode from Ionian to Mixolydian or Aeolian). The melodic data, therefore, argue that IA is the tune originally associated with the ballad text, and its representation in all major textual groups supports the claim.

The tune thus arrived at, it is not surprising to learn, belongs to one of the seven dominant tune families in Anglo-American tradition recognized by Samuel Bayard ("American Folksongs"); he has called it the "Butcher-Bateman" tune. When Bronson chose this tune as the vehicle for his analysis of tune transmission ("Melodic Stability"), he was able to draw his variants from the tune traditions of Child 4 "Lady Isabel and the Elf-Knight" (eighty exemplars), Child 73 "Lord Thomas and Fair Eleanor" (fifty), Child 74 "Sweet William and Lady Margaret" (twenty), Child 75 "Lord Lovel" (sixty), Child 105 "The Bailiff's Daughter of Islington" (twenty), and Child 155 "Little Sir Hugh" (thirty-six). Since it has already been ascertained that another tune tradition associated with "Little Sir Hugh" resembles a common variation in this one (groups IC, IIA), it is not surprising either that the two ballads have "crossed," or that the "prickly bush" refrain should have become attached to both; the rarity of the occurrence, however, indicates that the influence of similar tunes is negligible in this narrative tradition.

Bronson traces this tune to the tenth century of the Christian era. Oddly enough, although it is associated with no fewer than thirteen different ballad texts in the Polish collection published by Jan Bystroń,[29] I have found it with no "Gallows Tree" analogue in the European collections I have examined (see chap. vi). The exemplar published by Bronson is representative of the Polish corpus:

Example 1. Polish tune (Jan St. Bystroń, *Pieśni Ludowe*, p. 61)

The original text, then, was set to a tune already popularly sung.

Example 2. Tune no. 1, Ireland, c 1840 (*JAF*, 24 [1911], 337)

117

'Oh Georg - ie, hold- up— your- head, And

hold it fur a while. I think I see your

fa - ther com - ing o - ver 'bout one hun - dred miles.'

Example 3. Variant A5, North Carolina, 1941

Example 4. Variant C29, Mississippi, c. 1920

Certain deliberate changes in the text-tune complex can be identified. At some time after "stay thy hand" had been eroded to "wait," and "Judge" had been supplanted by "hangman," a Scottish adaptation was set to a plagal tune in the Mixolydian mode; this became the base tune for the amalgamated "Lord Joshua" text:

Example 5. Variant C2, Tennessee, 1916

In England, the tune shifted to a mid-cadence on II and a phrase 1 sequence III II I, roughly corresponding with but not necessarily attributable to a verbal shift from "Judge" to "hangman" and "stay thy hand" to "hold thy hand," and accompanied by the introduction of the "prickly bush" refrain (see Example 6).

Of Irish provenance, like tune no. 1, a two-strain version found its way to the United States and was remodeled and stylized for use in the Kentucky Settlement Schools (see Examples 7, 8, 9).

Finally, a very much simplified text-tune complex, localized in Virginia and featuring "beneath the willow tree" in its text, was re-created in a unique two-strain version in the Aeolian mode. In much the same manner in which the Settlement School stylization took place, this version was converted into the widely disseminated but essentially nontraditional model whose text features an inverted injunction to "slack the rope, hangman" (see Examples 10, 11, 12).

As with the ballad's texts, it seems clear that even massive innovations are not only heavily dependent upon received traditions but also seem to exert relatively little influence upon subsequent traditional singers: that is to say, each becomes a part of the tradition without achieving dominance over it. Commercially promulgated tunes, generally speaking, have fared no better than have those of noncommercial origin and dissemination, and have not necessarily driven out the latter. The tunes differ from the texts, however, in that few traces of direct conflict between one tune and another are observable. What seems to be typical is logical piecemeal deviation from the original tune, the end product of which is a new melody that nevertheless retains definitive touches of the old.

It follows from this melodic analysis that the text of the ballad originated in England. Textual findings showed that Scots tradition is responsible for much innovation ("slack the rope," "wait," "gold to pay my fee," "gold and fee," and

Example 6. Variant A7, Wiltshire, 1908

Example 7. Tune no. 2, Ireland, c. 1910 (*JIFSS*, 13 [1913], 14)

Example 8. Variant B89, Ohio, 1939

Example 9. Variant B41, Kentucky, 1916

Example 10. Variant D34, Virginia, 1935

116

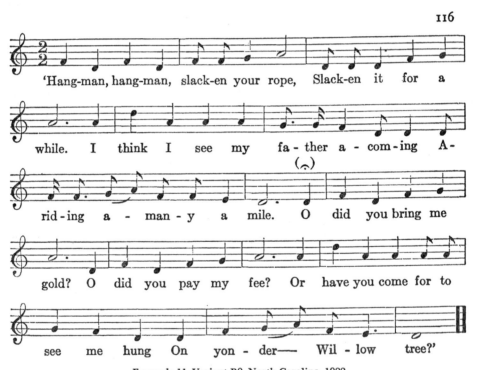

'Hang-man, hang-man, slack-en your rope, Slack-en it for a while. I think I see my fa-ther a-com-ing A-rid-ing a-man-y a mile. O did you bring me gold? O did you pay my fee? Or have you come for to see me hung On yon-der— Wil-low tree?'

Example 11. Variant B9, North Carolina, 1922

Example 12. Variant B21, South Carolina, 1925

"silver and gold") and that Scottish emigrants were the most lively and influential bearers of the tradition in the Western Hemisphere. The melodic findings are the reverse: Scots and Irish modifications are identifiable as modal shift or the addition of a second strain to the primary tune, and are relatively rare. In the one instance in which the ballad text was set to a genuine Scottish tune (Child 68 "Young Hunting") the tune was stylized after the pattern of the dominant tradition.

V

THE SYMBOLS

THE HIGH DEGREE of concern for the symbolic potential of "The Gallows Tree" that has dominated English and American interest in the ballad was indicated in chapter i. My investigation of the texts has shown that the two major symbols upon which attention has been focused—the prickly bush and the golden ball— were more properly to be identified with extratextual materials than with the ballad itself. Those extratextual materials, a refrain and a series of stories and games, both developed late in the ballad's tradition and are associated with varying textual components. Curiously enough, the symbols manifestly and consistently present in the texts, the gallows itself and a cash-ransom formulation, have been almost universally ignored by previous investigators.

Assuming, nevertheless, that all four symbols are of equal relevance, there remains the question of whether the meaning usually attributed to the first two (loss of a maiden's virginity) is grounded in genuine folk tradition. This chapter will therefore be devoted to an exploration of the thorn bush, the golden ball, and rescue from the gallows in terms of their utilization in other traditional materials, including the poetry of the Middle Ages,[1] local legends, customs and beliefs, tales, and balladry.

Concerning the "prickly bush," it was noted in chapter i that James Reeves followed Anne Gilchrist and Lucy E. Broadwood in equating its symbolic value with that of the "golden ball," both representing (in Reeves's words) "a fatal love entanglement." Frank Kidson was somewhat more cautious in attributing specific content to the symbol, observing only that the refrain was "undoubtedly very old" and "of the mystic class."[2] The refrain has been recovered with Child 155 "Little Sir Hugh" as well as with "The Gallows Tree," a phenomenon that, it was suggested in chapter iv, might be accounted for in terms of melodic relationships. But James Woodall's study of "Little Sir Hugh" and its symbols is corroborative of Reeves's interpretation: although he discounted the possible sexual overtones of the hero's loss of his ball in the Jew's garden, thus failing of the kind of total interpretation urged by Gilchrist and Broadwood, he concluded that "Little Sir Hugh" was an allegory of sexual ravishment.[3] That a refrain centering on a "prickly bush" symbolizing the agonies of a victim of seduction should become attached to two narratives concerned with precisely such agonies seems plausible enough.

But when we seek elsewhere in oral tradition for evidence of the use of such a symbol for this purpose we meet with some difficulty. Immediate reference can be made to a popular English song of unrequited passion, "The Seeds of Love," as represented in the following variant stanzas:

> My gardener he stood by,
> He told me to take great care,
> For in the middle of a red rose-bud
> There grows a sharp thorn there.
> I told him I'd take no care
> Till I did feel the smart,
> And often I plucked at the red rose-bud
> Till I pierced it to the heart.[4]

96

> She stooped down unto the ground
> To pluck the rose so red,
> The thorn it pierced her to the heart,
> And this fair maid was dead.[5]

> I put my hand into the bush,
> And thought the sweetest rose to find,
> But pricked my finger to the bone,
> And left the sweetest rose behind.[6]

> For often have I plucked at the red rosebud
> Till it pierced me to the heart.[7]

> I put my hand into one soft bush,
> Thinking the sweetest flower to find,
> I pricked my finger right to the bone
> And left the sweetest flower behind.[8]

> In June the red rose buds,
> And that is the flower for me,
> But on laying my hands on the red rose bush
> I thought of the willow tree.[9]

> I oftentimes have plucked that red rose-bush
> Till I gained the willow-tree.[10]

> Oftentimes I snatched at the red-a-rosy bud
> Till I gained the willow tree.[11]

> Wi' lightsome heart I pu'd a rose,
> Fu' sweet upon its thorny tree;
> But my fause lover stole my rose,
> And ah! he left the thorn wi' me.[12]

According to Child, the characteristic stanza here, beginning "I put my hand into the bush," was composed toward the end of the seventeenth century by a Mrs. Habergham (Child, V, 259); William Chappell identified it as the composition of Martin Parker some fifty years earlier (Chappell and Ebsworth, *Roxburghe Ballads,* I, 278). The speaker in each of these variants is a girl; what may be noted, however, is that in only one instance, the last (composed by Robert Burns), is the rose actually plucked, not "plucked at," unless a willow tree replaces the pricking thorn.

The central symbol in these lyric stanzas, the plucking of a rose as evidence of a womans' readiness to surrender her virginity, is of verifiable antiquity in European tradition. Scott Eliott has documented the use of flower plucking as such a symbol in Child 4 "Lady Isabel and the Elf-Knight," 5 "Gil Brenton," 39 "Tam Lin," 41 "Hind Etin," 52 "The King's Dochter Lady Jean," and 90 "Jellon Grame."[13] In these ballads, the chosen lover is usually a supernatural being and the pulling of the flower constitutes a trespass upon a fairy province.[14] A similar configuration occurs in the early Irish poem *Imramh Brain,* when (uniquely so far as Irish medieval traditions about other world journeys are concerned) a fairy mistress appears to summon Bran upon his journey after he has broken off the branch of a mysterious apple tree and taken it into his house.[15] Such supernaturalization of the tradition, however, is of the kind attributed by Pohl and Vargyas to Scots-Scandinavian oikotyping; not only is the *Imramh Brain* atypical in Irish tradition,[16] but the equation of rose gathering with nubility, quite devoid of supernatural overtones, is well documented in Continental European traditions from the classical period to the present.[17]

The concomitant figure, in which the would-be plucker of the rose is pricked instead by thorns, is not so easy to relate to the plight of a maiden who has surrendered her chastity: as has been noted, both the failure to pluck the rose at all and the substitution of a willow tree, notorious as a symbol of grief,[18] are more prevalent in the "Seeds of Love" tradition than is the interpretation provided by the poet Burns. But the situation is more clear in versions in which the speaker is male, not female:

> I put my hand into the bush,
> Thinking the sweetest rose to find,
> But I pricked my fingers to the bone,
> And left the sweetest rose behind.
>
> If roses be such a prickly flower,
> They should be gathered when they are green,
> So he that finds an inconstant love,
> I'm sure he strives against the stream.[19]
>
> The fairest flow'r in Nature's field
> Conceals the rankling thorn,
> So thou, sweet flow'r! as false as fair,
> This once kind heart has torn.[20]
>
> But, gloveless, alack! with my hands in the thorn,
> No roses I got, though I got my hands torn.[21]
>
> I saw a rose with a ruddy blush,
> And thrust my hand into the bush,
> I pricked my fingers to the bone,
> I would I'd left that rose alone![22]
>
> I wish my love was a red rose,
> And in the garden grew,
> And I to be the gardner;
> To her I would be true.
>
> There's not a month throughout the year,
> But love I would renew,
> With lilies I would garnish her,
> Sweet William, thyme, and rue.[23]
>
> I put my finger to the bush
> To pluck the fairest rose;
> I plucked my finger to the bone,
> But ah! I left the rose behind.
> So must I go bound and you go free?
> Must I love the lass that wouldn't love me?[24]

The symbolic content here is as lucid as it is demonstrably traditional. The rose represents the desired maiden herself (here inseparable from her sexual surrender), as it does in the *Roman de la Rose* of Guillaume de Lorris;[25] the *Rose and the*

Nightingale of Mohammed Fasli;[26] and numerous other classical and medieval works.[27] Nor is corroborative material lacking in modern folklore: e.g., a nineteenth-century French song laments that   ,

> My lover has left me
> Because of a rosebud
> That I gave him too quickly.[28]

German superstitions associate red roses with loss of chastity. If a rose blooms in autumn there will be a wedding. To test a girl's virtue, blindfold her and offer her a bouquet of mixed red and white roses; the state of her innocence will be revealed by the color of the flower she grasps first.[29] All of this coheres with the symbolic tradition discussed earlier; when a girl plucks a rose, it is implied that it is her intention to proffer it to the lover she has chosen, in token of the surrender of her own person. But a very clear distinction can be made between the willing and inviting female who plucks such a rose and the reluctant one who, as the rose herself, maintains a thorny defense. The male wooer of the second set of song stanzas encounters thorns *instead of* the rose he seeks; his desire is not consummated, and the thorns represent rejection and failure, not the aftermath of successful seduction. This is the meaning of the thorns of the *Romance of the Rose* (Robbins, pp. 34–37, 59) and the *Rose and the Nightingale* (Wilson, *Turkish Literature*, pp. 306–311), of *Orlando Furioso* ("The young virgin is like the rose that neither flock nor shepherd draws near to while it rests alone and secure in a beautiful garden on its native thorn"),[30] and of a lyric by "Der Wilde Alexander" ("A rose there is—I weep her yet! / Within so dense a thicket set, / No joys may come anear").[31]

This coherent and enduring symbolic interpretation reconciles the rose, signifying a desirable woman, with pricking thorns, traditionally protectors of forbidden precincts not at all related to love. M. J. Schleiden has described the use of wild-rose hedges for such protection in medieval legend (*Die Rose*, pp. 134–135, 195); Angelo de Gubernatis, Hanns Bächtold-Stäubli, and Lutz Mackensen have documented the potency of thornbushes against witches and evil spirits, as well as against human aggressors, from even earlier times.[32] The hedge of thorns which protects the castle of the Sleeping Beauty (AaT 410, *KHM* 50) is derived from this traditional association, although, as Bächtold-Stäubli, Mackensen, and Johannes Bolte have pointed out, it does not belong to the normative tradition of the tale.[33] That it is an ancient one is suggested by Pliny the Elder's notices that a holly tree planted beside a house will ward off evil influences, and that it is disastrous for a thornbush to be struck by lightning.[34] Modern traces are observable in the English custom of decorating with holly at the Christmas season (Folkard, *Plant Lore*, p. 376) and the German one of planting thorn hedges around homesteads and commons.[35] In this connection, the branch broken by Bran in the medieval Irish poem assumes a different significance; for, as Wilhelm Mannhardt has shown, non-thorn-bearing trees have also been long honored as protective emblems in European tradition, and in many parts of Europe it is still a grave offense to break off a branch from such a tree.[36]

The rose-thorn-tree complex is thus a complicated one, but by no means obscure. Plucking or pulling roses is traditionally symbolic of nubility in a girl or woman, and may be ultimately related to the offense against a sacred precinct that is committed when one breaks a branch from a protective tree. Such a tree, in turn, is directly related to the thorns of the rosebush, which also have a protective function traditionally equated with the woman's intention to preserve her chastity.

Since roses are conspicuously absent from the "prickly bush" refrain with which we are concerned, it follows that the rose-thorn symbol, with its sexual referent, is irrelevant to the "Gallows Tree" situation. What is relevant is the "prickly bush" as the protector of a forbidden area, and the fact that attempted trespass upon such an area (i.e., *any* attempted violation by *any* person of *any* social tabu) is likely to impose its own punishment.[37] If the sexual implications of rose plucking be insisted upon, it must be borne in mind that pricking by thorns in the erotic poetry of tradition is symbolic of failure to gain the forbidden precinct. Moreover, the reversal of the traditional sex roles in this respect initiated by Martin Parker (or Mrs. Habergham) has been stubbornly resisted by traditional singers in England, who almost invariably substitute a willow tree for a thorn in songs about lovelorn women and a male for a female if the line "I pricked my fingers to the bone" is retained. Among those traditional singers, of course, must be numbered those who accompany "The Gallows Tree" with the "prickly bush" refrain, not one of whom has proposed that the protagonist of the ballad is a girl (see chapter iii, "Conclusions").

The quest for sexual imagery encounters similar difficulties when it concerns itself with the "golden ball." Hedwig von Beit offered an etymological interpretation of the ball's significance in folklore corresponding to that of Gilchrist and Broadwood: from the Sanskrit word for "play," the Greek word for "boy-prostitute," and the German word for "desire," she derived the conclusion that in ancient times balls were viewed as the toys of Eros. When that deity tossed a ball to someone, it constituted an invitation not only to love, but to death—"to immortality, the mystery containing both love and death."[38]

Such an interpretation coincides rather precisely with the *incipit* of Baring-Gould's story utilizing "The Gallows Tree":

There were two lasses, daughters of one mother, and as they came home from t'fair, they saw a right bonny young man stand i't' house-door before them. He had gold on t'cap, gold on t'finger, gold on t'neck, a red gold watch-chain—eh! but he had brass. He had a golden ball in each hand. He gave a ball to each lass, and she was to keep it, and if she lost it, she was to be hanged.

["Golden Ball," p. 333]

But gifts of this sort in contemporary Germanic legend are bestowers of material prosperity, not love and death. Three reported by Max Lüthi are representative:

Two citizens engage in a bowling match with a party of dwarfs, and each receives a ball as a parting gift. One of them decides his ball is too heavy to carry, and throws it away. The next day, the other ball has turned into gold.

A little man in a green cloak and a red pointed hat hides in the fleece of a poor man's goats balls which turn into gold, silver, pearls, and other precious stones; the poor man has only to leave something sweet each day at the doorstep for the little man and to keep the secret.

A poor shoemaker makes shoes for the dwarfs, and receives each Friday as payment a snake, in whose stomach is a hare, in whose stomach is a golden ball. He is thereby kept prosperous until he boasts of his good fortune in the tavern, when the arrangement immediately comes to an end.[39]

Another traditional function for balls bestowed by supernatural beings, golden or otherwise, is that of rolling ahead of the folktale hero to guide him on a quest;

this occurs, for example, in "The Well of D'Yerree-in-Dowan"[40] and "The Little Red Hairy Man"[41] as well as in French and German legends (*HDA*, V, 756, and Lüthi, *Die gabe*, p. 87).

Closer to the tradition exemplified in most "Gallows Tree" variants, however, is a ball that is lost. Giraldus Cambrensis included in his *Itinerarium Kambriae* the story of Eliodorus, who, running away from his schoolmaster, was escorted to a land beneath the earth by two diminutive blond creatures. He was able to journey back and forth at will until, in response to a request from his mother, he stole the golden ball that was the plaything of the underworld king's son. When he reached his home, he stumbled over the threshhold and the ball rolled out of his hands, to be instantly retrieved by two fairies who had followed him. Spitting and cursing at him, they carried it off, and he was never able to find his way to their country again.[42]

In the tale of "Gille nan Cochla Craicionn," a boy is enmeshed in difficulties when his ball falls into a courtyard, destroying the work of a woman silver craftsman; she restores the ball, but lays a spell upon the offender.[43] And in a Danish ballad, a similar incident places the boy in the power of a princess who forbids him to sleep or rest until he has performed for her an impossible task.[44]

To these last two tales, overlooked by Reeves, the situation of Child 155 "Little Sir Hugh" can certainly be related. But of the three patterns thus established for the "golden ball" of tradition (as the gift of a supernatural being which confers prosperity until the donor is slighted in some way; as a magical guiding object; and as a personal possession whose loss places its owner in the power of the finder), none is applicable to the situation of "The Gallows Tree." Baring-Gould's account departs from traditional legend in that the penalty for loss of the ball is death, not simply the loss of concomitant benefits.

Other tales of the "golden ball" group (see table 5) lack the supernatural character assigned by Baring-Gould to the donor of the ball:

E1 Two girls are each given a golden ball to play with. Their mother says that if they lose them they will be hanged. The elder accidentally sends hers into a blacksmith's shop (cf. n. 43). The blacksmith returns the ball, but warns her that he will not do so again. She loses it in the same way a second time, and receives a second warning. The third time the blacksmith keeps the ball, and she is sentenced to be hanged.

E2 A certain king had three children, one son and two daughters, to each of whom he presented a ball made of gold; whoever lost the ball was to be hanged. The elder daughter lost hers in a neglected garden thickly overgrown with weeds and brambles. Search proved unavailing, and she prepared to meet her fate.

E5 A rich lady possessed a golden ball, which she held in high esteem. A poor girl, her servant, had to clean the ball each day, under penalty of death if she lost it. One day when she was cleaning the ball near a stream it disappeared. The girl was condemned to die.

E14 A king had three daughters. He gave each a golden ball to play with, which they were never to lose. The youngest lost hers, and was to be hung on the gallows-tree if it were not found by a day named.

E20 There were three sisters named Pepper, Salt, and Mustard. Their father went on a journey and promised to bring back whatever they asked for; each asked for a golden ball. Their mother threatened to hang them if they lost their balls. Pepper lost hers, and her mother hanged her. [In this unusual version, the dead girl and her lover are turned into birds, after which she is restored to life and they resume human shape.]

Here the golden ball is the gift of human parents, so that the parallel is closer to the ball-lost-in-courtyard syndrome. But the punishment is imposed by the donor, not the finder, and it is death, not involvement in subsequent adventures. For such a configuration there is no traditional analogue.

Still another inconsistent aspect is the sex of the loser of the ball, who in the traditions cited earlier was always male. Here, however, a parallel is immediately available in four eastern European variants of "Iron Henry" or "The Frog Prince" (AaT 440, *KHM* 1). A king gives his daughter a golden ball to play with, as in E2 and E14; the ball rolls away from her into a fountain, and is restored to her by a frog, who exacts in return a promise that he may sleep in her bed and dine off her plate (as in the dominant lost ball tradition). This version of the tale is extremely rare in oral tradition, for the lost object is usually a ring or a handkerchief;[45] in an even more generally known version, the one known to Sir Walter Scott,[46] the girl is sent to get water from the well. Nevertheless, the then-unique "lost golden ball" version was the one chosen by the Brothers Grimm for inclusion in the first edition of their *Kinder- und Hausmärchen*, and it appeared in the English translations of that work by Edgar Taylor,[47] Lucy Crane,[48] Mrs. H. B. Paull and Mr. L. A. Wheatley,[49] and Mrs. Edward Lucas.[50]

Since the losing of a ball has in the legend and tale traditions outside the ballad complex been invariably associated with a male protagonist, and since this version of "The Frog Prince" is as exotic in oral tradition as it is widely circulated in print, Grimm's *Household Tales* in English translation is inescapably the most probable source for the lost golden ball, given to a daughter by her parents, of our "Gallows Tree" variants. Like Gilchrist and Broadwood, Hedwig von Beit attempted to interpret the ball in the Grimm tale as a symbol of lost virginity (*Symbolik*, II, 36–37). Even if the version were genuinely traditional, however, her interpretation could apply only to the lost ball as the equivalent of the rose-gathering syndrome discussed earlier, that is, as emblematic of the *readiness* to abandon virginity.

Surrounding tradition makes it quite clear that the relationship of golden balls to sexuality is at most a tenuous and secondary one.[51] Psychologically balls in folklore can be said to represent in broad terms the individuality or selfhood of a human being (von Beit, *Symbolik*, II, 36–37; *HDA*, V, 757). Guiding and wealth-conferring balls bestowed upon mortals by supernatural beings may in these broad terms stand for the release of unsuspected powers in the personality, and balls that are lost can only mean a corresponding loss of control over subsequent events.

The lost key of three group E variants (E6, E8, E9) was also equated by Broadwood with loss of virginity. She cited "an old song" containing the lines, "Oh, if my love were a coffer of gold, / and I the keeper of the key" in evidence; but another "old song" shows that the referent for the key is not quite what she considered it to be:

Kytt hath lost her key, her key,
Good Kytt hath lost her key;
She is so sorry for the cause,
She wotts not what to say.

Good Kytt she wept, I ask'd why so
That she made all this mone?
She sayde, alas! I am so woo,
My key is lost and gone.

Kytt, why did you lose your key,
For sooth you were to blame,
Now every man to you will say,
Kytt Loss-key is your name.

Good Kytt she wept and cried, alas!
Her key she could not find,
In faith I trow in bowers she was
With some that were not kind.

Now, farewell, Kytt, I can no more,
I wott not what to say,
But I shall pray to God therefore
That you may find your key.

Kytt hath lost her key,
But I have one will fit
Her lock, if she will try.
And do not me deny,
I hope she hath more wit.

My key is bright, not rusty,
It is so oft applied
To locks that are not dusty,
Of maidens that are lusty,
And not full filled with pride.

Then, Kytt, be not too proud,
But try my ready key,
That still hath been allowed
By ladies fair a crowd
The best that ere they see.

You can but try, and then,
If it fits not, good bye;
Go to some other man,
And see if any can
Do better, Kytt, than I.

But never come back to me,
When you are gone away,
For I shall keep my key
For others, not for thee;
So either go, or stay.[52]

This manifestly bawdy symbol suggests that, properly understood, the thorns of the "Seeds of Love" song and the golden ball of the "Gallows Tree" variants might well refer not to the loss of virginity, but to an unwelcome chastity imposed by the male lover's withdrawal of his sexual favors. However, such an interpretation carries us very far indeed from the situation of "The Gallows Tree"; a more plausible, if disappointingly prosaic, explanation for the key figure may be found in its association in one text with "silken cloak." Both *silkekjole* "silken cloak" and *guldkjae'* "golden chain" are found among the possessions sought for ransom in the ballad's Scandinavian analogues, and the hypothesis of secondary, late, and sporadic borrowing from that tradition, with "key" a natural (and rhyming) substitution for *kjae'*, is sufficient to account for the phenomenon (*DGF*, VIII, 481).

Károly Kerényi and Clyde Kluckhohn have warned against the ascription of meaning to phenomenological symbols without taking careful account of the cultural and traditional context that alone can provide the articulation of that meaning.[53] In the materials here brought together we can see the value of their warning. Although the "prickly bush" is a verifiable symbol for rejection in love (at least when a rose bush is meant), the only connection that can be said to exist between the "golden ball" and sexuality is that which may occur if the finder of a lost golden ball should claim marriage as the price of its restoration. It may be argued that the nineteenth century, with its particularly repressive sexual taboos, could have given both symbols new meanings in the British Isles (see chap. iii, n. 65); but we have no record that this is true save that of the assertions of twentieth-century scholars, none of whom has furnished tangible supporting evidence. Again, it is perfectly true that individuals are capable of investing objects with meanings of considerable import to themselves (see Barry, "Folksinger," pp. 59–76); but such meanings are private, and cannot be described as traditional unless they can be shown to be shared with a substantial number of individuals in precisely the same relationship to their referents.

The informants for "Gallows Tree"—"golden ball" variants have borrowed heavily and indiscriminately from independent narrative traditions. Variant E1 is closely related to "Gille nan Cochla Craicionn"; E2 and E14, to the Grimm version of "The Frog Prince"; E7, to German legendry and to "The Youth Who Went Forth To Learn Fear"; and E20, to some versions of AaT 425 (*KHM* 88) "Beauty and the Beast," in which a departing father promises to bring his daughters anything they may request. In each of these instances, the lost golden ball figures quite simply as an attractive rationalization for the ballad situation, borrowed from a printed source rather than from oral tradition and patently lacking in specific symbolic content for the narrators.[54] On the other hand, E5, in which a servant loses the ball belonging to her mistress, is thematically very close to the variants in group C in which the imputed crime is theft; if the ballad can be said to have a tradition in this regard, then the ball in E5 has the same symbolic value of the cup, comb, watch, and thimble of those variants, namely that of a purportedly stolen object serving as a mechanism for justifying the death sentence.

A modern Irish folktale preserves the essence of the Welsh legend reported by Giraldus Cambrensis in the same death-penalty context:

A girl is kidnapped by the fairies and given the task of caring for their golden hurley-ball, but she loses it when a neighboring farmer discovers it in his field and walls it up in his chimney. Searching for the ball, she encounters the farmer, who woos and marries her. She dies a few days after the wedding, having fruitlessly explored the house for the missing ball. A mysterious tall man comes three times during the wake to ask the corpse if she has found the object; the third time, the priest asks what it is that he wants, the stranger explains, and the husband retrieves the ball from its hiding place and returns it to him. The priest demands that the stranger release the woman from her enchantment, and she is restored to life; the stranger disappears with the ball.[55]

It is obvious from these Celtic examples that supernatural beings whose golden balls are stolen or lost by mortals are both independent in folk tradition and quite capable of devising their own punishments without recourse to institutionalized legal procedures.

It is appropriate, then, to turn to the only symbols that are constant and inarguable in the ballad's texts: the gallows and the terms of ransom. It has been proposed that the tradition is not really concerned with ransom at all, but with the belief that a condemned man may be saved from the gallows if a woman can be found that is willing to marry him.[56] Ballads based on just such a theme can be found in both English[57] and German[58] tradition, together with variations in which a sister saves a brother by running naked three times around the gallows,[59] the executioner offers to marry the victim and is refused,[60] or the rescue is effected by an offer to substitute for the condemned person.[61] As Wilhelm Heiske and Hinrich Siuts have pointed out, the theme is an imaginative one—Siuts considered it "purely literary"—and based upon no actual custom.[62] In England, however, it is frequently bound up with precisely the situation of "The Gallows Tree": in "The Merchant of Chichester" (Chappell and Ebsworth, *Roxburghe Ballads*, I, 320–325) the lady saves the victim by marrying him only after

> The merchants of the town,
> From death to set him free,
> Did proffer there two thousand pound,
> But yet it would not be.

The same failure is reported in "The Downfall of William Grismond" (Chappell and Ebsworth, *Roxburghe Ballads*, VIII, 70–71, 145):

> But then my loving father his gold he did not spare,
> To save me from the Gallows; he had of me great care:
> But it would not be granted, the Gallows was my share.

Ballads in the Child corpus offer similar negative testimony. In Child 72 "The Twa Clerk's Sons o' Owsenford" (A and C texts) the father's query, "Will ye grant me my two sons' lives / Either for gold or fee?" is denied; Child 182 "The Laird o' Logie," 187 "Jock o' the Side," 191 "Hughie Grame," and 194 "The Laird o Wariston" all have variants in which "a' the gold o fair Scotland," "a' the monie o fair Scotland," "a peck of gold and silver," "five hundred pieces of gold," or "white monie and gold" are mentioned as insufficient to obtain the release of the culprit. Child 209 "Geordie," however, centers upon the pardoning of a condemned criminal through the payment of a ransom. In this respect it is echoed by Laws Q37 "The Turkish Factor" (a young woman condemned to die for striking her mistress is released when a hundred pounds are paid);[63] by "The Confession and Repentance of George Sanders" (Chappell and Ebsworth, *Roxburghe Ballads*, VIII, 72–75) in which a father three times casts himself into debt to save his son from the gallows; and by the stage song "Blueskin":

> When to the Old Bailey this Blueskin was led,
> He held up his hand; his indictment was read;
> Loud rattled his chains; near him Jonathan stood,
> And full forty pounds was the price of his blood;
> > Then hopeless of life
> > He drew his penknife,
> To make a sad widow of Jonathan's wife,
> But forty pounds paid her, her grief shall appease,
> And every man round me may rob if he please.[64]

It is not only in latter-day balladry, moreover, that executions may be averted by a payment in cash; the thirteenth-century *Havelok the Dane* twice refers to the possibility:

> Utlawes and theves made he bynde,
> Alle that he michte fynde,
> And heye hengen on galwe-tre;
> For hem ne yede gold ne fee.
>   [11.41–44]

> For yif ich havede ther ben funden,
> Havede ben slayn, or herde bunden,
> And heye ben henged on a tre,
> Havede go for him gold ne fe.
>   [11.1427–14.30][65]

And a unique manuscript of *The Seven Sages of Rome* includes a tale that has been found in no other written source and hence must have been supplied directly from oral tradition:

> Hyt was a squyer of thys contre,
> And full welle louyd was he;
> In dedys of armys and yn justyng
> He bare hym beste yn hys begynning.
> So hyt befelle he had a systur sone,
> That for silver he had nome,
> He was put in preson strong,
> And schulde be dampned and be hong.
> The squyer faste thedur can gon,
> And askyd them swythe anon,
> What thyng he had borne away,
> And they answered and can say
> He had stolen syluer grete plente,
> Therefore hanged schulde he bee.
> The squyer hym profurd, permafay,
> To be his borowe tyll a certen day
> For to amende that hy mysdede,
> Anon they toke hym yn that stede,
> And bounde hym faste fote and honde,
> And cast hym in to preson stronge.
> They let hys cosyn go a way
> To quyte hym be a certen daye.
> Grete pathes then usyd he,
> And men he slewe grete plente,
> Moche he stole and bare away,
> And stroyed the contre nyght and day.
> But upon the squyer thoght he nothyng
> That he in preson lefte lyeing.
> *To that tyme came, as y yow say,*
> *But for the squyer came no paye.*
> *He was hanged on a galowe tree,*
> For hym was dele and grete pyte.[66]
>   [My italics]

Except for the substitution motif in this narrative,[67] the account is strikingly reminiscent of the situation most frequently represented in "Gallows Tree" texts: the culprit is condemned for theft, but can escape the gallows if restitution is made. The "Blueskin" song suggests a possibility also attested in legal annals, that a condemned murderer may escape punishment if an agreed-upon sum is paid to the victim's family. So runs a writ issued in Scotland during the thirteenth century "to the relatives and friends of B., commanding them to relieve him from the poverty into which he has fallen, and to free him from the fine which he incurred for the death of a certain person imputed to him 'quantum ad eadem pertinet,'" and such cases have been documented for the reigns of Edward III, James I, and George III of England.[68]

There is, then, not a little evidence that the concept of ransom from the gallows by the payment of a sum of money was a recognized folk tradition in Britain from quite an early date, and that it was based at least in part upon actual legal practice. Crimes with which it is associated are murder and theft, the latter prevailing in the "Gallows Tree" tradition. Our conclusion that "Judge" antedates "hangman" in the tradition is supported by such evidence, in that fines can be arranged only with the sentencing magistrate; the removal of the setting to the gallows itself is explicable on the ground of surrounding tradition, in which rescue by means other than the payment of money is effected.[69]

A final word should be added on the subject of the death penalty as punishment for loss of chastity, since "The Gallows Tree" has been compared to Child 65 "Lady Maisry" and the heroine of that ballad is executed by her male relatives for becoming pregnant by an Englishman.[70] Medieval romance, the popular ballad, and legal history agree that adultery and fornication have been traditionally considered to be familial, or at most ecclesiastical, crimes;[71] that the classical punishment in such cases is burning, not hanging;[72] and the civil crime for which wayward damsels might be put to death is infanticide, not illicit love.[73]

There is, then, no reason to suppose "The Gallows Tree" to be the vehicle of sexual symbolism. The ballad dramatizes a familiar situation, dating from the early Middle Ages, but still a matter of easy reference in the seventeenth and eighteenth centuries: a criminal convicted of murder or theft could avoid the death penalty if his relatives were able to raise an agreed-upon sum of money before the date set for his execution. Although the tradition normally related to a male protagonist, nothing prevents its adaptation to the case of a woman, provided the crime itself and the surrounding circumstances remained constant. But that such an adaptation has ever been capable of converting the tradition to one of lost and restored virginity is belied both by the absence of traditional verification for any such interpretation of the symbols involved and by the tenacity with which the identification of the victim as male and the terms of rescue as "gold," "silver," and "money" "to pay a fee" have persisted in the ballad's oral tradition as opposed to the "tradition" that has heretofore been ascribed to it.

VI

THE TRADITION IN EUROPE

ALTHOUGH IT is not feasible to undertake here a thorough investigation of the European traditions related to "The Gallows Tree," it is equally impracticable to ignore the contributions of European scholars in regard to the ballad complex. This chapter will, therefore, consider the analyses and conclusions of those who have concentrated upon the Scandinavian, German, and Italian analogues of "The Gallows Tree" and offer an alternative hypothesis.

Most closely related geographically to "The Gallows Tree" are the Scandinavian versions, "Faestemand løskøber Faestemø" and "Den Bortsalda." In the ten texts furnished in *DGF*, VIII, 466–475, a girl is in a boat; in four, she is being taken to "a heathen land" ("Hedenske Lande"), in two to "Frieseland," and in three her parents have sold her for "a little piece of bread" ("et Stykke Brød") or "two barrels of gold" ("tio Tønder Guld"). A Swedish variant cited by Kempinnen changes this to "They sold me away for silver and gold, / To go to the heathen land" ("De sålde mig bort för silfer och gold, / Att komma till det hedniska landet"). She asks the helmsman to "wait" (see chap. iii, n. 11) because "here comes" (A, C, D) or "I am expecting" (E, F, G, H) a relative. (As in English tradition, it may be either the father or the mother who arrives first.) One Danish text (B) has "yonder I see my father" ("hist ser jeg min kaer Fader"); two Swedish variants quoted by Kempinnen have "I see my father coming" ("Ja ser min fader komma"). The sequence of relatives follows: the formula is "Oh, my . . . , you hold me so dear, / Sell your . . . and set me free here" ("O, min . . . , du haver mig saa kier, / du saelger dine . . . og løser mig her"). In a table representing twenty-seven variants (*DGF*, VIII, 451–452), the properties are itemized, the father being asked most often for land (fields or forests), the mother and sister for wearing apparel or jewelry, the brother for horses, and the lover for rings, crowns, or ships. In the texts in which she is being carried off to "a heathen land," the reply is uniformly "I have two [of the items in question]; I shall use one, and leave the other one alone" ("Jeg har ikke . . . foruden to, / Den ene skal jeg bruge, den anden skal staa"). Where it is specified that the parents have sold her, the reply is "Yes, I have some, one, two, three, four, five; / but I will not sell any of them to set you free" ("Ja, . . . jeg have en, to, tre, fire, fem, / Men ingen jeg maa saelge for at løse dig igen"). Although Erik Pohl thought that the first phrasing (two items) was probably a secondary simplification of the type (*"Losgekaufte,"* p. 117), Grüner-Nielsen tended to agree with Julius Krohn ("Mädchen," p. 113) that the marked incongruity of the rationalizing introduction of the latter (five items) indicates that it is this version which is secondary; furthermore, it predominates in Swedish variants, but is not to be found in those from the Faroe Islands, Iceland, or Germany (Krohn, "Mädchen," p. 123). Pohl, Grüner-Nielsen, and Krohn were in agreement that all Scandinavian variants were derived from the German version, which traveled first to Denmark ("heathen land," "wait," "I have two"), then to Norway and Sweden, and finally to Finland and Estonia, reaching the last-named countries at the end of the seventeenth century.[1]

Pohl pointed out, however, that the earliest text of record (1700) is from Iceland, and the variant quoted by Kempinnen differs slightly from the others:

> Wait, Friselanders, and Friselanders, wait
> My relatives will ransom me.
> "My good father, and good my father,
> Ransom me from the Frisians!"
> "My good daughter, and good my daughter,
> With what can you be ransomed?"
> "My good father and good my father,
> Pledge your fields to set me free."
> "My good daughter and good my daughter,
> I would rather have them than you."[2]

Could "The Gallows Tree" have been derived from this tradition? On the one hand, crucial distinctions between the impending death for the victim of the first and the (presumably) impending slavery for the victim of the second, and ransom in cash and ransom to be obtained by selling personal property, are not easily to be brushed aside. On the other hand, "set me free" is regular in both versions; "wait," occurring sporadically in Anglo-American texts, is regular here, while "I see my . . . coming," "daughter," and "silver and gold" appear occasionally. What this pattern suggests is not so much development of one version out of the other as it is the mutual contamination of two distinct types, as is predictable on the ground of the close and continuing relationships between Scandinavians and Northern Britons documented by Liestøl. Since in the Scandinavian version the property is to be sold, it may be inferred that the direct payment tradition is antecedent; the "set me free" that is common to both versions is likely to belong to a parent tradition. It is evident, however, that minor texual elements are more readily borrowed in translingual situations than are characteristic basic concepts.

Turning to "Die Losgekaufte," the German ballad claimed by Krohn, Grüner-Nielsen, and Pohl to be antecedent to the Scandinavian tradition, we find greater textual variation. Five variants published in the *Deutsche Liederhort* of Ludwig Erk and Franz Magnus Böhme have injunctions to the skipper to "halt" (78a), "halt dein Schiff" (78b), "Lass das Schiff zu Lande gahn" (78c), and to let the ship turn around or sink (78d, e, an injunction that is rhetorical and anticipates the response of the relatives). Of the four variants published by Georg Heeger and Wilhelm Wüst,[3] one also has "halt das Schiff," the other three the "wait" of Scandinavian and Anglo-American versions ("warte," "erwarte"). A text published by Karl Simrock[4] has "Halt"; another, from Alexander Reifferscheid's collection,[5] has "lass das Schifflein stille stehen," and still another, cited by Kempinnen (*Lunastettava neito*, p. 15) and published with slight variation by Raimund and Elizabeth Zoder,[6] has "wake up." A relationship can be seen between "halt" and "halt das Schiff" and Anglo-American "stop" and "hold your hand" or "hold the rope"; but the pattern of variation seems to be that of secondary development. In none of these variants is there "here comes" or "I see . . . coming," the characteristic line being "I still have a father" ("Ich habe noch ein Vater"); but in four of the texts in the Erk-Böhme collection, and with considerable regularity in the others cited, the stanza concludes with "der Vater angegangen kam." A single text, Erk-Böhme 78e, has "daughter"; but "set me free" occurs regularly as "löse mich" or "erlöse mich," and an alternative tradition has "save my young life" ("rett' mein junges Leben").

Relatives are asked to "pledge" or "pawn" ("setze, versetze") a single possession, rather than to "sell" a number of them as in Scandinavian variants; examining sixty-three texts in the Deutsche Volksliedarchiv, Georgios Megas found this verb in all but six, which had "give."[7] A single exception is that of Erk-Böhme 78d, a variant of the text composed by Annette von Droste-Hülshoff and featuring the rescue of the doomed girl by virtue of the lover's selling himself to the galleys ("verkaufe dich ans Ruder")[8]

The ransom asked from the father is most frequently a "cloak," a "hat," or "house and land"; the last named corresponds to the uniform request in Scandinavian variants, and was considered by Pohl to be the primary tradition in German tradition as well (*"Losgekaufte,"* p. 38); because "cloak" is statistically dominant, however, Megas thought "house and land" to be an intrusion ("Losgekauften," p. 67).

The mother is also asked for a garment, the sister for a garment or a piece of jewelry (often a crown), and the brother for a horse (as in Scandinavian texts) or a sword. The lover's assets may be a horse, a sword, or a ring (Megas, "Losgekauften," p. 68; Pohl, *"Losgekaufte,"* p. 38).

Pohl argued that the persistence of horse and sword in in both German and Finnish-Estonian variants, while a sword never figures in Scandinavian texts, proved that the German ballad was the source for both Scandinavian and Finnish-Estonian types (*"Losgekaufte,"* p. 300). "Wait," "house and land," and the approach of the relatives to the place of jeopardy could also be considered original with German tradition. The "horse" and "sword" assigned so much importance by Pohl, moreover, suggest a means by which the tradition of ransom in cash might have been converted into ransom by pawning personal possessions ("setze," "versetze"), which in turn was converted into "sell" ("saelge") in Scandinavian texts. "Ross" and "Schwert" are colloquial terms for two silver coins that circulated in Germany, "Ross" from the beginning of the seventeenth century, and "Schwert" from the fifteenth; the epithets are descriptive of the characteristic emblems stamped upon the coins.[9] "Setze" is applicable to money as well as to possessions, although "versetze" refers only to the pawning of goods.[10] Early texts in which a number of "Rösser" or "Schwerter" were to be "setzen" could thus have been responsible for the entire cycle of North Germanic variants involving the pledging or pawning of objects.

This hypothesis is not one that can be insisted upon solely on the basis of the Germanic traditions with which we are now concerned. However, another puzzling feature of "Die Losgekaufte" is the consistent response of the victim's relatives to the effect that the ship is to be either turned around or sunk, and that the maiden is to be drowned: "lass das Schiff rumme [herum] gahn, / lass das Mädchen to [zu] Grunne gahn" (Erk-Böhme 78d, Reifferscheid, *Westfälische Volkslieder,* p. 5), or "Lass nur sinken! Die schöne ... die soll ertrinken" (Erk-Böhme 78b, c, e; Heeger and Wust, *Rheinpfalz,* p. 25; Zoder, "Das Volkslied,"

p. 397; Simrock, *Deutschen Volkslieder*, p. 39). There are traces, then, if not wholly comprehensible ones, of the ballad situation in "The Gallows Tree" that are present here and absent from Scandinavian variants: ambiguous names for coins ("silver") and the fact that the victim's life and not merely her freedom is at stake.

Because of the German ballad's dramatic quality and lack of a regular rhyme scheme, Henry Sager concluded that "Die Losgekaufte" owed its very existence to an original *Kunstlied* such as the version composed by poetess Annette von Droste-Hülshoff.[11] Such a possibility is supported by the investigations of Hinrich Siuts ("Volkslieder unserer Tage," pp. 67–84), Holger Nygard ("Middle Ages," pp. 85–96), and Branford P. Millar.[12] Megas ("Losgekauften," pp. 69–72) claimed a traditional origin for "Die Losgekaufte," but asserted that the German version was the source of the entire pan-European tradition and that both ransom in cash and the life jeopardy of the victim were secondary developments. Pohl ("*Losgekaufte*," pp. 315–323) and Grüner-Nielsen (*DGF*, VIII, p. 465) argued, however, that "The Gallows Tree" and "Die Losgekaufte" were both derived directly, and independently, from a Mediterranean pirate kidnapping tradition.

The most widely known version in the Mediterranean tradition is "Scibilia Nobili," honored by Child (II, 346) as "the best of the cycle." Its story is a complicated one. A woman is kidnapped in her husband's absence. He pursues her abductors and offers them her weight in gold, but they refuse to bargain with him. He is, however, permitted to speak with her, and consults her about the feeding of their child. When he departs, she refuses food and drink because of her worry over the infant, and finally leaps into the sea, but the pirates pull her aboard again. The ransom stanzas follow. When she is safely at home, her father dies and she puts on a red dress; for her mother's death she wears yellow, for her brother's green, and for her sister's white. Only when her husband dies does she consent to wear black (see chap. iii, n. 2).[13]

The opening stanza of the ransom sequence differs radically from those in the Germanic traditions thus far examined. The heroine asks if the wind is from the south or the north, in which case it will carry her to her father:

> Marinaru, marina marona
> Sammi a diri chi ventu fa,
> S'è sciloccu o tramuntana
> Nni mì patri mi purtirò.

There is no connection to be ascertained between the universal approach of the relatives ("I see ... coming," "her kommer," "... ergangen kam") in Germanic tradition and the approach of the victim and her captors ("nni mì patri mi purtirò") here.[14] Nor is there any sign of "hold your hand," "halt das Schiff," "stop," or "wait/tøfver/erwarte." Similarly, in the second stanza the heroine does not demand ("saelge," "versetze") her ransom, but inquires, "do you want to ransom me?" ("miu caru patri, mi vuliti riscattari?"). This is reminiscent of the English "have you any?" or "have you brought?"; but his reply, although it has the "daughter" found sporadically in all Germanic versions, is that heretofore found only in the Icelandic text: "My dear daughter, how much is your ransom?" ("mia cara figghia, quantu è lu ricàttitu tò?"). She answers, "three lions, three falcons, four columns of gold" ("tri liuna, tri farcuna, quattru culonni chi d'oru su' "). His final response is "I cannot lose so much money; it is better to lose you!" ("non pozzu perdiri ssi dinari, quantu e megghiu ti perdi tu!").

The only difference between this text and the one from Iceland is in the "wait; my relatives will ransom me" of the injunction and the "pledge your fields" of the request. The two versions show that a quite literal translation is feasible even between Italian and Icelandic; but they show, too, that it is in minor features that relationships are to be sought. "Pledge your fields," then, indicates that Megas was wrong about the place of "Haus und Hof" in the history of the German ballad, and that "versetze" and "Haus und Hof" belong to an early stage of that version. The correspondence seen here argues that in a still earlier stage the ransom was in cash.

"Scibilia Nobili" cannot be cited as wholly representative of that earlier stage, for the coins named in its text are both ambiguous and strange. "Lions" may refer to a Venetian silver coin first issued in the late seventeenth century (Frey, *Numismatic Names,* p. 133); to golden coins issued much earlier in England, Scotland, and France (Frey, *Numismatic Names,* pp. 135–136); or to coins of little worth ("Löwenpfennige," "Löwenheller") struck in Germany during the fifteenth century. "Falcons" are probably the golden "Falkendukat" or the silver "Falkenthaler" struck in Brandenburg in the eighteenth century (Frey, *Numismatic Names,* p. 81). "Columns of gold" can only be the sixteenth-century Spanish coin (of silver, not gold) stamped with two crowned pillars rising from the sea (Frey, *Numismatic Names,* p. 51). "Four columns of gold," therefore, would be two such coins, although the more valuable metal is substituted; however the names are interpreted, the resemblance of this enumeration to the "gold and silver and money" of "Gallows Tree" texts A26 and A28 is striking, and indicative of secondary elaboration.

Bronzini has demonstrated precisely to what extent "Scibilia Nobili" was a derived tradition. An Albanian legend tells of a woman enticed on board a ship by the promise of silken garments for sale; in despair over her shame and the separation from her child, she leaped overboard and drowned herself (Bronzini, *Canzone Epico-lirica,* pp. 279–288, with several variants cited). Except for the silk-selling motivation, the narrative corresponds in detail with the narrative introduction to "Scibilia Nobili," and explains why, in that ballad, an initial offer of ransom on the part of the victim's husband is refused although the pirates seem quite willing to bargain later—an illogicality like that of the parents' sale of their daughter in the Swedish type. The Albanian legend, in turn, is a version of a tradition of wide distribution in the Balkans and traced to medieval France by Vargyas: to escape her captors, who threaten to ravish her, a girl throws herself into the water (usually the Danube river) and drowns herself (Vargyas, *Medieval History,* pp. 42–47). It has been shown that this tradition was adapted to a Maltese local legend of the fourteenth century, and set in ballad form from one to two hundred years later;[15] the ransom stanzas, belonging to an independent tradition, could only have been added afterwards, and the "Falkendukat," not coined before the eighteenth century, suggests that the amalgamation occurred at a point when the independent tradition was already well developed.

Three Spanish ballads show the mutual attraction of these motifs, and provide another analogue to the Icelandic version. In one, the heroine is enticed aboard ship by the promise of silks for sale, is carried off, asks to be returned to shore because she is seasick ("Mariner, bon mariner—portaume á terra; que á mi 'ls ayres de la mar—me 'n donan pena"), but discovers that her captor is the son of the King of England, who has sailed the seas for seven years looking for her.[16] In the second the quest for silks figures again, as does the seasickness ("Mariner, bon mariner, portàume en terra, que las onas de la mar me donan pena"). As in "Scibilia Nobili," however, this text asks the kidnappers to take her where her father is, turning the ship to do so ("Voltàu la nàu que plorant và; duisme en el port hont pare està"). The ransom stanzas are as in "Scibilia Nobili" and the Icelandic version: "My father, do you want to ransom me? The Moors are selling me" ("mon pare, hem voleu quitá? Moros me venen"). "My daughter, tell me, tell me, for how much are they selling you?" ("ma filla, digàu, digàu, per cuant vos venen"). "My father, for a hundred escudos [golden coin, first issued in the sixteenth century (Frey, *Numismatic Names*, p. 79)] I am yours" ("mon pare, per cent escuts vostra seria"). "My daughter, for one menudo [copper coin, first issued in the middle of the seventeenth century (Frey, *Numismatic Names*, p. 148)] I would not ransom you" (ma filla, per un menut no us quiteria").[17]

The third variant from Spain is exactly like the second, except that the introductory stanzas defining the situation are absent; it begins, "turn the ship, turn it, go toward the shore that is receding" ("volta barqueta, voltarás ma, veurás la platja, que llunyantse va").[18]

Icelandic and Romance traditions are therefore very close, in their question-and-answer sequence and in the suggestion that the child is not worth the amount asked. The "wait" and "pledge your fields" of the Icelandic version, however, indicates that, as with British and Scandinavian types, an interpenetration of two versions has occurred; when these are compared with an Estonian variant in which the girl also asks that she be taken to where her parents are, and the ransom is three different objects from each relative (with no "house and land"),[19] one realizes that the Northern European tradition is not so simple as it might at first appear.

Twenty-three Italian variants published in 1929 by Michele Barbi offer still other alternatives.[20] Two of them (A and Z) attest the ballad attached to "Scibilia Nobili"; the ransom is, respectively, "due leoni con due falconi e una borsa [purse] di oro sta" and "du liuna, du farcuna, e tant' oru ch'è bello di ochiù [as much gold as is good to see]."[21] A third demonstrates the process of substituting livestock for names of coins meaningless to the singer; the B-text asks for "three roosters, three capons, three columns of gold" ("tre gallini, tre caponni, tre colonne d'oro fa"). But instead of an address to the ship's personnel, this variant, like the remaining twenty, has the line, "She sent word to her father/mother" (the order varies in the same way that it does in other traditions): "manda a dire," "manda a chiama." There is no indication of the approach of the relatives, and the verb is not "set me free" but "take out" ("cavare") or "take away" ("levare"). Similarly, no ransom is specified, although in four texts (C, L, O, V) the relatives reply that "per lei quattrini [copper coin, first noted in the fifteenth century (Frey, *Numismatic Names*,

p. 195)] non ha," and in two (N, S) it is a "denar" [equivalent to French "denier," Roman "denarius," but always a debased coin of little worth (Frey, *Numismatic Names*, pp. 63–64)] that they cannot spare for her benefit.

In A, the relatives tell the mariners to "turn" the ship ("volgetela"), in B, E, and K to "pull it away" ("tiratela"), corresponding to the "rumme gahn" of some German variants. C, D, and I, however, have a command corresponding to the "lass sie ertrinken" found in all German texts, "throw her in the sea!" ("spingetela," "Buttatela"). A variant collected in the United States in the twentieth century suggests the origin of such a response, and indicates that the German texts in which the ship is also to sink are secondary to the tradition represented by turning the ship and letting the girl drown.

The informant for the American version reported that the girl's jeopardy was due to her inability to pay her fare.[22] The text, however, not only reflects the ransom-formula of "Scibilia Nobili" ("tre leoni, tre vapori [steamships?], tre colonni di oro cià") and the "manda a dire" of all Italian texts unrelated to "Scibilia Nobili" but also features "let her drown" ("affondátelà"). The address to her persecutors is as significant as it is unique in reported tradition: "Sailors, don't drown me, for the storm is not coming now!" ("marinari, non mi affondati, che la tempesta non viene adesso!"). The tradition represented in these Italian and German variants, then, is recognizable as the one that figures in Child 24 "Bonnie Annie," Child 57 "Brown Robyn's Confession," Laws K22 "Captain Glen," and Laws N10 "The Silk Merchant's Daughter": a threatening storm can be averted by the sacrifice of someone aboard the ship to the waves.

In a study of the motif (D2136.8 in S. Thompson's *Motif-Index*), Lutz Röhrich distinguished two types, in one of which the storm is invoked by the presence on the ship of a person guilty of an unconfessed crime (of this type is the Old Testament account of Jonah as well as that of "Brown Robyn's Confession" and "Captain Glen"); in the second ("Bonnie Annie," "The Silk Merchant's Daughter") any human sacrifice, chosen by drawing lots or by the appointment of the youngest or most important person, will appease the elements.[23] In Röhrich's opinion, the first type is the consequence of Judaeo-Christian rationalization of a more ancient belief in the appeasement of malevolent nature deities through human sacrifice, since in these legends and ballads the guilty person regularly confesses, accepts his immolation, and is saved by divine intervention. A trace of the older tradition lingers in the identification of the guilty person by casting lots (Jonah 1:7); in "The Silk Merchant's Daughter" and in a Byzantine Greek romance,[24] an innocent person is selected by the same procedure. In the early medieval Japanese *Kojiki*, a wife volunteers to drown in her husband's place to avert a storm.[25] (According to Esther Hibbard, such a substitution motif was as conventional in Japanese literature of this period as it was in the West;[26] see chap. v, nn. 66–67.)

A version of the ballad in which this is the basis for the victim's jeopardy and the ransom is in cash may, therefore, be legitimately inferred as the origin of all German variants ("let her drown!") in which the victim is ransomed by the pawning of personal possessions, as well as of all Romance variants in which the drowning motif has been supplanted by a localized pirate-kidnapping tradition but the ransom remains in cash. The Scandinavian tradition thus appears to be a late one, and to have come under three separate influences: the pirate capture of Spain and Italy (most clearly distinguishable in the Icelandic version); the ransom by pledging personal possessions of Germany (that the "saelge" universal in Danish and Swedish variants is secondary to German "versetze" is also indicated by Icelandic "gjalter"); and certain verbal formulations from Scots-English tradition ("wait a while," "I see . . . coming").

Returning to the Italian tradition, we find still unexplained the "manda a dire" that is characteristic and has no analogue thus far; it is the more puzzling since these texts regularly place the heroine "nel mezzo al mare." Eleven others, however, place her not on a ship but "in prigione"; in K, L, M, R, S, she does not know "per qual ragione" or "cagione" ("for what reason"), but also in M as well as in L and V it is for "a bunch of violets" or "a bunch of rings" that she has presumably stolen. Two of these also refer to the "quattrino" that the girl is not worth (L, V); but V has the first parallel to "The Gallows Tree" in the phrasing of the request: "She sent to ask her father if he had a quadrinello to take her out from there" ("manda a chiama lo suo padre, se aveva un quadrinello per cavarie un po' di là"; compare "have you any gold, gold to set me free?").

Both the "drowning" texts and the "prison" texts in Barbi's collection invariably feature the "refusal to mourn" stanzas that made up the third section of the "Scibilia Nobili" amalgamated text. Since in many of them the ransom stanzas are perfunctory, it seems certain that, while "Scibilia Nobili" borrowed from this tradition, it, too, is an amalgamation, and the ransom stanzas were again borrowed from elsewhere (Bronzini, *Canzone Epico-lirica,* pp. 290, 296).[27]

Erik Pohl proposed the German "Edelman und Schäfer" (Erk-Böhme 43) as the probable source (Pohl, *"Losgekaufte,"* p. 310); Megas (*"Losgekauften,"* p. 70) considered "Edelmann und Schäfer" to be a derivative of "Die Losgekaufte." In a pattern by now all too familiar, Pohl and O. J. Brill, whose study of "Edelmann und Schäfer" embraced sixty-five variants,[28] agreed that the ransom stanzas were intrusive in the "Edelmann und Schäfer" tradition. As has been noted (see chap. iii n. 53), one form that the ballad situation may take is that the relatives do not refuse the ransom, but offer it willingly; this is true of all eight of the Erk-Böhme texts and of one published by Leopold Haupt and Johan E. Schmaler.[29] In two others in the Haupt and Schmaler collection, however, the usual situation obtains. Although both ask for property ("Versetz' ein Halbhundert der Schafe, zwei Kühe, ein Goldfuchs [again the ambiguous coin],[30] ein lündischer Rock, ein Korallenschnur," "Verkaufe zwei Rappen [black steeds], zwei Kühe, ein lündischer Rock, ein silberne Ring" [Haupt and Schmaler, *Wenden,* I, 107–110]), one also has the "I would rather have them than you" formula of "Scibilia Nobili" and the Icelandic text ("Der Shaf' ein Halbhundert viel lieber mir sind / Als du mir bist, mein ungehorsam Sohn"). The other includes a reflection on the worthlessness of the victim paralleling that of other Italian and Spanish variants ("Wenn du, mein Söhnlein, was nütze wärst, / Würdst du im Dresdener Gefangniss nicht sein").

The story in these texts is of a young man who is thrown into prison by a nobleman for dressing above his station. One text agrees with Italian tradition in that "junker Bursch schrieb seinem Vater daheim" ("he wrote home to his father"), but in most of them (with no regular formulation) it is said in impersonal narrative that the parent (father or mother) learned of the son's trouble and went ("gieng," "fuhr") to the prison. One of the texts in which the relatives refuse the ransom, however, has "Ich sehe, ich höre, mein Vater kommt hier," another startlingly precise correspondence with "The Gallows Tree" ("I see, I hear, my father comes here"). The other ends when the sweetheart (asked to sell a silver ring) hurried to the prison and "löst ihn mit Silber und löst ihn mit Gold." All of these texts have "to set me free," here "auslösen."

The ballad text that became associated with "Edelmann und Schäfer," therefore, was very like the ballad text that became associated with the refusal-to-mourn tradition in Italy—and may have been even more like the one that became associated with "Mary Hamilton," "Hugh of Lincoln," and "The Tale of the Golden Ball" in England and Scotland. The common denominator is imprisonment. Ransom in cash, missing from Italian prison variants, "Die Losgekaufte," and Scandinavian tradition, is present in Italian and Spanish pirate-kidnapping versions and in the Anglo-American tradition. The circumstance that the relatives come to the victim, rather than having to be sought out, is missing from all Mediterranean versions but present in all Germanic ones. (That is to say, the logical development of pirate-capture versions, that the ship must return to the shore in order for ransom to be obtained, is omitted from most Northern ballads in which a ship figures.) Although each of the localized traditions we have considered has achieved a *Normalform* in which no massive resemblance of one to another can any longer be discerned, a type can with assurance be extrapolated from them in which a man is in prison and about to be hanged, his relatives come to the prison (probably in response to a letter), and he asks them for "gold and silver to set me free."[31]

This far no commentator on the ballad cycle has been willing to go. In his headnote to "The Gallows Tree," Child cited three Slavic ballads in which an imprisoned man writes to his relatives for ransom; in two of them the ransom is in differentiated property, and in one of these the sweetheart's ransom is her "white hand" (Child, II, 349–350). Another of the same general description is added in a supplementary note (Child, II, 514). To these, however, he attached no importance.

Grüner-Nielsen collected eleven such variants from eastern European tradition; eight of them ask for differentiated properties, but "white hand" occurs as the mother's (refused) request in one, and three, from Lithuania and Yugoslavia, ask for sums of money (two hundred Thaler, four hundred pieces of gold, three hundred pieces of gold [*DGF*, VIII, 461]). Grüner-Nielsen commented upon the similarity of this group to the English and Italian ballad situations, and that a male rather than a female seemed to be characteristic of the type (*DGF*, VIII, 463), but concluded that the syndrome was secondary (*DGF*, VIII, 465). Although Megas noted that "Die Losgekaufte" was not found in the western coastal provinces of Germany, he could not accept either eastern provenance or an antecedent prison setting for it ("Losgekauften," pp. 70–72). Erik Pohl was prepared to acknowledge that the seven variants (one Polish, six Russian) collected by him in which ransom from prison was effected by the payment of a sum of money could not have been derived from surrounding traditions with ransom by differentiated properties

("*Losgekaufte*," pp. 288–289). Nevertheless, he, too, found it impossible to enter-
tain the hypothesis that the situation was precisely the opposite.

A Slovakian variant deserves translation:

> "A cow out there in the meadow killed your finest peacock."
> And without delay the lords hastened to hold trial.
> Johann—so the judgment commanded—was cast immediately into a dungeon.
> Into the prison they took him, surrounded him with high walls;
> There he lay in strict custody; the water below him was deep.
> In haste he wrote to his father, a letter with these lines:
> "God's blessing on you, Father, set me free from here!"
> "Dear son, if I only knew how much I must pay for you."
> "Four hundred pieces of red money, as many of white."[32]

This text displays the "trial scene, with judge and jury" insisted upon by one
"golden ball" informant (see Gilchrist and Broadwood, "Children's Game-Songs,"
p. 233) and implied by "Judge" and its derivatives in other "Gallows Tree" texts;
the "set me free" found almost universally in the cycle, no matter what variant
forms are associated with it; "gold and silver," explicitly present in "The Gallows
Tree" and implicitly so in the coin differentiation of "Scibilia Nobili"; and the
letter-writing syndrome of "Edelmann und Schäfer" and Italian "prison" and
"drowning" variants. Other Eastern European versions may be summarized as
follows:

1. Ransom in differentiated properties

   a. Latvian

   A young man writes to his father and asks him to sell his horse and buy him
   out of military service (mother, her cow; brother, his land; sister, her dowry;
   sweetheart, her wreath).[33]

   b. Persian

   A girl sits upon a bench in a room, surrounded by Tatars. "Father, my
   father, set me free here!" "Daughter, my daughter, with what should I set
   you free?" "Father, my father, with your horse!" "Daughter, my daughter,
   you are not worth a horse!"[34]

   c. Slovenian

   A poor soldier lies imprisoned in a tower. "Father, my dearest, set me free
   from the prison!" "Son, my beloved, what must be given for you?" "It is not
   much to give: your three black horses." "Son, my beloved, it is too much to
   give!" (mother, three white castles; brother, three bright rifles; sister, three
   fair tresses; sweetheart, her white hand).[35]

2. Ransom unspecified

   a. Russian

   A boy sits in prison and writes to his father and mother. "Oh, my good
   master, beloved father, Oh, my mistress, beloved mother! Buy your son free,
   your own son, your beloved child!" His father and mother refuse, his relatives all say to him, "There have never been thieves in our family, never

thieves, never robbers." He writes to his sweetheart and gives the letter to a swallow to be delivered. She immediately stirs herself: "Up, mother, father, my faithful maidservant! Quickly bring me the golden key, open the ornamented box, take out all my bright gold, and buy my friend free!"[36]

b. Russian

The boy sits in a dark tower, in chains. He leaps up from his bed and writes to his friends. "Bold friends, dear friends, true comrades, Up! and loose my bands, Up! and break my chains, Up! and loosen my bonds; release me, oh, release me with money, give, oh, give me freedom!" They laugh and say, "Little fool, why do you write such stupid lines, foolish words, a useless letter? You call us friends in vain, your comrades quite in vain. We, as free men, have nothing in common with prisoners." His sweetheart rejects him on the same terms; but his mother assembles all her possessions and gives him freedom.[37]

c. Serbian

A well-dressed young girl is captured. When they come to the sea, she bathes herself, and her face begins to shine like the sun. Sime Latinine looks at her and beckons her to him, but she says, "Hold your hand, you Rumanian shepherd. Maidens are not reared for you, but for the Pash of Bosnia." He answers, "My dear soul, I will sell my white towers, and I will buy you with my companions, and I will take you to white Venice, and I will sell you to the Doge." She responds, "You soldier, you Sime Latinine, don't sell your white towers and buy me with your companions, for there will come three ransoms for me: one from my father, one from my uncle, and one from my beloved Pash of Bosnia." A letter comes from her father: "My daughter, gypsy, don't depend upon me, your father cannot buy you free." So with her uncle; but her sweetheart writes: "Dear brother in God, Sime Latinine, if you have not kissed the maiden I will send you three loads of goods and a chair of pure gold, and when we meet, my brother, we shall exchange better gifts."[38]

d. Lithuanian

The young man is imprisoned in a castle or tower. He asks his father, mother, brother, and sister to redeem him. They refuse to help him, because they love their fortune more than him. Sometimes they are trying to redeem him, but without success. The sweetheart only is ready to redeem him by selling her ring or wreath.[39]

e. Turkish

Mahmud is condemned to prison; his parents refuse to buy him free, but his wife gives her pearls for him.[40]

3. Ransom specified

a. Hungarian Gypsy

A woman walking in the forest with her child meets four robbers, who demand that she sleep with all four of them before the next sunrise. She has a pet raven, and says to it,

> "Raven, raven, fly home!
> Tell the house of my father
> That four robbers have captured me,
> They want one hundred *Gulden*.

> "Father, father come quickly!
> For captured is your child.
> And four robbers want to have
> One hundred *Gulden* by tonight!"

> "Raven, raven, fly quickly,
> Say to my poor child:
> One hundred *Gulden* is a lot of money,
> And my house is not well provided."

Her mother also refuses, but her husband comes and kills the robbers.[41]

b. Serbian

A sister sends word to her brother, "Brother! I have been taken by the Turks, buy me free from Turkish slavery! The ransom they demand is small, three *Litra's* [ancient Sicilian coin corresponding to the Roman pound (Frey, *Numismatic Names,* p. 136)] of gold, two sacks of pearls." The brother sends in answer: "I need the gold to furbish my horses, so they will do me honor when I ride. I need the pearls to adorn my sweetheart, so that she will be beautiful when I kiss her." The sister writes again: "I am not a Turkish slave, but a Turkish Sultana, Brother!"[42]

The range of distribution of this ballad type (captivity, exchange of messages, ransom) shows that its provenance must be eastern European: Italy, Germany, Czechoslovakia, Poland,[43] Russia, Lithuania, Latvia, Yugoslavia, and Turkey. It is not, however, the only eastern European type. Erich Seemann found eleven different versions of the theme (jeopardy, successive appeals to relatives in vain, rescue by beloved) in Lithuania alone;[44] Erik Pohl distinguished two principal groups in addition to the ransom type, rescue from drowning and rescue by removing a snake from the victim's bosom ("*Losgekaufte,*" pp. 241–242), and to these Grüner-Nielsen added a third, relief from thirst by bringing water (*DGF,* VIII, 461–462).

Western European traditions are not so varied. Spanish balladry yields two, rescue-from-pirates-by-cash-payment and relief-from-thirst.[45] Italy has three (excluding the refusal-to-mourn syndrome, which as we have seen [see chap. iii, n. 2] is of independent derivation): rescue-from-pirates-by-cash-payment, rescue-from-drowning, and rescue-from-prison. Germany has two, rescue-from-drowning-by-pawning-possessions and rescue-from-prison with both cash-payment and pawning/selling-possessions. Anglo-American and Scandinavian traditions have one each: rescue-from-execution-by-cash-payment and rescue-from-pirates-by-selling-possessions. Spanish and Italian exemplars show that the drowning and thirst motifs indigenous to eastern Europe did circulate in the West if only to a limited extent. But all western European versions in which ransom figures (pirate, execution, or imprisonment, and whether the ransom is directly in cash or obtained by pawning or selling posessions) can only have been derived from the rescue-from-prison-by-cash-ransom that is one of several developments in the Slavic- and Finno-Ugric-speaking area. "The Gallows Tree," as Grüner-Nielsen came very near acknowledging, is, with its male victim, punishment at official hands, approach of the relatives, and appeal for "gold and silver to set me free," more closely related in detail to the parent tradition as it can be extrapolated from both Eastern and Western variants than is any other manifestation of the tradition in the West, and on both verbal and structural evidence is extremely unlikely to have been derived from any intermediary western European version.[46]

There is but one plausible explanation for the Western distribution of these three forms of the eastern European tradition (thirst, drowning, ransom): the invasion of western Europe by Gypsies, who came to the Balkans at the beginning of the fourteenth century and fled that area to escape Turkish persecution during the fifteenth.[47]

The dearth of a native narrative song tradition among Gypsies has been commented upon by many investigators.[48] The ease with which they acquire the languages of the peoples among whom they travel has also been attested.[49] When Laura Smith went in search of ballads among the English Gypsies, she found Romany versions of "Little Sir Hugh," "The Cruel Mother," and "Shule Aggrah."[50] Herrmann collected a prose version of the rescue-from-snakebite ballad in their own tongue from Gypsies in Siebenbürgen ("Liebesprobe," pp. 41–42); Rosenfeld reported that the Gypsies of Bukowina sang, again in their own tongue, almost precisely literal translations of Bulgarian and Rumanian ballads ("Lieder der Zigeuner," p. 830).

Gypsies were first taken notice of in Germany in 1414, in Italy in 1422, and in France in 1427 (Clébert, *Tziganes,* pp. 103, 55, 64). It is believed by some that Gypsies had appeared in the British Isles by the middle of the fifteenth century,[51] but the first clear documentation of their presence is to be found in Scottish annals for April 22, 1505, and Henry T. Crofton has observed that this date coincides with the expulsion of the nomads from Spain in 1492, from Germany in 1500, and from France in 1504.[52]

The prison-ransom ballad could, then, have been carried by Gypsies from the Balkans directly to Italy, Germany, and England at any time during the fifteenth and sixteenth centuries, to be amalgamated with or converted into oikotypal traditions in the manner that we have seen. In England, however, as elsewhere, the visitors appear to have been shunned or isolated before the beginning of the seventeenth century.[53] At that time, coincidentally with heightened persecution and repression on the Continent,[54] the English attitude toward Gypsies became a hospitable one.

Eric Winstead's examination of the records for the County of Hertford for the period 1581–1698 showed that Gypsies *qua* Gypsies were prosecuted in that region only once, toward the end of the century, and that prosecutions for vagrancy in general were "astonishingly few."[55] In 1650, Matthew Hales commented that the only case known to him of Gypsies' having been condemned to death had occurred some twenty years earlier in Suffolk.[56] In 1608, Thomas Dekker published *Lan-*

thorne and Candlelight, which included a dictionary of Gypsy slang;[57] most of its terms were utilized by Ben Jonson in his masque *The Metamorphosed Gypsy* in 1621,[58] and two years later another play appeared romanticizing the Gypsy people, Middleton and Rowley's *The Spanish Gypsy.*[59]

Corresponding relaxation of popular attitudes did not take place in other European countries until the following century. I propose, therefore, that "The Gallows Tree," adaptable as it was to native tradition regarding the evasion of execution by payment of a fee or a bribe and perhaps contributing to the emerging tendency among traditional ballad singers to use the device of incremental repetition (see chap. iii, nn. 68–69) was translated from Romany into English about the middle of the seventeenth century, having been previously translated into Romany from (probably) Serbian, and that the only other such translation was made in Northern Italy, perhaps from one to two hundred years earlier.[60]

VII

THE SOURCE

It has been shown that what is constant in the western European versions of the ballad is rescue from jeopardy, successively refused by family members and offered by the protagonist's beloved, by the payment of ransom in some form. Variations may occur in the sex of the victim, the order of appearance of the relatives, the expressed attitudes or motivations of the relatives (in some versions an offer on their part is refused by the victim's persecutor), or in the denouement (in some versions, again, the rescue is not effected at all). Such features, therefore, are peripheral, as are the narrative settings to which the ballad core may be attached.

It has also been indicated that rescue through the payment of ransom is only one of a number of types in which the fundamental situation obtains to be found in eastern Europe, of which rescue from possible snakebite and rescue from drowning are salient. This proliferation of types has been assumed by Child, Pohl, Grüner-Nielsen, and Megas to be an insignificant and modern development. But such an assumption is ill-founded, as this chapter will attempt to show.

One possible explanation for the persistence of the ballad's narrative core in a number of different dramatic settings is that offered by Bronzini and Coirault. According to Bronzini, "Iteration, as a stylistic form, by its very adaptability to new incidents and sentiments, is without doubt among the most common, elementary, and archaic forms of the popular poetry of all peoples and of all times" (*Canzone Epico-lirica*, I, 306). Coirault asserted that "the popular tendency to compose enumerative structures . . . is very nearly comparable to that of the association of ideas, and it is well known with what absorbing intensity the latter dominates the psychology of the primitive" (*Chansons folkloriques*, p. 27). Cecil Sharp called the "climax of relatives" formula proof of the ancient provenance of "The Gallows Tree";[1] although Archer Taylor was reluctant to go so far, he agreed that the ballad "may be an example of a primitive technique."[2]

On this principle, the theory of "convergence" is sufficient to account for the stability of the "climax of relatives" in the ballad; it resides in the structure of the "primitive" mentality, and, once the situation of jeopardy arises in any narrative song, the possibility of rescue and the enumerative structure follow of themselves.

Coirault himself concluded, however, that this supposedly primitive tendency did not manifest itself in French balladry until the seventeenth century (see chap. iii, n. 68). It may also be observed that most of the "primitive" enumerative structures cited by Reed Smith in American Negro hymnody (*South Carolina*, pp. 85–86) and by Erich Seemann in Lithuanian balladry ("Volksliedbeziehungen," 196–199) do not correspond in essential structure to the sequence found in "The Gallows Tree" and its cousins, which normally culminates in a reversal of the established pattern. Equally pertinent, of course, is the question of why this "primitive" and presumably spontaneous development has been so selective as it has in western European traditions—why, for example, it is not to be found in all gallows rescue ballads.

Another kind of primitivism, akin to that discussed in chapter v, was proposed by Alexander H. Krappe and Iivar Kempinnen: assuming with other investigators that versions with a female victim who has been captured by pirates represented the basic form of the ballad, they rejected the pirate motif as a rationalization and concluded that its origin was mythic, and that the helmsman was none other than Charon, the Greek ferryman of the dead.[3]

In 1871, Bernhard Schmidt collected on the island of Zakynthos two popular ballads representing death as a journey in Charon's boat, and cautiously suggested that "the Ship of Death is not actually altogether forgotten in modern Greece."[4] Another ballad collected by Schmidt is remarkably close to the German traditions represented in "Die Losgekaufte" and "Edelmann und Schäfer":

> "Your boat that's carrying you off, oh, stop it now, your boat!
> Won't you sell the little boy that you are taking with you?
> A thousand I would give to see him, a thousand more to talk,
> And a thousand would his mother give, and a thousand too his sister!"

> The child opened his sweet mouth and thereupon replied:
> "Spend if you will your γρόςια, your φλωριά you should save!
> But only when the blackest crow to whitest dove shall turn,
> May you, beloved mother, expect your son again."[5]

Present are the boat, the threat of death, and the ransom (in the equivalent of "silver" and "gold"),[6] combined with a sequence of relatives willing to buy the child's life;[7] but there is no mention of Charon, and the ballad is one of a class called by the Greeks *Myrologia*, composed and sung by women as funeral elegies (Schmidt, *Griechische Märchen*, pp. 40–43). Reference to Charon is more explicit in a similar ballad collected by Emile Legrand during the same period:

> A ship loaded with youths sets sail,
> In the stern are the sick, in the prow the wounded,
> And beneath the sails are those who have drowned in the sea.
> It seeks a port to enter,
> A harbor in which to drop its anchor,
> At last it ties up in a favorable place.
> And the word goes around to the villages,
> And it is announced by everyone:
> "Widows, your husbands are for sale;
> Mothers, your children are for sale;
> Sisters, your brothers are for sale."
> Mothers run with their φλωριὰ, sisters with their σόςι,
> And the widows, the poor bereaved widows,
> With their ηλειδιὰ in their hands,
> And those who had nothing came with their hands clasped.
> But suddenly Charon changed his mind and cut the ropes.
> And the mothers crossed the mountains again,
> The sisters turned to the hills,
> And the widows, the poor bereaved widows,
> To the lonely valleys.[8]

There is some evidence, then, for the association of the pirates of "Scibilia Nobili" and "La Donzella" with the figure of Charon; there is also evidence that our eastern European ballad featuring ransom was not unknown to the quasi-professional composers of these elegiac narrative songs. Much earlier attestation for the ferryman as a symbol of death was collected in the form of iconography by Otto Waser and F. von Duhn, who found a number of funerary representations featuring a woman or a child being led away from loved ones by a figure bearing or resting upon an oar.[9] Nevertheless, Waser agreed with Dirk Hesseling and their pioneering predecessor Julius Ambrosch: the attachment of the name Charon to a nautical figure symbolizing death owes nothing to Greek mythology or folklore.[10]

The name Charon itself, shown by Ambrosch to be of Tuscan derivation, meant in classical Greek "fierce, grim,"[11] and was applied to the Nemean lion and the Cyclops as well as to the ferryman of literary legend. The Etruscan figure who bore the name rode on a black horse, carried a hammer (Ambrosch, *De Charonte*, p. 10) or a falcon, bow, and arrows (Waser, *Charon*, p. 93), and was a "grim" and "fierce" messenger of death; his image merged with that of the Greek Thanatos before the fifth century B.C.[12] As such a figure (armed, on horseback) he appears in popular Greek poetry from the fifteenth through the nineteenth centuries.[13] One of a number of examples may be quoted:

> Listen, listen, to what Charon proclaims to mothers sorrowing;
> "Who has children, hide them,
> Who has brothers, look out for them,
> You wives of brave husbands, hide your mates!
> For Charon is on the prowl for booty."
> And see, there he came, high on his horse, across the field.
> Black he was, black as a crow, and rode upon a black horse.
> To pierce hearts and to cut off heads.
> I stood with my hands folded and said to him, weeping,
> "Why, O Charon, won't you let yourself be bribed?
> Take from the rich their φλωριὰ,
> Take from the poor their γρόcια,
> Take away from them even their little vineyards!"
> Angry as a dog, he gave me a rough answer:
> "The rich may keep their φλωριά,
> The poor their γρόcια,
> They may enjoy their little vineyards!
> I take only the beautiful, in form like angels,
> To cause misery and woe to sisters and mothers,
> And to break the bonds of holy matrimony."[14]

Charon as a ferryman, in contrast, has been exclusively a literary symbol from the time the concept was first introduced in Greece from Egypt.[15] There is no mention of such a deity in Homer, Hesiod, or Pindar, nor is there any record of a cult devoted to him at any time (Ambrosch, *De Charonte* p. 34). Waser pointed out that where a ferryman appears as a death-symbol literary influence, e.g., that of Aristophanes' *Frogs,* is readily discernible (*Charon*, pp. 90–91). Hesseling noted that the Latin poets who were fond of the symbol nevertheless represented him as the fearsome and horrible being of Italian folk tradition (*Charos*, pp. 15–16), and that the ferryman-of-the-dead has not appeared in folk traditions (as opposed to literary ones) outside Greece (*Charos*, p. 7). Schmidt reported that even in Greek oral tradition the representation of Charon as a ferryman is rare indeed compared to his representation as an armed horseman (*Neugriechen*, p. 222).

The "myth" of Charon, then, is like the "myth" of the lost golden ball; oral tradition offers no convincing support for the symbolism ascribed to them by those seeking to interpret "The Gallows Tree."[16]

If the innate tendencies of the "primitive" mind cannot be held wholly responsible for the successive appeals to relatives in that ballad, and if the ferryboat to the other world of Egyptian mythology and classical literature cannot satisfactorily account for the shipboard setting of many of its Western analogues, there is, nonetheless, a secure foundation for the assertions of Albin Lesky, Georgios Megas, Erik Pohl, Alexander Krappe, and Iivar Kempinnen that the ballad's ultimate source is to be looked for in the Greek legend of Alcestis. In the play produced by Euripides in 438 B.C., Apollo tells the story:

Zeus killed my son, Asclepius, and drove the bolt of the hot lightning through his chest. I, in my anger for this, killed the Cyclopes, smiths of Zeus' fire, for which my father made me serve a mortal man, in penance for my misdoings. I came to this country, tended the oxen of this host and friend, Admetus, son of Pheres. I have kept his house from danger, cheated the Fates to save his life, until this day, for he revered my sacred rights sacredly, and the fatal goddesses allowed Admetus to escape the moment of his death by giving the lower powers someone else to die instead of him. He tried his loved ones all in turn, father and aged mother who had given him birth, and found not one, except his wife, who would consent to die for him, and not see daylight any more.[17]

A fable attributed to Hyginus preserves the essential features:

Many suitors sought in marriage Alcestis, daughter of Pelias and Anaxibia, Bios's daughter; but Pelias, avoiding the proposals, rejected them, and set a contest promising that he would give her to the one who yoked wild beasts to a chariot and bore her off. Admetus asked Apollo to help him, and Apollo, because he had been kindly received by him while in servitude, gave to him a wild boar and a lion yoked together, with which he carried off Alcestis. He obtained this, too, from Apollo, that another could voluntarily die in his place. When neither his father nor his mother was willing to die for him, his wife Alcestis offered herself, and died for him in vicarious death. Later Hercules called her back from the dead.[18]

Apollodorus gives a fuller account than either of these:

When Admetus reigned over Pherae, Apollo served him as his thrall, while Admetus wooed Alcestis, daughter of Pelias. Now Pelias had promised to give his daughter to him who should yoke a lion and a boar to a car, and Apollo yoked and gave them to Admetus, who brought them to Pelias and so obtained Alcestis. But in offering a sacrifice at his marriage, he forgot to sacrifice to Artemis; therefore when he opened the marriage chamber he found it full of coiled snakes. Apollo bade him appease the goddess and obtained as a favor of the Fates that, when Admetus should be about to die, he might be released from death if someone should choose voluntarily to die for him. And when the day of his death came neither his father nor his mother would die for him, but Alcestis died in his stead. But the Maiden [Persephone] sent her up again, or, as some say, Hercules fought with Hades and brought her up to him.[19]

Allusions in Aeschylus' *Eumenides* and Plato's *Symposium* referring to traditions connected with the legend not found in the play of Euripides (that Apollo obtained the privilege for Admetus by making the Fates drunk,[20] and that Alcestis was restored to life by divine edict rather than by the intervention of Hercules)[21] show that the story was a familiar one that had already undergone some variation by the middle of the fifth century B.C. It can be differentiated from the traditional theme of voluntary self-sacrifice on behalf of another (see chap. v, nn. 66–67, and chap. vi, n. 26) by precisely what distinguished the ballad with which we are concerned from contiguous traditions: the father and mother refuse the sacrificial offer before it is made by the wife.

In 1925, Albin Lesky sought to establish a connection between this old Greek story, a group of exempla from medieval Hebrew tradition, and the German ballad "Die Losgekaufte."[22] In 1933, one year after the publication of his own study of the German ballad, Georgios Megas returned to the subject. The introductory remarks to his "Die Sage von Alkestis" are better quoted than summarized:

I believe that I have already shown that the basic idea of the Alkestis legend underlies this whole ballad-cycle; however, in respect to the situation of the protagonist and the particular motifs the modern ballads depart considerably from the ancient Greek legend. While Alkestis offers her life in place of her husband's, the price of rescuing the beloved from the pirate ship or from imprisonment in modern ballads is fixed in terms of personal possessions; the love-motif has obviously not developed here into the motif of sacrificial death. There are indeed versions, especially among the Slavs, in which it is not a question of ransom, but of saving the loved one from drowning or from a snake concealed—often only supposedly—in his bosom, or of rescuing a wife from bandits, in which a personal sacrifice is demanded of the rescuer, but here there is no personification of death and the basic situation is quite different. It is therefore scarcely possible to determine the pre-literary form of the Alkestis legend on the basis of these materials. This is perhaps why Lesky's argument has not been generally accepted.... Therefore I believe it justifiable to assemble a more complete body of materials in order to undertake a further investigation of the old tradition.[23]

Megas turned to folk tales rather than to folk songs for the materials he sought, and to Slavic, Oriental, and African sources rather than to western European ones. There he found, more or less consistently represented, the following narrative tradition:

A. A young man is by the Fates doomed at his birth to die on his wedding day. In one Greek tale, his death is to be by snakebite; in several variants from Greece and Bulgaria, by drowning on the way to the wedding.

B. An intermediary obtains for him the proviso that his life can be saved if someone is found to take his place or surrender to him some portion of the other's own life-expectancy.

C. His father and mother (occasionally other relatives as well) refuse to make the sacrifice; his bride offers it.

D. The volunteer is miraculously restored to life.

Combining the data thus obtained with the testimony of classical literature, Megas reconstructed the story as Aeschylus, Euripides, and Plato must have known it: A long-wished-for child is born, but the Fates decree that he will die on his wedding day. A faithful servant, overhearing the pronouncement, undertakes a successful pursuit of the Fates to their own precinct, where he makes them drunk and extracts from them the qualification that it will not be necessary for his master to die if someone else is willing to take his place. At the wedding feast, the messenger of death appears. When his father and mother demur, his bride volunteers to die for him, and is sent back from the other world as a reward for her courage and fidelity.

According to Megas, this story became a local legend in Thessaly, attached to the persons of Admetus and Alcestis; the faithful servant became the god Apollo because of an independent tradition to the effect that he had been sentenced to do penance by serving a mortal, as he himself reports in the lines quoted above from Euripides.

The fact that there seems to be little immediate connection between this prose narrative tradition and the European ballad cycle should not be permitted to obscure, as it has done even in Megas's studies, the very remarkable tendency for certain of its components to persist in combination as others are lost. Thus the tale of the youth fated to die on his wedding day is extant in modern Greek, Serbo-Croatian, Indian, Hungarian, Czech, Lithuanian, Estonian, Finnish, Swedish, and Irish tradition (AaT 934B), and may be suspected to underlie such Scottish ballads as Child 215 "Rare Willie's Drowned in Yarrow" and Child 259 "Lord Thomas Stuart"; the subversion of a curse laid upon a child at its birth is recognizable in AaT 410;[24] the intervention of a servant and the threat of death by drowning and snakebite on the hero's wedding journey are still found together in AaT 516; the medieval epic hero Digenes Akritas was represented as winning for himself, in a wrestling match with Death, the right to prolong his life at the expense of another.[25]

Two Turkish folk tales preserve a great deal of the old story:

A young man faithfully serves his master for seven years, after which he receives a sack full of gold, a horse, and a handful of earth which will restore sight to his blinded parents; the master reveals himself to be Azrael, the angel of death, and tells him that he is to die on his wedding day. On the wedding night, Azrael appears, but offers to take another in the hero's place. His father and mother refuse, but his wife consents; Azrael kills the old couple and permits the bride and groom to live.[26]

Azrael comes for a young man, who asks his father and mother if they will substitute for him. They reply that they can always get another son. His wife volunteers, although he tries to prevent the sacrifice from being carried out. The pair are turned into birds; God restores them to life, and takes the parents.[27]

An exemplum published by Moses Gaster also features the angel of death:

A father rebukes a poor man, and is to be punished by the death of his son. He asks for a respite so that his son may marry before he dies, and the angel agrees. The son is visited by the prophet Elijah, who advises him of his impending death and suggests that he show kindness to a poor man, who will be the angel in disguise. All goes as predicted; the poor man appears at the wedding, and the son does him honor. Father and mother offer to take their son's place, but flinch and retract the offer at the moment of their execution. The bride does not flinch; both she and her husband are granted seventy years of life.[28]

Other exempla from Hebrew manuscripts show only traces of the tale:

A man invited guests to the wedding of his son, who however was bitten by a snake and died that very day. The man did not disturb the wedding feast but after the dinner he announced the sudden death of the bridegroom.

Rabbi Meier hearing a voice that ordered a serpent to kill Judah ha-Nassi ran ahead of it, reached the house, closed the doors and windows and prayed intently. The serpent, unable to enter, coiled round the house till a voice from Heaven proclaimed Rabbi Meier's prayer to be granted, when it departed.

Rabbi Akiba's daughter, destined to die on her wedding day, had given alms to the poor and was saved from a snake which was coming through a hole in the wall, by covering it with a sieve.[29]

In a Greek tale, it is the victim's sister who saves her brother:

A son is born to a King and his wife, who already have a daughter. On the third day after the birth, the sister hears the Fates prophesying: the first one says that at the age of three he shall fall into the fire and be burnt, the second that at the age of seven he shall fall off a cliff, and the third that when he is twenty-one and celebrates his marriage he shall be bitten by a snake. The sister snatches him out of the fire, pulls him back from the edge of the cliff, and kills the snake.[30]

An episode from the medieval *Livre de Caradoc* is related to the tradition:

Karados is tricked into reaching into a box containing a snake, which twines itself around his arm. He is placed in a barrel of vinegar, his sweetheart in a barrel of milk a short distance away. She offers her breast to the snake, which abandons Karados to bite off her nipple. Her brother kills the snake, and the wound is healed by the application of the boss of a magic shield.[31]

It is not astonishing, therefore, to find the following ballad in Rumanian tradition:

"Why dost thou cry, groan, scream? Hast thou spent thy money, or spoilt thy clothes, or did thy steed grow old, or is it time for you to get married?"

"As I lay sleeping under the pear-tree the wind blew the pear-blossoms upon me, and among them was a little serpent-dragon with three tails of gold. It is twisted about my heart; will you wrap your hand in my handkerchief and draw it away?"

"It is better to be without you than a mother without a hand; I can bear other sons."

The sweetheart reaches into his bosom and draws out a bag of gold coins.[32]

It is to the old tale, into which the motif of death specifically by snakebite and on the wedding day must have been incorporated by Apollodorus' time, that I submit all these narrative traditions are indebted.[33] And it is certainly to this version of the ballad that "prison-ransom" variants owe the "white hand" that is sporadically requested or offered (see chap. vi).

The same kind of fragmentary development is observable in the "drowning" tradition, of wider European distribution but certainly of later provenance. This time a Russian tale preserves most of the basic elements of the old story:

A boy's mother curses him before his birth. After he is grown and married, he suddenly disappears. A beggar reports to his parents that, taking shelter in a hut, he had been disturbed by a horseman who also spent the night there, muttering incessantly, "May the Lord judge my mother, in that she cursed me while a babe unborn!" The father goes to the hut to spend the night, and recognizes his son, who leads him to a hole in the ice formed on the river. The son rides into the hole, but the father will not follow him. The next night his mother has the same experience. The third night his wife goes; he instructs her to remove her cross before entering the hole. She does, and finds herself in a large hall with Satan presiding. He asks who she is, and sends them both back, since married couples should not be parted.[34]

Nothing but the drowning motif and the refusal of the relatives to help remains in a Little Russian ballad:

> On the broad Danube river,
> Very far from the land,
> Ah! there the young Cossack is sinking.
>
> Weeping, he demands to be saved.
> "Father, oh, save me!
> For I, the young Cossack, am going under."
>
> The father went for a boat,
> But found neither boat nor sieve.
> "Oh, you will drown, my son, you will drown!"

Mother, brother, and sister make the same response, but his sweetheart saves him.[35]

The wedding motif remains salient in a Serbian custom. As the bride is about to leave her father's house, she mounts a horse, bows to her relatives, and sings with her bridesmaids,

> "O maiden, swimming in the white Danube,
> The farther thou swimmest, the more wilt thou cry!
> O father, save me from the waters of the Danube!"

Her father replies,

> "Since thou art mine no longer, I will not save thee!
> He to whom thou belongest, let *him* save thee!"

The entire sequence of relatives follows.[36]

One version of the drowning motif suggests, as do a few ransom ballads, that the cause of the refusal is inability:

> As the maiden sank, she called to her father,
> "O father dear, do not let me drown!"
> "My dear child, I cannot swim,
> I dare not go into the river."[37]

> Dofinka rose early to wash linen in the Danube.
> She washed the cloths, and beat them with a golden club.
> The Danube began to be troubled,
> It washed away the cloths,
> It swallowed up the lovely Dofinka.
> Her mother came to the bank and said to Dofinka,
> "Swim, swim, Dofinka so you can reach the bank,
> And I can pull you out!"
> "I cannot, mama, I cannot,
> For my hair is caught in the willow roots.
> Go and tell papa!"
> Her father did not dare.
> When Nicolas heard it, all clothed he leaped into the Danube.
> Dofinka was brought back alive.[38]

Another features the rejection of the victim characteristic of many prison-ransom variants:

> A maiden swims across the water,
> She swims not so that she will drown,
> She swims only in order to see
> If her mother will trouble herself.
> And the mother goes to the bank,
> Throws a stone into the water,
> "Sink, you bad one! sink,
> You're not mine and never have been!"[39]

Even on the basis of this admittedly incomplete and fragmentary assemblage of variant texts, it is wholly reasonable to accept Megas's conclusions regarding the *Urform* of this narrative tradition, and to suppose that the snakebite and drowning motifs entered the tale tradition relatively early by way of the parallel tale represented in modern narratives by AaT 516. During the Middle Ages that part of the story having to do with the jeopardy itself and the father-mother-bride sequence of rescue appeals became in the Balkans a narrative song tradition, while the surrounding narrative structure persisted in prose narrative as AaT 934B. Perhaps during the Tatar invasions of the thirteenth century, perhaps in the repressive period that followed, a new version was composed in which the condition of jeopardy was removed from the realm of nature (snakes and rivers) to the realm of social relationships (imprisonment). The mitigation in this version of the terms of rescue, from the risk of the rescuer's own life to the payment of ransom, is paralleled by the reduction of the terms of substitution from the surrender of a whole life to the surrender of only a portion of it in other branches of the tradition.

The "climax of relatives," however, appears from this evidence to be distinctly a non-Western concept.[40] It is ancient, if not precisely "primitive," and it has taken many forms. "The Gallows Tree" as it is sung in the United States in the twentieth century may fairly be regarded as a modern survival of the form that bridged the gap between the Alcestis legend of the fifth century B.C. and the pirate-kidnapping legend of contemporary Europe.

VIII

CONCLUSIONS

I T W A S P R O P O S E D in chapter i that certain theoretical questions might be illuminated in this study. To these questions we may now address ourselves.

1. The narrative core of "The Gallows Tree" has been embedded in a great number of dramatic situations. In its oldest known setting, the popular tale attached to the legend of Admetus and his wife Alcestis, the victim was male and his life was in jeopardy unless someone could be found to substitute for him, a theme which exists independently; his father and mother refused to sacrifice themselves, but his wife was willing and was rewarded by being herself restored to life. The male sex of the victim persisted in Hebrew narrative and in both prose and song attached to modifications of the substitution motif involving the surrender of only a portion of the rescuer's life (Megas, "Alkestis," p. 262); the risking, not substituting of the rescuer's life (in "snakebite" and "drowning" versions); and the payment of ransom. A marked tendency to reverse the traditional sex, however, is observable in all but the first of these, and is characteristic of all Western "ransom" versions except "The Gallows Tree," in which such reversal is late and sporadic. Other aspects of the oldest narrative setting, the stipulation of the victim's manner of death by the Fates, death on the victim's wedding day, and the intervention of a faithful servant, are also to be found independently in oral tradition. The pattern is therefore one of continuous fragmentation and recombination, with some old traits persisting in combination with each other, others finding radically new associations. There is no evidence for a mythic or symbolic interpretation of these narrative settings, with the possible exceptions of the appeasement of the elements by a human sacrifice suggested by some Italian and German variants and a Serbian wedding custom that implies that with marriage responsibility for the individual's welfare is transferred from the natural family to the spouse. Refrains are rare and invariably secondary to previously established versions. Verbal traits tend to persist in variants adopting new narrative settings ("gold and fee" and "gold and silver" in "Gallows Tree" texts, "wait a while" and "I see . . . coming" in Scandinavian versions, "manda a dire" in Italian prison-rescue and shipboard-rescue variants).

2. The most stable feature of the tradition is a sequence of refusals, climaxed by a reversal. Change in the sex of the victim, the order of appearance of relatives and spouse or lover, and the circumstances of the refusal are fairly frequent and attributable to "complex demand" and individual idiosyncracy. Such essentially rationalizing elements seldom show relationships between variants and types, although they may in some cases reveal unsuspected individual culture-contacts; more reliable for analysis of the tradition *qua* tradition are nonrational elements like the precise terms of rescue, the means of establishing communication between victim and potential rescuer, and the address to the persecutor ("wait a while," "turn the ship"). It may be said that similarities between variants and types have four possible causes:

a. Direct borrowing or imitation of one by the other.

131

b. Descent from a common source.

c. Spontaneous convergence arising from similar cultural contexts.

d. Spontaneous convergence arising from individual response to "complex demand."

The last two tend to be ideational or rationalizing in nature, as when rescue fails to be effected or when relatives respond favorably or explain the reason for their refusal, although both depend to a large extent upon the first two (i.e., continuity in the basic structure is a prerequisite for such developments). Cultural context is likely to be responsible for the acceptance of the "prison-ransom" theme in Britain and the "pirate-ransom" theme in Scandinavia, but cannot seriously be maintained to be the sole reason for the similarity in this respect between British and Slavic, Scandinavian and Mediterranean versions. Direct borrowing and descent from a common source, on the other hand, are determinable from precise verbal formulations such as "traveling," "yonder," "beneath," "gold and silver," "horse," "sword," "land," "to set me free," ". . . is worth more to me than you are." There is, however, seldom a perfect correspondence between such formulations and total situation in variants of the ballad; most texts show both ideational and verbal affiliations with more than one competing tradition, regardless of language barriers.

3. In the history of this ballad cycle, cultural context has undoubtedly exerted some influence over the selection of ideational elements. Reversal of the sex of the victim and variation in the order of appearance of the relatives, occurring throughout the continuum of variants, appear to be historical phenomena independent of oikotyping. On the other hand, innovations like the removal of the scene of jeopardy to the deck of a ship or to the foot of the gallows can only be ascribed to oikotypal cultural preferences. So far as can be determined, mass media dissemination of an innovation has had no greater effect upon the ballad's tradition than has creative "unofficial" innovation.

4. Very seldom does a stable text-tune complex manifest itself. To the extent that it has been possible to identify the tunes to which versions outside the Anglo-American tradition are sung (German, Spanish, Polish), it can be said that textual relationships are not predicative of tune relationships. Closer study of the Anglo-American melodic tradition demonstrated that tune types tended to be distributed throughout the textual groupings. This is frequently attributable to "convergence" (e.g., the substitution of a mid-cadence on II or III for one on V); but there is evidence that just as new "ballad ideas" become associated with traditional verbal formulas, so do new tune modifications.

5. The basic idea of rescue from jeopardy by the payment of ransom has proved stable in all Western versions of the ballad cycle, although narrative settings, rhythmical structures, and rhyme schemes vary according to preestablished patterns in each language group. Nevertheless, the retention of verbal commonplaces is far more frequent than might be supposed. It can be safely asserted that the transmission of the ballad has been primarily through direct and close translation, modifications in narrative setting and stanzaic form being secondary. For example, the Northern development into ransom by pawning or selling differ-

entiated properties may well have resulted from an earlier differentiation into coins representing the original "gold and silver" (Italian "lions," "falcons," "columns of gold," Greek φλωριά, γρόσια, German "Ross," "Schwert," "Goldfuchs").

Whether one is concerned with the ballad as a genre, the origin and history of a particular ballad, or the social or psychological function of either, therefore, it is not sufficient to consider the "ballad idea" in its broadest terms or to rely upon the interpretation of selected texts. It is in the distribution of its relatively minor and unobtrusive verbal formulas that the essence of an oral tradition resides. And what the tradition of "The Gallows Tree" "means" is more surely that it *is* a tradition, demonstrating its transcendence over all barriers imposed by language, geography, or social caste through the preservation of such verbal formulas, than it is the "meaning" that may be ascribed to such accidental properties as it may have attracted to itself in sundry places and times.

NOTES

[1] Child, II, 346–355, 514; III, 516–517; IV, 481–482; V, 296.

[2] *DGF*, VIII, 445–475.

[3] Erik Pohl, *Die deutsche Volksballade von der "Losgekaufte,"* FFC 105 (Helsinki, 1934).

[4] Iivar Kempinnen, *Lunastettava neito: Vertaileva Balladi-Tutkimus* (Helsinki, 1957).

[5] Giovanni Bronzini, *La Canzone Epico-lirica nell'Italia Centro-Meridionale*, 2 vols. (Rome, 1956), I, 269–322.

[6] Anne Gilchrist and Lucy E. Broadwood, "Notes on Children's Game-Songs: The Prickly Bush (The Maid Freed from the Gallows) and Its Connections with the Story of the Golden Ball," *JFSS* 5 (1915), 228–239.

[7] Alexander H. Krappe, "The Maid Freed from the Gallows," *Speculum* 16 (1941), 236–241.

[8] Ingebord Urcia, "The Gallows Tree and the Golden Ball: An Analysis of 'The Maid Freed from the Gallows' (Child 95)," *JAF* 79 (1966), 463–468; Tristram P. Coffin, "The Golden Ball and the Gallows Tree," in *Folklore International: Essays in Traditional Literature, Belief, and Custom in Honor of Wayland Debs Hand*, ed. D. K. Wilgus (Hatboro, Pa., 1967), pp. 23–28.

[9] A description of the circumstances under which this predilection for deductive rather than inductive scholarship came to hold sway over British and American ballad study is to be found in D. K. Wilgus's *Anglo-American Folksong Scholarship since 1898* (New Brunswick, N.J., 1959), pp. 3–122.

[10] Sabine Baring-Gould, "The Story of the Golden Ball," in an appendix to William Henderson's *Notes on the Folk Lore of the Northern Counties of England and the Borders* (London, 1866), pp. 333–335. The appendix was omitted from the second edition in 1879.

[11] See chap. v for detailed discussion.

[12] *KHM* 1, *KHM* 4. The *Kinder- und Hausmärchen* were first issued in Munich and Leipzig in 1812; the number of subsequent and revised editions make it impracticable to give page references. The two tales in question may also be identified as nos. 440 and 326 in the revised and enlarged edition of Antti Aarne's *Verzeichnis der Märchentypen*, FFC 3 (Helsinki, 1910) by Stith Thompson, *The Types of the Folktale*, FFC 184 (Helsinki, 1961) [AaT].

[13] Sabine Baring-Gould, *Curiosities of Olden Times* (Edinburgh, 1896), pp. 287–288.

[14] Gilchrist and Broadwood, "Children's Game-Songs," 231–232.

[15] "Julius Krohn," "Das Lied vom Mädchen, welches erlöst werden soll," *JSFO* 10 (1892), 124 (translated from *Virittäjä*, 2 [n.d.], 36–50).

[16] Anne Gilchrist, "Conventional Ballads," *JFSS*, 3 (1907), 75.

[17] Dorothy Scarborough, *On the Trail of Negro Folk-Song* (Cambridge, Mass., 1925), p. 38.

[18] Phillips Barry, Fanny H. Eckstorm, and Mary W. Smyth, *British Ballads from Maine* (New Haven, Conn., 1929), pp. 212–213. For a discussion of the medieval tradition see Kenneth Jackson, *The International Popular Tale and Early Welsh Tradition* (Cardiff, 1961), pp. 25–29.

[19] James Reeves, *Idiom of the People* (London, 1958), p. 155. Compare Gilchrist and Broadwood, "Children's Game-Songs," p. 234.

[20] Francis B. Gummere, *The Popular Ballad* (Boston, 1907), pp. 101–105.

[21] Helen Child Sargent and George Lyman Kittredge, *English and Scottish Popular Ballads* (Boston, 1904, 1932), pp. xxv–xxvii.

[22] Joseph Jacobs, *English Fairy Tales* (London, 1895), pp. 259–260; Martha Beckwith, "The English Ballad in Jamaica," *PMLA* 39 (1924), 469.

[23] Baring-Gould, "Golden Ball"; as published in *Notes on the Folk Lore of the Northern Counties*, the portion of the story corresponding to "The Youth Who Went Forth to Learn Fear" was bracketed, and noted as having been obtained from another informant. In *Curiosities*, Baring-Gould revealed that he had himself read the story as a child in a chapbook (p. 287), and again used brackets to indicate its intrusive nature. Joseph Jacob's reprint in *More English Fairy Tales* (London, 1894), pp. 12–15, omits the brackets.

[24] Herbert J. Halpert, "The Cante-Fable in Decay," *SFQ* 5 (1941), 191–200, and "The Cante-Fable in New Jersey," *JAF* 55 (1942), 133–143; Kenneth Porter, "Some Examples of 'The Cante-Fable in Decay,'" *SFQ*, 21 (1957), 100–103. At least one of Halpert's examples, which he asserted to be

"obviously a remnant of the *cante-fable*," was described as "just a song [that] told the story" by the informant. The informant should have been trusted, for the original of his version had been printed as "The Merchant and the Fiddler's Wife" by Thomas d'Urfey in *Wit and Mirth, or Pills to Purge Melancholy,* 6 vols. (London, 1719), V, 77–80, and by John S. Farmer in *Merry Songs and Ballads prior to the year A.D. 1800,* 5 vols. ([London?], 1897), IV, 152–155—with "no talking in it," precisely as the informant insisted.

[25] Dan Ben-Amos, "The Situation-Structure of the Non-Humorous English Ballad," *MF* 13 (1963), 163–176; Roger D. Abrahams, "Patterns of Structure and Role Relationships in the Child Ballad in the United States," *JAF* 79 (1966), 448–462.

[26] Although its structure and situation are remarkably similar to those of "The Gallows Tree," and Erik Pohl suspected a Flemish variant of being a bridge (although a weak one) between the English ballad and a lost French tradition ("*Losgekaufte,*" pp. 315–316), this ballad, as I hope to show elsewhere, belongs to an independent narrative song tradition peculiar to Germany, the Low Countries, and Ireland.

[27] Another study purporting to deal with the idiosyncrasies of the American folk in contrast to their British counterparts was that of Brownie McNeil ("The Child Ballad in the Middle West and lower Mississippi Valley," in *Mesquite and Willow, PTFS* 27 [Dallas, 1957], 23–77), who found that Americans rejected what was morally offensive, rationalized what was supernatural, and were fond of treating tragic materials in comic style.

[28] Arthur Kyle Davis, *Traditional Ballads from Virginia* (Cambridge, Mass., 1929), p. 367.

[29] Russell Ames, "Art in Negro Folklore," *JAF* 56 (1943), 242; John Greenway, "Folksong as an Anthropological Province," in *A Good Tale and a Bonine Tune, PTFS* 32 (Dallas, 1964), 216; William A. Owens, *Texas Folk Songs* (Austin, 1950), p. 27.

[30] Olive Dame Campbell and Cecil J. Sharp, *English Folk Songs from the Southern Appalachians* (New York and London, 1917), p. 108 (the discrepancy was noted by Davis, *Virginia,* p. 369); Scarborough, *Negro Folk-Song,* p. 37.

[31] Compare, for example, Louise Pound, "New-World Analogues of the English and Scottish Popular Ballads," *MWQ* 3 (1916), 171–187; Stanley Edgar Hyman, "The Child Ballad in America: Some Aesthetic Criteria," *JAF* 70 (1957), 235–239; Tristram P. Coffin, "The Folk Ballad and the Literary Ballad: An Essay in Classification," *MF* 9 (1959), 5–18.

[32] Quoted by Sona Rosa Burstein, "Moses Gaster and Folklore," *Folk-Lore* 68 (1957), 289.

[33] Archer Taylor, "Precursors of the Finnish Method of Folk-Lore Study," *MP* 25 (1927–1928), 481–491.

[34] Tristram Coffin, "The 'Braes of Yarrow' Tradition in America," *JAF* 63 (1950), 335.

[35] John Greenway, "The Flight of the Grey Goose: Literary Symbolism in the Traditional Ballad," *SFQ* 18 (1954), 174, 166. Greenway's contention was borne out by S. J. Sackett's investigation of "Metaphor in Folksong," *FFMA* 6 (1963), 6–15, which yielded rather meager and banal results. Reviewing Reeves's collections (*Idiom* and *The Everlasting Circle* [London, 1960]), Allen Rodway pointed out the difference between the traditional ballad and the street-ballad in this respect (*EC* 11 [1961], 215–219); when Donal O'Sullivan published his *Songs of the Irish* (Dublin, 1960) he made a similar distinction between traditional Irish material and the poetry of a literary figure like William Butler Yeats, whose symbolism, he declared, "owe[d] nothing to anything he might have heard from the country people when he was a boy in Sligo" (p.11). R. C. Stephenson attributes the poverty of imagery in the traditional ballad to the nature of the ballad and the folktale as auditory, rather than visual, genres ("Dialogue in Folktale and Song," *PTFS* 27 [1957], 129–130).

[36] D. K. Wilgus, "Shooting Fish in a Barrel: The Child Ballad in America," *JAF* 71 (1958), 161–164.

[37] MacEdward Leach, "The Singer or the Song," in *Singers and Storytellers, PTFS* 30 (Dallas, 1961), 30–45.

[38] George Herzog, "The Study of Folksong in America," *SFQ* 2 (1938), 59–64.

[39] Greenway, "Anthropological Province," pp. 209–217; Richard M. Dorson, "A Theory for American Folklore," *JAF* 72 (1959), 197–215; Melville Jacobs, "A Look Ahead in Oral Literature Research," *JAF* 79 (1966), 413–427.

[40] Anna Birgitta Rooth, "Scholarly Tradition in Folktale Research," *Fabula* 1 (1957–1958), 193–200. Her own study of *Loki in Scandinavian Mythology* (Lund, 1961) is illustrative of the comparative method favored by Rooth.

[41] W. Edson Richmond, "The Comparative Approach: Its Aims, Techniques, and Limitations," in *A Good Tale and a Bonnie Tune*, PTFS 32 (1964), 217–227.

[42] In 1955, D. K. Wilgus expressed his regret that practical considerations enforced the separate study of texts and tunes ("Ballad Classification," *MF* 5 [1955], 95); not the least of the factors contributing to a more favorable condition at the present time is the publication of Bertrand H. Bronson's *The Traditional Tunes of the Child Ballads*, 3 vols. (Princeton, 1959–1967), which brings together much previously unpublished material and serves as a working model for classification procedures.

[43] Kaarle Krohn, *Die folkloristische Arbeitsmethode* (Oslo, 1926). See also Antti Aarne, *Leitfaden der vergleichenden Märchenforschung*, FFC 13 (Hamina, 1913); for a historical account of the development of the method, see Taylor, "Precursors."

[44] Walter Anderson, "Geographische-historische Methode," *HDM*, II; recapitulated by Walter Anderson in *Zu Albert Wesselski's Angriffen auf die finnische folkloristische Forschungsmethode*, *ACUT (H)* 38 (1936), and by Richmond in "Comparative Approach," p. 221.

[45] Walter Anderson, *Eine neue Arbeit zur experimentellen Volkskunde*, FFC 168 (Helsinki, 1956), 22–23. Reference is to Anderson's study of the traditional narrative represented in Child 45 "King John and the Bishop," *Kaiser und Abt*, FFC 42 (Helsinki, 1923). [Except where otherwise indicated, all translations furnished are my own.]

[46] In its original Oriental form, the story featured neither the threefold encounter in disguise nor the identification of the heroine by means of a lost object which became characteristic of the narrative in Europe.

[47] Marta Pohl, *Gemeinsame Themen englisch-schottischer und französischer Volksballaden*, *SVF* 4 (Berlin, 1940), 50–54; Lajos Vargyas, *Researches into the Medieval History of Folk Ballad* (Budapest, 1967), pp. 258–259; Holger Nygard, *The Ballad of Heer Halewijn*, FFC 169 (Helsinki, 1958).

[48] Term coined by Carl W. von Sydow in 1927 ("Folksagorforskningen," *FF* 14 [1927], 105–137) to define special versions of narratives owing their distinctive qualities to national, political, or geographical idiosyncrasies.

[49] Some of the oikotypes distinguished by Swahn are the heroine's use of a public bathhouse for the purpose of obtaining information about her lost husband in Turkish and Greek tradition, eavesdropping as a mechanism fulfilling the same function in the Mediterranean area, and release from enchantment by decapitation in the North Germanic region.

[50] In addition to the comments of Greenway, Dorson, and Jacobs cited above (n. 39), see Anderson, *Albert Wesselski's Angriffen*, pp. 10–11; Nygard, *Heer Halewijn*, pp. 9–11; and Albert Wesselski, *Das Märchen des Mittelalters* (Berlin, 1925).

[51] See chap. iii, nn. 71–72; chap. iv, n. 24; and Ethel Stanwood Bolton, "Immigrants to New England, 1700–1775," *EIHC* 63 (1927), 177–192, 269–284, 365–380; 64 (1928), 25–32, 257–272; 65 (1929), 57–72, 113–128, 531–546; 66 (1930), 411–426, 521–536; 67 (1931), 89–112, 201–224, 305–328.

[52] See Vladimir Propp, *The Morphology of the Folktale*, trans. Laurence Scott (Bloomington, Ind., 1958).

[53] As did Nygard, Taylor demonstrated in this study the necessity for examining variants not widely circulated in print and for attending carefully to seemingly minor and insignificant verbal elements.

[54] Bertrand Bronson, "Mrs. Brown and The Ballad," *CFQ* 4 (1945), 129–140. Attention was called here to the effect of individual preferences and styles upon the singing of variants.

[55] Bertrand Bronson, "The Interdependence of Ballad Tunes and Texts," *CFQ* 3 (1944), 185–207. Of marked interest for my investigation are Bronson's hypotheses that stability and relative homogeneity of melodic tradition are indications of greater age in the tune-text complex, and that "crossing" verbal materials may be related to corresponding melodic elements.

[56] A major concern for both Barry and Wilgus has been the relationship between oral tradition and the compositions of professional and quasi-professional artists.

II: The Schema

[1] "Crossing" is the name given to the phenomenon in which one ballad text is inserted into, or added to, that of another, often giving a new turn to the narrative. "The Gallows Tree" has been most conspicuously "crossed" with Child 173 "Mary Hamilton," Child 155 "Little Sir Hugh," and Laws I 4 "The Coon-Can Game."

[2] Tristram P. Coffin, *The British Traditional Ballad in North America* (Philadelphia, 1963), p. 97.

[3] It has been necessary to depart slightly from the definitions proposed by W. Edson Richmond ("The Comparative Approach: Its Aims, Techniques, and Limitations," in *A Good Tale and a Bonnie Tune. PTFS* 32 [1964], 217, 224–226) and D. K. Wilgus (*Anglo-American Folksong Scholarship since 1898* [New Brunswick, N.J., 1959], p. 438) because of the nature of the analysis. Richmond would reserve "version" for "a shift in the *narrative* pattern [my italics]" and Wilgus distinguishes between "version" (representing a distinctive complex of variants) and "type" (representing a distinctive complex of versions). Within its own tradition, "The Gallows Tree" contains both "versions" and "types," which could be defined either in terms of characteristic verbal traits or in terms of narrative patterns; in its relationship to the pan-European tradition, however, it constitutes both a "version" and a "type," depending upon the range of focus implied in the definition.

III: The Texts

[1] William Chappell and J. Woodfall Ebsworth, eds., *The Roxburghe Ballads*, 8 vols. (Hertford, 1871–1899), VIII, 721.

[2] Giovanni B. Bronzini, *La Canzone Epico-lirica nell'Italia Centro-Meridionale*, 2 vols. (Rome, 1956), I, 32; Lajos Vargyas, *Researches into the Medieval History of Folk Ballad* (Budapest, 1967), pp. 93–96. Italian, Greek, and Hungarian parallels are cited by Bronzini and Vargyas. In the medieval Irish poem *Buile Suibne* ("The Frenzy of Suibne"), dating from before the thirteenth century, the hero goes mad in the forest and is unmoved by successive reports of the deaths of his relatives until he is told that he has lost his son (J. G. O'Keeffe, ed., *Buile Suibne* [*The Frenzy of Suibne*], *ITS* 12 [London, 1913], pp. 53–59).

[3] "Johnnie Law" is an American slang term for any law enforcement officer; see *DAS*.

[4] Friedrich Ranke, *Der Erlöser in der Wiege* (Munich, 1911).

[5] J. G. von Hahn, *Griechische und albanische Märchen*, 2 vols. (Munich, 1868, 1918), I, lix-lxv.

[6] Archer Taylor, "The Pertinacious Cobold," *JEGP* 31 (1932), 1–9.

[7] Eleanor Gordon Mlotek, "International Motifs in the Yiddish Ballad," *For Max Weinreich on His Seventieth Birthday* (The Hague, 1964), p. 210, n. 3.

[8] Walter Anderson, *Zu Albert Wesselski's Angriffen auf die finnische folkloristische Forschungsmethode, ACUT (H)* 38 (1936), 16. Anderson's purpose was not so much to discover the *Urform* as to determine what he called the *Zentrum*, around which all variants, both early and late, "oscillate." The same procedure is applicable to both ends.

[9] Child 4 "Lady Isabel," Child 39 "Tam Lin," Child 46 "Captain Wedderburn's Courtship," Child 47 "Proud Lady Margaret," Child 53 "Young Beichan," Child 64 "Fair Janet," Child 65 "Lady Maisry," Child 66 "Lord Ingram and Chiel Wyet," Child 69 "Clerk Saunders," Child 83 "Child Maurice," Child 89 "Fause Foodrage," Child 91 "Fair Mary of Wallington," Child 94 "Young Waters," Child 96 "The Gay Goshawk," Child 97 "Brown Robin," Child 103 "Rose the Red and White Lily," Child 109 "Tom Potts," Child 110 "The Knight and the Shepherd's Daughter," Child 158 "Hugh Spencer's Feats in France," Child 159 "Durham Field," Child 173 "Mary Hamilton," Child 176 "Northumberland Betrayed by Douglas," Child 178 "Captain Car," Child 182 "The Laird o Logie," Child 185 "Dick o the Cow," Child 186 "Kinmont Willie," Child 187 "Jock o the Side," Child 191 "Hughie Grame," Child 192 "The Lochmaben Harper," Child 194 "The Laird of Wariston," Child 200 "The Gypsy Laddie," Child 203 "The Baron of Brackley," Child 204 "Jamie Douglas," Child 214 "The Braes of Yarrow," Child 215 "Rare Willie Drowned in Yarrow," Child 217 "The Broom of Cowdenknowes," Child 222 "Bonny Baby Livingston," Child 226 "Lizie Lindsay," Child 227 "Bonny Lizie Baillie," Child 228 "Glasgow Peggy,"

Child 229 "Earl Crawford," Child 231 "Andrew Lammie," Child 236 "The Laird of Drum," Child 238 "Glenlogie," Child 243 "James Harris," Child 264 "The White Fisher," Child 270 "The Earl of Mar's Daughter," Child 280 "The Beggar Laddie," Child 293 "John of Hazelgreen," Child 294 "Dugall Quin," Child 297 "Earl Rothes," Child 304 "Young Ronald."

[10] W. Anderson, *Albert Wesselski's Angriffen*, p. 36. "When in variant materials two different motifs occur in the same place, of which one is found nowhere outside this narrative and the other normally occurs in other narratives known in the same area, the first one is more likely to belong to the narrative." "Stay thy hand" is, of course, attested in ordinary sixteenth-century usage (*NED, IX,* 876).

[11] *DGF,* pp. 466–475. The wording is, "I tøfver en liden Stund," "I tøve endnu lidt," "du tøver en Tid," "I tyve nu en Stund," "I tøve her en Stund," "I drejer vel en Stund," "Biða, Biða min, Frísar." The Swedish text published by E. G. Geijer and A. A. Afzelius in *Svenska Folkevisor* (Stockholm, 1880), has "ni vänten liten Stund."

[12] *MED,* III, 430; *NED,* IV, 127–128.

[13] Child 4 "Lady Isabel," Child 9 "The Fair Flower of Northumberland," Child 22 "St. Stephen and Herod," Child 24 "Bonnie Annie," Child 30 "King Arthur and King Cornwall," Child 48 "Young Andrew," Child 58 "Sir Patrick Spens," Child 59 "Sir Aldinger," Child 68 "Young Hunting," Child 72 "The Clerk's Twa Sons o Owsenford," Child 73 "Lord Thomas and Fair Annet," Child 88 "Young Johnstone," Child 89 "Fause Foodrage," Child 93 "Lamkin," Child 99 "Johnie Scot," Child 101, "Willie o Douglas Dale," Child 107 "Will Stewart and John," Child 109 "Tom Potts," Child 110 "The Knight and the Shepherd's Daughter," Child 116 "Adam Bell, Clim o the Clough, and William of Cloudesly," Child 122 "Robin Hood and the Butcher," Child 123 "Robin Hood and the Curtal Friar," Child 126 "Robin Hood and the Tanner," Child 138 "Robin Hood and Allen a Dale," Child 140 "Robin Hood Rescuing Three Squires," Child 158 "Hugh Spencer's Feats in France," Child 178 "Captain Car," Child 188 "Archie o Cawfield," Child 244 "James Hatley," Child 267 "The Heir of Linne," Child 286 "The Golden Vanity."

[14] Knut Liestøl, "Scottish and Norwegian Ballads," *SN* 1 (1946), 10. "Gold and fee" does occur in one late seventeenth-century English ballad that is not included in the Child canon: "The Most Pleasant Song of Lady Bessy," published in Llewellyn Jewitt, ed. *The Ballads and Songs of Derbyshire* (London, 1867), p. 39.

[15] *DAE,* II, 948–949; *DA,* I, 593.

[16] Child 39 "Tam Lin," Child 41 "Hind Etin," Child 43 "The Broomfield Hill," Child 58 "Sir Patrick Spens," Child 64 "Fair Janet," Child 68 "Young Hunting," Child 83 "Child Maurice," Child 93 "Lamkin," Child 100 "Willie o Winsbury," Child 114 "Johnie Cock," Child 154 "A True Tale of Robin Hood," Child 178 "Captain Car," Child 194 "The Laird o Wariston," Child 217 "The Broom of Cowdenknowes," Child 236 "The Laird o Drum," Child 245 "Young Allan," Child 268 "The Twa Knights," Child 269 "Lady Diamond," Child 279 "The Jolly Beggar," Child 305 "The Outlaw Murray."

[17] Matthew 10:9 (*NED,* IV, 127–128).

[18] Child 54 "The Cherry Tree Carol," Child 61 "Sir Cawline," Child 81 "Little Musgrave and Lady Barnard," Child 108 "Christopher White," Child 109 "Tom Potts," Child 122 "Robin Hood and the Butcher," Child 125 "Robin Hood and Little John," Child 142 "Little John a Begging," Child 154 "A True Tale of Robin Hood," Child 178 "Captain Car," Child 187 "Jock o the Side," Child 207 "Lord Delamere," Child 237 "The Duke of Gordon's Daughter," Child 283 "The Crafty Farmer," Child 289 "The Mermaid."

[19] Chappell and Elsworth, *Roxburghe Ballads,* I, 50, 103, 134, 343, 489, 555; II, 351, 394, 504, 533, 566; III, 262, 274, 281, 284, 454, 519, 655; IV, 117, 373, 386, 412; VI, 275, 294, 329, 337, 421, 459, 480, 633, 656; VII, 51, 106, 181, 231, 234, 280, 346, 354, 370, 383, 495, 539; VIII, 30, 127, 129, 146, 172, 433; VIII (Part 2), lxxiii, cxlv, clxv, 494, 536, 563, 600, 634.

[20] Child 24 "Bonnie Annie," Child 81 "Little Musgrave and Lady Barnard," Child 100 "Willie o Winsbury," Child 108 "Christopher White," Child 136 "Robin Hood's Delight," Child 138 "Robin Hood and Allen a Dale," Child 185 "Dick o the Cow," Child 209 "Geordie," Child 214 "The Braes of Yarrow."

[21] Child 49 "The Twa Brothers," Child 53 "Young Beichan," Child 58 "Sir Patrick Spens," Child 87 "Prince Robert," Child 97 "Brown Robin," Child 99 "Johnie Scot," Child 110 "The Knight

and the Shepherd's Daughter," Child 157 "Gude Wallace," Child 182 "The Laird o Logie," Child 190 "Jamie Telfer," Child 192 "The Lochmaben Harper," Child 194 "The Laird o Wariston" Child 229 "Earl Crawford," Child 237 "The Duke of Gordon's Daughter," Child 247 "Lady Elspat," Child 252 "The Kitchie-Boy," Child 267 "The Heir of Linne," Child 268 "The Twa Knights."

The *NED* cites one instance of "money" as "property convertible into coin" in the thirteenth century (VI, 603); in general usage, however, both as "white money" and as "money" it remained a synonym for "silver" until the nineteenth century (see also Joseph Wright, *The English Dialect Dictionary*, 6 vols. [London, 1923], IV, 149). The use of the formula outside the Child canon is attested in William Hugh Logan, *A Pedlar's Pack of Ballads and Songs* (Edinburgh, 1869), p. 127 (from a chapbook published in 1796); John Bell, *Rhymes of Northern Bards* (Newcastle, 1812), p. 7; and George Farquhar Graham, *Songs of Scotland,* 3 vols. (Edinburgh, 1861), III, 131 (a song composed by Robert Burns in 1787).

[22] A note is in order here regarding the authenticity of Peter Buchan's materials, of which A13 is an exemplar. The text has certainly been tampered with by the addition of narrative elements, a practice for which Buchan is well known. But the same kind of *narrative* tampering is observable in A8, A9, A11, and A14. The correspondences in verbal traits between A13 and A25 corroborate the contention of Alexander Keith (Gavin Greig and Alexander Keith, *Last Leaves of Traditional Ballads and Ballad Airs Collected in Aberdeenshire by the Late Gavin Greig* [Aberdeen, 1925], pp. xix–xxxv) and Sigurd B. Hustvedt (*Ballad Books and Ballad Men* [Cambridge, Mass., 1930], pp. 69–71) that Buchan's texts are far more trustworthy in verbal detail than are those of many of his contemporaries. The "gold and fee" of A1, for instance, perhaps the most widely reprinted of Child's variants but the only one of its kind to be reported from Southern England, is very likely attributable to the effect of "romantic nationalism" on Bishop Percy (see W. Edson Richmond, "Romantic Nationalism and Ballad Scholarship: A Lesson for Today from Norway's Past," *SFQ* 25 [1961], 91–100). The instances of "stand," "wait," and "slack the rope" found in texts collected by Peter Buchan are not so attributable.

[23] As with "Judge" and "George," the recorded transcriptions of A16, A17, and A24 explain the development of "prickle holly bush." The informants for A16 and A24 do not pronounce the "h" visible in the printed word "holly." Consequently, their "'olly" corresponds phonetically to A17's pronunciation of the final syllable of "prickle-*lie*," a common manifestation of Anglo-American folk song. Similarly, A24's " 'igh gallis tree" becomes "idler's spree" in A17.

[24] Edward R. Russell, "A Folk Song," *Athenaeum*, 3510 (February 2, 1895), 248, and H. M. Charters-Maitland, *Athenaeum*, 3511 (February 9, 1895), 184.

[25] Cecil Sharp, *English Folk Song: Some Conclusions,* 4th rev. ed., ed. Maud Karpeles (Belmont, Calif., 1965), p. 114. All references are to this edition.

[26] Gordon Hall Gerould, *The Ballad of Tradition* (New York, 1932, 1957), pp. 117–124; Joseph W. Hendren, *A Study of Ballad Rhythm, with Special Reference to Ballad Music, PSE* 4 (1936), 20, 100–126.

[27] W. Anderson, *Albert Wesselski's Angriffen*, p. 26.

[28] Hinrich Siuts, "Die Volkslieder unserer Tage," *ZV* 55 (1959), 67–84.

[29] William Bascom, "The Main Problems of Stability and Change in Tradition," *JIFMC* 11, (1959), 11.

[30] James H. Jones, "Commonplace and Memorization in the Oral Tradition of the English and Scottish Ballads," *JAF* 74 (1961), 97–112.

[31] Albert B. Friedman, "The Formulaic Improvisation Theory of Ballad Tradition—A Counterstatement," *JAF* 74 (1961), 113–115.

[32] *NED*, IX, 164; see also *EDD*, V, 492.

[33] This unique instance illustrates the reliability of Peter Buchan as a collector (see n. 22) The stanza may be regarded as intrusive upon the text of "Lang Johnny More" like the instances of "stand" and "wait" documented earlier, but later collections from England and the United States show that either Buchan or his informants knew these traditions, which could have originated only in "The Gallows Tree" since they do not regularly appear in any other ballad text.

[34] Neither Greig and Keith's *Last Leaves* nor Greig's *Folk Song of the North-East* (2 vols., (Peterhead, 1914) includes a single text of "The Gallows Tree," and Bertrand Bronson reported

that it is also missing from the unpublished materials of such earlier collectors as Motherwell, Mrs. Harris, C. K. Sharpe, Kinloch, Mrs. Brown, Alexander Campbell, and Walter Scott (Bertrand H. Bronson, "On the Union of Words and Music in the 'Child' Ballads," *WF* 11 [1952], 234). William Montgomerie, however, claimed that it was used by children as a game song in Forfarshire around 1840 ("Sketch for a History of the Scottish Ballad," *JEFDSS* 8 [1956], 40).

[35] American collectors have not infrequently contributed the texts published in the Child collection to the repertories of their informants; see A. H. Scouten, "On Child 76 and 173 in Divers Hands," *JAF* 64 (1951), 131–132. Notable in B1 and A28, however, is the combining of elements from A1 with other traditions not available in Child.

[36] As has been noted, this formula is ordinarily found with "gold and silver" or "gold and money" as ransom, not "gold and fee."

[37] See D. K. Wilgus, "The Rationalistic Approach," in *A Good Tale and a Bonnie Tune, PTFS* 32 (1964), 227–237.

[38] Compare Child variants F, G, and H (my E6, E9, and E7).

[39] Leonhard Schultze, *Aus Namaland und Kalahari* (Jena, 1907), pp. 434–436. Other African versions may be found in Leo Frobenius, "Volkserzählungen und Volksdichtungen aus dem Zentralsuden," *Atlantis* 9 (1924), 103; Bruno Gutmann, *Volksbuch der Wadschagga* (Leipzig, 1914), p. 122; Moïse A. Landeroin and Marie A. J. Tilho, *Grammaire et Contes Haoussas* (Paris, 1909), p. 279; Hermann Oldenburg, *Die Literatur des alten Indien* (Stuttgart and Berlin, 1903), pp. 169–171; R. S. Rattray, *Akan-Ashanti Folktales* (Oxford, 1930), reprinted in Susan Feldmann, *African Myths and Tales* (New York, 1963), pp. 186–189; and A. J. N. Tremearne, *Hausa Superstitions and Customs* (London, 1913), p. 340.

[40] Robert L. Rands and Carroll L. Riley, "Diffusion and Discontinuous Distribution," *AA* 60 (1958), 274–297.

[41] See the essays by Bronislaw Malinowski and Herbert J. Spinden in *Culture: The Diffusion Controversy*, ed. G. Elliott Smith, *et al.* (New York, 1927).

[42] See Robert Conot, *Rivers of Blood, Years of Darkness* (New York, 1967), p. 381.

[43] Henry M. Belden and Arthur Palmer Hudson, eds., *Folk Songs from North Carolina*, Frank C. Brown Collection of North Carolina Folklore III (Durham, N.C., 1952), 301–302, 308, 348; Vance Randolph, *Ozark Folksongs*, 4 vols. (Columbia, Mo., 1946–1950), IV, 265.

[44] Belden and Hudson, *North Carolina*, III, 332–334; Child 191 "Geordie."

[45] Genesis 44:1–34 and 45:1–15; Robert Graves and Raphael Patai, *Hebrew Myths* (New York, 1963), pp. 268–270. The motif is entered as H151.4 in Stith Thompson, *A Motif-Index of Folk Literature*, 6 vols. (Bloomington, Ind., 1955–1958), and also occurs in Grimm 54a "Hans Dumm" variants (Johannes Bolte and Georg Polívka, *Anmerkungen zu der Kinder- und Hausmarchen der Brüder Grimm*, 5 vols. [Leipzig, 1912, 1932], I, 489).

[46] In addition to "A most miraculous, strange, and trewe Ballad, of a younge man of the age of 19 yeares, who was wrongfully hanged at a town called *Bon* in the *lowe Countreyes* since Christmas last past 1612; and how god preserved him alive, and brought his false accuser to deserved destruction" (*The Shirburn Ballads*, ed. Andrew Clark [Oxford, 1907], pp. 158–163), a lengthy narrative in song based upon the international folktale AaT 873 and utilizing the "cup-theft, false accusation" motif is to be found in the Douce and Roxburghe collections (Chappell and Ebsworth, *Roxburghe Ballads*, III, 22, and III, 328, respectively), dated 1750 (VIII, 180). It was reprinted in Joseph Ritson's *Bishoprick Garland* ([London.], 1784; see *Northern Garlands* [Edinburgh, 1887], pp. 17–26) and in a chapbook dated 1780 (see James O. Halliwell, *Yorkshire Anthology* [London, 1851], pp. 245–256). It was usually entitled "The Durham Garland." The case of the notorious Mary Carleton, who after a career that included trial and acquittal for bigamy, appearance in the leading role of a play written about herself ("The German Princess"), and transportation to Jamaica, was hanged for stealing plate in December, 1672 (Chappell and Ebsworth, *Roxburghe Ballads*, VII, 66), is probably not an atypical example of real-life episodes reinforcing the tradition.

[47] Sharp, *Conclusions*, pp. 12–15, 38; Phillips Barry, "American Folk Music," *SFQ* 1 (1937), 29–30. The emphasis of these two collectors is, of course, quite different from Anderson's; Sharp concerned himself with a theoretically ideal end product resulting more from the "selection" of the audience than from "selections" made by singers, and Barry looked upon "communal re-creation"

primarily as a function of individual creativity. Such creativity must certainly be held responsible for each massive innovation, even when its materials are drawn from prior tradition.

[48] A ballad designated as I4 in Laws, *Native American Balladry;* rubrics A-I are found in this volume, rubrics J–Q in his *American Ballads from British Broadsides.* Wilgus has suggested that the omission of the relative-sequence in variant C40 may have been the result of a time limitation imposed on the performer by the company for whom he recorded it.

[49] Tristram Coffin, "An Index to Borrowing in the Child Ballads of America," *JAF* 62 (1949), 156–161. Eleven years earlier, Mellinger Henry was advised by Phillips Barry to regard it as a version of "The Gallows Tree" (Mellinger Henry, *Folk-Songs from the Southern Highlands* [New York, 1938], pp. 94–95), and even Coffin seems not to have realized that the "borrowing" of which he spoke was representative of a new and distinct tradition.

[50] Marina Bokelman, "The Coon-Can Game: A Blues Ballad Tradition" (University of California, Los Angeles, 1968).

[51] The *NED* lists "rasp-house" as meaning "a place of confinement" (VIII, 159); W. H. Logan explained the term as referring to the fact that men committed to the "Raspelhuis" in Holland were forced to work at rasping Brazil-wood (*Pedlar's Pack*, p. 138). The definition given here was provided by E. Verwijs and J. Verdam, *MNW*, VI, 1043–1044, and is based upon the word's derivation in both instances ("raspel" and "rascal") from OF "raspalge" or "lower stratum."

[52] Three texts in group A (A4, A6, A31), however, nineteen in group B (B3, B13, B26, B36, B37, B40, B43–47, B50, B51, B55, B84, B86, B87, B91), thirteen in group C (C1–5, C7, C10, C11, C13, C17, C18, C26, C48), and six in group D (D4, D12, D13, D15, D23, D33) feature "take you home" or an equivalent in the sweetheart's response. C2 has "I have come to win your neck," C10 "to deliver you," C48 "to see you saved." "To take me off the tree" thus seems to have migrated from the request stanzas to the final stanza in the same manner that "yonder" migrated from the third line to the final phrase of the request stanza ("yonder tree") as the original text was being simplified and stylized.

[53] P. von Goetze, *Serbische Volkslieder in's deutsche uebertragen* (Leipzig, 1827), pp. 110–112.

[54] "Spare my life" occurs in Child 90 "Jellon Grame," Child 93 "Lamkin," Child 155 "Little Sir Hugh," and Child 173 "Mary Hamilton." The number of variants that utilize it in the "Lamkin" corpus represented in Child (three, from Scotland and Ireland) implies that this is likely to have been its original setting; its association with "Mary Hamilton" and "Little Sir Hugh," both of which which have been reported to "cross" with "The Gallows Tree," is interesting (see Belden and Hudson, North Carolina, II, 160, for an American variant of "Little Sir Hugh" with "spare my life").

[55] See John Robert Moore, "Omission of the Central Action in English Ballads," *MP*, 11 (1914), 391–406; J. Oates Smith, "The 'Fifth Act' and the Chorus in the English and Scottish Ballads," *DR* 42 (1962), 329–340; R. C. Stephenson, "Dialogue in Folktale and Song," in *Mesquite and Willow*, *PTFS* 27 (1957), 129–137; Tristram P. Coffin, " 'Mary Hamilton' and the Anglo-American Ballad as an Art Form," *JAF* 70 (1957), 208–214 (reprinted in *The Critics and the Ballad*, eds. MacEdward Leach and Tristram P. Coffin [Carbondale, Ill., 1961], pp. 245–256).

[56] The game song referred to by Montgomerie (see n. 34) was probably that entered here as E6; other reports of the ballad's use in a game or a dramatization have been made with reference to the Faroese version (*DGF*, VIII, 447–448) as well as in the collections of Arthur Kyle Davis (*Traditional Ballads from Virginia* [Cambridge, Mass., 1929], pp. 360–361) and Arthur Palmer Hudson (*Folksongs of Mississippi and their background* [Chapel Hill, N. C., 1936], p. 56). Despite the reservations of Phillips Barry (Phillips Barry, Fanny H. Eckstorm, and Mary W. Smyth, *British Ballads from Maine* [New Haven, Conn., 1929], p. 210), the probability that this represents the degeneration of a narrative song, since it is so often accompanied by a degeneration of its text, is high. See also Benjamin A. Botkin, *The American Play-Party Song*, *USUN* 37 (1937), and "The Play Party in Oklahoma," in *Follow the Drinkin' Gou'd*, *PTFS* 7 (1928), 7–24; William A. Owens, *Swing and Turn: Texas Play-Party Games* (Dallas, 1936); and Leah Jackson Wolford, *The Play-Party in Indiana* (Indianapolis, 1916).

[57] The single text for Erk-Böhme no. 97, reprinted from Ludwig Achim von Arnim's *Des Knaben Wunderhorn*, 3 vols. (Heidelberg, 1808) II, 285–289, appears as the first of three variants in *DVM*, III, 219–226. As Archer Taylor has pointed out, the ballad theme is also found in Spanish and

Portuguese tradition ("Una comparación tentativa de temas de baladas inglesas y españolas," *FA*, 4 [1956], 5–27); see also his "German Folksongs in Spain," *HR* 27 (1959), 49–55, and "Themes Common to English and German Balladry," *MLQ* 1 (1940), 23–25.

⁵⁸ Jonas Balys, *Lithuanian Narrative Folksongs* (Washington,D.C., 1954), pp. 55–57.

⁵⁹ See chap. i, n. 24. Siuts noted that the phenomenon is common in Germanic oral narrative, and that it is due to forgetting of the ballad text "Volksleider unserer Tage," p. 73).

⁶⁰ Again we have the "false accusation" motif characteristic of *cante-fables* with "gold and silver" and "silver and gold."

⁶¹ The motif is F211 in Thompson's *Motif-Index* and in Tom Peete Cross's *Motif-Index of Early Irish Literature*, Indiana University Publications, Folklore Series, 7 (Bloomington, Ind., [n.d.]). It appears sporadically in Icelandic and Lithuanian tradition. See also Hyder Rollins Patch, *The Other World According to Descriptions in Medieval Literature* (Cambridge, Mass., 1950).

⁶² Motif D31; there are scattered references in Danish folklore, but the bulk of the tradition is centered in Spanish, Arabic, and Jewish tales.

⁶³ Mrs. Barnes and Mrs. Tuck of Chidcock, Dorset, as recorded by Peter Kennedy, 19 October 1952 (BBC 18694).

⁶⁴ W. Anderson, *Albert Wesselski's Angriffen*, p. 30; D. K. Wilgus, "Ballad Classification," *MF* 5 (1955), p. 100; Bertrand H. Bronson, "About the Commonest British Ballads," *JIFMC* 9 (1957), 22–27.

⁶⁵ Willa Muir, *Living with Ballads* (London, 1965), pp. 171–174.

⁶⁶ See Phillips Barry, "The Part of the Folksinger in the Making of Folk Balladry," in Leach and Coffin, eds., *The Critics and the Ballad*, pp. 59–76.

⁶⁷ Reed Smith, *South Carolina*, p. 93.

⁶⁸ Patrice Coirault, *Formation de nos chansons folkloriques* (Paris, 1953), I, 26–27; Holger Nygard, "Ballads and the Middle Ages," *TSL* 5 (1960), 85–96.

⁶⁹ Louise Pound, "On the Dating of the English and Scottish Ballads, "*PMLA* 45 (1932), 10–16; E. Joan Wilson Miller, "The Rag-Bag World of Balladry," *SFQ* 24 (1960), 217–225; David C. Fowler, "Toward a Literary History of the Popular Ballad," *NYFQ* 21 (1965), 123–141. When Ewald Flügel undertook the task of dating the Child ballads in 1899 ("Zur Chronologie der englischen Balladen," *Anglia* 21 [1899], 312–358), he found only twenty-three that could be traced earlier than the seventeenth century, none of them featuring enumerative or incremental structure.

⁷⁰ W. Anderson, *Albert Wesselskis Angriffen*, pp. 35–41.

⁷¹ See Thomas Addis Emmett, "Irish Emigration during the Seventeenth and Eighteenth Centuries," *JAIHS* 2 (1899), 70; Wesley M. Gewehr, *The Great Awakening in Virginia, 1740–1790* (Durham, N. C., 1930), p. 25; Edwin C. Guillet, *The Great Migration: The Atlantic Crossing by Sailing-Ship since 1770* (London, 1937), p. 1; J. P. MacLean, *An Historical Account of the Settlements of Scotch Highlanders in America Prior to the Peace of 1783* (Glasgow, 1900), passim; George Shepperson, "Writings in Scottish-American History: A Brief Survey," *WMQ* (ser. 3), 11 (1954), 163–178. The evidence of the "Gallows Tree" texts supports the contentions of Shepperson and Herschel M. Gower ("How the Scottish Ballads Flourished in America," *SR* 6 [1960], 7–11) that the cultural influence of the Scottish emigrants of this period has been unjustly overlooked.

⁷² Emmett, "*Irish Emigration*," p. 61; J. Holland Rose et al., *The Cambridge History of the British Empire*, I (New York, 1929), 136–180; John Camden Hotten, *The Original Lists of Persons of Quality; Emigrants; Religious Exiles; Political Rebels; Serving Men Sold for a Term of Years; Apprentices; Children Stolen; Maidens Pressed; and Others Who Went from Great Britain to the American Plantations 1600–1700*," (London, 1874); Clifford K. Shipton, "Immigration to New England, 1680–1740," *JPE* 44 (1936), 225–229. I am assuming with J. W. Hendren ("The Scholar and the Ballad Singer," *SFQ* 18 [1954], 142) that ballads would have been sung primarily by the "Serving Men Sold for a Term of Years" and "Apprentices" rather than by "Persons of Quality."

IV: THE TUNES

¹ Bertrand H. Bronson, "On the Union of Words and Music in the 'Child' Ballads," *WF* 11 (1952), 233–234; Samuel P. Bayard, "American Folksongs and Their Music," *SFQ* 17 (1953), 124.

² For a conspicuous exception, see George List, "An Ideal Marriage of Ballad Text and Tune," *MF* 7 (1957), 95–112.

[3] Bronson, "Words and Music," p. 239; Bayard, "American Folksongs," p. 126 (Bayard comments that "singers almost invariably set new poems to tunes already in common use"); Philip Gordon, "The Music of the Ballads," *SFQ* 6 (1942), 147.

[4] Cecil J. Sharp, *English Folk Song: Some Conclusions,* ed. Maud Karpeles, 4th ed., rev. (Belmont, Calif., 1965), pp. 24–38; Phillips Barry, "American Folk Music," *SFQ* 1 (1937), 32, 35; Bertrand H. Bronson, "Folksong and the Modes," *MQ* 22 (1946), 44–45; Sirvart Poladian, "The Problem of Melodic Variation in Folk Song," *JAF* 55 (1942), 204–206.

[5] Sharp, *Conclusions,* pp. 68–108; Barry, "American Folk Music," pp. 42–43; Bronson, "Words and Music," p. 248; Bertrand H. Bronson, "The Morphology of the Ballad Tunes," *JAF* 67 (1954), 1–13; Bayard, "American Folksongs," p. 134; Anne Gilchrist, "A Note on the Modal System of Gaelic Tunes," *JFSS* 4 (1911), 150–153; W. B. Reynolds, "The Irish Folk Scale," *JIFSS* 10 (1911), 12–15; George Boswell, "Some Characteristics of Folksongs in Middle Tennessee," *TFSB* 15 (1949), 63–69; Victor A. Grauer, "Some Song-Style Clusters—A Preliminary Study," *Ethnomusicology* 9 (1965), 265–271.

[6] Bertrand H. Bronson, "Melodic Stability in Oral Transmission," *JIFMC* 3 (1951), 50–51; Bayard, "American Folksongs," p. 129.

[7] George Herzog, "Musical Typology in Folksong," *SFQ* 1 (1937), 51–52.

[8] Bertrand H. Bronson, "Mechanical Help in the Study of Folk Song," *JAF* 62 (1949), 81–82.

[9] Jan Schinhan, *The Music of the Ballads,* Frank C. Brown Collection of North Carolina Folklore, IV (Durham, N. C., 1957), p.xx.

[10] Donald Winkelman, "Musicological Techniques of Ballad Analysis," *MF* 10 (1960–1961), 197–205; George List, "An Approach to the Indexing of Ballad Tunes," *FFMA* 6 (1963), 7–16.

[11] George R. Stewart, Jr., "The Meter of the Popular Ballad," *PMLA* 40 (1925), 933–962.

[12] See Joseph W. Hendren, *A Study of Ballad Rhythm, with Special Reference to Ballad Music, PSE* 4 (Princeton, N. J.) (1936), p. 28; Herzog, "Typology," p. 53; Philip Gordon, "Music," p. 148; Bertrand H. Bronson, "The Interdependence of Ballad Tunes and Texts," *CFQ* 3 (1944), 186; Samuel P. Bayard, "Two Representative Tune Families of British Tradition," *MF* 4 (1954), 13–33; and Tristram P. Coffin, "Remarks Preliminary to a Study of Ballad Meter and Ballad Singing," *JAF* 78 (1965), 149–151.

[13] Sigurd Bernhard Hustvedt, "A Melodic Index of Child's Ballad Tunes," *PUCLALL* 1 (1936), 51–78.

[14] William J. Entwistle, "Notation for Ballad Melodies," *PMLA* 55 (1940), 61–72; Samuel P. Bayard, "Ballad Tunes and the Hustvedt Indexing Method," review of Hustvedt, "Melodic Index," in *JAF* 55 (1942), 148–154.

[15] Mieczyslaw Kolinski, "The Structure of Melodic Movement: A New Method of Analysis," in *Miscelanea de estudios dedicados a Fernando Ortiz,* 3 vols. (Havana, 1956), II, 879–918. A. O. Vaïsänen has proposed still another system ("Suggestions for the Methodical Classification and Investigation of Folk Tunes," *JIFMC* 1 [1949], 34–35), but it is too highly compressed for analytical purposes. See also Gustav O. Arlt, "The Status of Research in Folk Melodies," M.A. thesis (University of Chicago, 1929).

[16] Oswald Koller, "Die beste Methode, Volks- und volksmässige Lieder nach ihrer melodischen Beschaffenheit lexicalisch zu ordnen," *SIM* 4 (1902–1903), 1–15.

[17] Bronson, "Mechanical Help," p. 83. As George Foss has observed, it is probable that most tune transcriptions adjust the pitch and key to the convenience (or the capacity) of the transcriber, so that the loss of accuracy is not likely to be crucial ("The Transcription and Analysis of Folk Music," in *A Good Tale and a Bonnie Tune, PTFS* 32 [1964], 241–242).

[18] According to Sharp (*Conclusions,* p. 81) and Bronson ("Modes," p. 42), this is statistically and psychologically the preferred mid-cadence throughout Anglo-American folk song.

[19] See John A. and Alan Lomax, *Negro Folk Songs as Sung by Lead Belly* (New York, 1936).

[20] Similar five-phrase tunes do, of course, accompany the texts of Child 75 "Lord Lovel" and Child 155 "Little Sir Hugh," both of which are melodically related to the tunes now under consideration, and "Sir Hugh" has been sung with a "prickly bush" refrain. The uniqueness of this variant in our "prickly bush" tradition, however, suggests that it is not here a case of a tune tradition controlling a text (see George Boswell, "Reciprocal Controls Exerted by Ballad Texts and Tunes," *JAF,* 70 [1967], 169–174), but simply a whimsy of the singer.

[21] Gavin Greig and Alexander Keith, *Last Leaves of Traditional Ballads and Ballad Airs,* (Aberdeen, 1925), p. 47. Keith commented that two-strain tunes are extraordinarily rare in Scots tradition, and attributed their occurrence to the fondness of musicians, "even more than versifiers [for] 'perfecting' such material as comes within their reach."

[22] See Jean Ritchie, *Singing Family of the Cumberlands* (New York, 1956).

[23] Published anonymously in *JIFSS* 13 (1913), 14, as "MS No. 479, being No. 109 from Paddy Conneely." The text referred to ("Oh, stop your hand, Lord Judge," entered in this study as E23) is cited as "MS No. 355."

[24] Just as the heaviest period of Scots emigration did not begin until well into the eighteenth century (see chap. iii, n. 71), so the greatest Irish influx did not come until the nineteenth; see Donald Lines Jacobus, "Irish in New England before 1700," *NEHGR* 90 (1936), 165–167; William Forbes Adams, *Ireland and Irish Emigration to the New World from 1815 to the Famine* (New Haven, 1932), pp. 69–70, passim; W. A. Carrothers, *Emigration from the British Isles* (London, 1929), pp. 41–46; Edwin C. Guillet, *The Great Migration: The Atlantic Crossing by Sailing-Ship since 1770* (London, 1937), pp. 34, 183; Stanley C. Johnson, *A History of Emigration from the United Kingdom to North America 1763–1912* (London, 1913), pp. 14–15. G. Malcolm Laws, Jr., "Anglo-Irish Balladry in North America," *Folklore in Action,* ed. Horace P. Beck (Philadelphia, 1962), pp. 172–183, and Edith Fowke, "British Ballads in Ontario," *MF* 13 (1963), 133–162, have attested that the later Irish emigrants took few traditional ballads with them. However, the instances in American tradition of "stop the rope," "money to pay my fee," and tunes related to tune no. 2 suggest that the limited Irish "Gallows Tree" tradition was not without its effect on American versions. Such instances are probably due to emigrations prior to the Great Famine of the late 1840s.

[25] The tune has been published in William A. Owens, *Texas Folk Songs* (Austin, 1950), p. 181; Carl Sandburg, *The American Songbag* (New York, 1927), pp. 310, 456; and John A. and Alan Lomax, *Our Singing Country* (New York, 1941), p. 309.

[26] W. A. Craigie and A. J. Aitken, *DOST,* trace the word to ON *handselja* "to make over formally by shaking hands." John Jamieson, *EDSL,* and Joseph Wright, *EDD,* concur as to its general application: gift, money, or bread received at the outset of a year, a day, or an undertaking as a token of good luck.

[27] John Meier and Erich Seemann, "Volksliedaufzeichnungen der Dichterin Annette von Droste-Hülshoff, *JVF* 1 (1928), 79–118. In a personal communication dated March 30, 1968, Professor Jan P. Schinhan has corroborated the affiliations of B9 with the "willow tree" group, and advises that the cylinder recording made in 1922 by Dr. Brown of Duke University "was never made available to anyone else."

[28] With these examples in mind, it may be conjectured that a first-strain I *(VI)* V I *(VI)* V is likewise indicative of a best quasi-traditional status. The informant for B75 reported two different texts, one (B34) lacking a tune, in addition to a tune without a text (tune no. 3). The informant for D39 was himself a folklore collector.

[29] Jan Bystroń, *Pieśni Ludowe z Polskiego Śląska,* I (Krakow, 1934), 61–62, 173, 178–181 (seven variants), 187–188, 246, 271, 280, 297, 316, 349, 374, 515, 527. Most of these tunes have a fifth phrase, absent from "Gallows Tree" narrative variants. A single "Gallows Tree" analogue in this collection, in which a boy asks his relatives for water because he has a headache, is sung to a quite different tune. The tunes furnished in Erk-Böhme and by Fred Quellmaltz ("Die Melodie zur ballade von der Losgekauften," *JVF* 3 [1932]), 74, 86) for the German analogue "Die Losgekaufte" are similarly, if disappointingly, unrelated.

V: THE SYMBOLS

[1] As Kenneth Jackson (*The International Popular Tale and Early Welsh Tradition* [Cardiff, 1961], pp. 2–4) and others have frequently had occasion to remark, a dichotomy between "folk" tradition and "learned" tradition developed only with the European Renaissance in post-Classical Western literature; Geoffrey Chaucer and Chrétien de Troyes are only two of the many poets whose work shows an intimate acquaintance with the oral traditions that are still in circulation among the descendants of their contemporaries.

[2] Frank Kidson and Mary Neal, *English Folk-Song and Dance* (Cambridge, 1915), p. 58.

[3] James R. Woodall, " 'Sir Hugh': A Study in Balladry," *SFQ* 19 (1955), 77–84.

[4] J. H. Dixon, *Ancient Ballads and Songs of the Peasantry of England,* Percy Society Publications, 17 (London, 1846), 223.

[5] Sabine Baring-Gould and H. Fleetwood-Sheppard, *Songs and Ballads of the West* (London, 1892), p. 227.

[6] Harold Boulton, *Songs of the Four Nations* (London, 1893), p. 102.

[7] Lucy Broadwood and H. Fuller-Maitland, *English County Songs* (London, 1893), p. 59.

[8] Cecil J. Sharp and Charles E. Marson, *Folk Songs from Somerset,* III (London, 1906), 32–33.

[9] J. Collingwood Bruce and John Stokoe, *Northumbrian Minstrelsy* (Newcastle, 1882; facsim. ed., Hatboro, Pa., 1965), pp. 90–91; reprinted in John Stokoe and Samuel Reay, *Songs and Ballads of Northern England* (London, 1899), pp. 80–81.

[10] Sharp and Marson, *Folk Songs from Somerset,* I (London, 1904), 2.

[11] *Ibid.,* V (London, 1909), 19.

[12] George Farquhar Graham, *The Songs of Scotland,* 3 vols. (Edinburgh, 1861), II, 5. This version is from a poem, "Ye Banks and Braes o' Bonnie Doon," composed by Robert Burns.

[13] Scott Elliott, "Pulling the Heather Green," *JAF* 48 (1935), 352–361.

[14] See also E. S. Hartland, *The English Fairy and Other Folk Tales* (London, 1890), pp. 19–20; Thomas Keightley, *The Fairy Mythology* (London, 1873), p. 304.

[15] Kuno Meyer and Alfred Nutt, *The Voyage of Bran Son of Febal,* Grimm Library, IV (London, 1895), 2–5. In *Echtra Cormac,* the only other "voyage" text in which such a branch appears, it is brought by a warrior and has the property of inducing sleep, like the broom of Child 43 "Broomfield Hill" (Whitney H. Stokes and E. Windisch, *Irische Texte* [ser. 3, vol. 1], III [Leipzig, 1891], 193–195, 211–213); cf. n. 33.

[16] See James Carney, *Studies in Irish Literature and History* (Dublin, 1955), pp. 280–295. Given the ecclesiastical and generally learned bent of the author of *Imramh Brain,* it would not be going too far to suppose that he borrowed his branch from the sixth book of the *Aeneid* (see Patrick W. Joyce, *A Short History of Ireland* [London, 1894], pp. 155–158), but see n. 36.

[17] Angelo de Gubernatis, *La mythologie des plantes,* 2 vols. (Paris, 1872–1882), II, 323; Charles Joret, *La rose dans l'antiquité et au moyen âge* (Paris, 1892), pp. 305–344; Richard Folkard, *Plant Lore, Legends, and Lyrics,* 2nd ed. (London, 1892), p. 522.

[18] See, e.g., Charles M. Skinner, *Myths and Legends of Flowers, Trees, Fruits, and Plants* (Philadelphia, 1911), pp. 293–298. It may be noted, however, that this, too, is a relatively recent and quais-sophisticated development of an ancient association of the willow with death.

[19] W. Christie, *Traditional Ballad Airs,* 2 vols. (Edinburgh, 1876), I, 227. A very slightly different variant is in William Hugh Logan, *A Pedlar's Pack of Ballads and Songs* (Edinburgh, 1869), pp. 336–337.

[20] J. Pittman, Colin Brown, and Myles B. Foster, *Songs of Scotland,* 3 vols. (London, 1877), II, 10.

[21] Baring-Gould and Fleetwood-Sheppard, *Songs and Ballads,* p. 125.

[22] *Ibid.,* p. 185.

[23] Lucy Broadwood, *English Traditional Songs and Carols* (London, 1908), p. 65.

[24] Herbert Hughes, *Irish Country Songs,* 4 vols. (London, 1909), I, 69.

[25] Reference is to the English translation of Harry Robbins, *The Romance of the Rose by Guillaume de Lorris and Jean de Meun* (New York, 1962).

[26] Reference is to the English translation of J. von Hammer-Purgstall and Epiphanius Wilson, in *Turkish Literature,* ed. Epiphanius Wilson (New York, 1901), pp. 231–357.

[27] See, in addition to Joret, *La Rose,* pp. 305–344, M. J. Schleiden, *Die Rose: Geschichte und Symbolik* (Leipzig, 1873), pp. 46, 142, 153–154.

[28] Eugène Rolland, *Recueil de chansons populaires* (Paris, 1883), p. 202.

[29] E. Hoffmann-Krayer and Hanns Bächtold-Stäubli, *HDA,* VII, 779.

[30] Allan Gilbert, trans., *The Orlando Furioso of Ariosto,* 2 vols. (New York, 1954), I, 8.

[31] Frank Nicholson, trans., *Old German Love Songs* (Chicago, 1907), p. 163. (For this reference I am indebted to Barbara Seward, *The Symbolic Rose* [New York, 1960].) The German poets Herder and Goethe gave the theme a sophisticated twist in "Heidenröslein," a purported folk ballad: in their poems, the rose's defense is of no avail, and she must suffer herself to be broken by a youth

who does not mind the pricks (Franz Magnus Böhme, *Volksthümliche Lieder der Deutschen im 18. und 19. Jahrhundert* [Leipzig, 1895], pp. 96–97).

[32] Angelo de Gubernatis, *Mythologie des Plantes* I, 127–130; *HDA*, II, 358; *HDM*, I, 408.

[33] *HDA*, II, 359; *HDM*, I, 409–410; Johannes Bolte and Georg Polívka, *Ammerkungen zu den Kinder- und Hausmärchen der Brüder Grimm*, 5 vols. (Leipzig, 1912–1932), I, 434–442. Mackensen suggests that it entered the tradition through an association with the "sleep-thorn" of Scandinavian tradition (see n. 15 and Inge Boberg, *Motif-Index of Early Icelandic Literature* [Copenhagen, 1966], D1364.2); Schleiden further associated the "sleep-thorn" with the "sleep-apple," a growth sometimes found on the stems of wild roses (*Die Rose*, p. 181).

[34] H. Rockham, et al., trans., *Natural History of Pling the Elder*, 10 vols., Loeb Classical Library (London, 1938–1942), IV, 326–327, VI, 84–85 (Books XV, xvii, and XXIV, lxxii).

[35] Heinrich Marzell, *Die Pflanzen im deutschen Volksleben* (Jena, 1925), pp. 48–53.

[36] Wilhelm Mannhardt, *Wald- und Feldkulte*, 2nd ed., 2 vols. (Berlin, 1904–1905), I, 34–38, 50–51, 60–61, 70–71, II, 5, 33, 37. In an otherwise perceptive and illuminating article ("An Oral Canon for the Child Ballads: Construction and Application," *JFI* 4 [1967], 75–101), J. Barre Toelken dismisses this pan-European tradition as "a sophisticated and far-off concept" (pp. 96–97); I submit that the "breaking of a little bush" that motivates fratricidal murder in many variants of Child 19 "Edward" is more intelligible in these terms than it is as a figurative representation of incest, as Tristram P. Coffin argued ("The Murder Motive in 'Edward,'" *WF* 8 [1949], 314–319). Toelken's position, that oral tradition in balladry must be distinguished from the "non-oral," is a sound one; nevertheless, it cannot be assumed that ballad imagery occupies a world divorced from other kinds of folk tradition, which deserve to be investigated before they are disclaimed.

[37] The proverb, "no rose without a thorn," is related but distantly to the complex under discussion. Its implications are those exploited by Herder and Goethe in their "Heidenröslein" poems (see n. 31), as is demonstrated by numerous parallel proverbs in all western European languages: "no fire without smoke," "no grain without chaff," "no honey without poison," and so on. In the sense of this proverb, the thorn, like smoke, chaff, and poison, represents not failure but the necessary and quite tolerable disadvantages that are likely to accompany any positive good. See *SGRS*, I, 480–484, and *DSL*, II, 677–681, IV, 1723–1730.

[38] Hedwig von Beit, *Symbolik des Märchens*, 2 vols. (Bern, 1957), II, 37.

[39] Max Lüthi, *Die Gabe im Märchen und in der Sage* (Zurich, 1943), pp. 39–44. Even this interpretation is by no means universal; balls, combs, rings, spinning wheels, and other objects more frequently appear as gifts entailing no special significance at all, according to Lüthi.

[40] Douglas Hyde, *Beside the Fire* (London, 1910), pp. 129–141. In this tale, the ball is a silver one and guides the hero to the magic water his father needs to restore him to health.

[41] Sidney O. Addy, *Household Tales, Collected in the Counties of York, Lincoln, Derby, and Nottingham* (London, 1895), pp. 50–53. Copper, silver, and golden balls are rolled by a grateful "little red hairy man" to lead the hero to giant-killing adventures. This corresponds in the main to AaT 431A, with two Irish variants reported. The motif is D1313.1, reported in Arabic, Indian, and Irish tradition, and occasionally occurs in AaT 425 as well.

[42] James F. Dimock, ed. *Itinerarium Kambriae, Giraldi Cambrensis Opera*, VI (London, 1868), 75–76 (lib. 1, cap. 8). In this very old British tale concerning a golden ball, the motif is theft—just as it is in the majority of "Gallows Tree" variants that seek to account for the victim's jeopardy.

[43] John Gregorson Campbell, *The Fians: Stories, Poems, and Traditions*, Argyllshire Series, IV (London, 1891), 260, 274 (two different variants).

[44] *DGF* 70 (II, 238–254, and III, 841).

[45] Bolte and Polívka, *Anmerkungen*, I, 5–7. Of the four variants known to Bolte in which the object lost by the princess is a golden ball, the other three were collected in the last quarter of the nineteenth century, two in eastern Germany and one, corresponding almost word for word to the Grimm selection, from a Latvian informant (E. Veckenstedt, *Wendische Sagen, Märchen und aberglaubische Gebräuche* [Graz, 1880], p. 254; E. Kühn, *Der Spreewald und seine Bewohner* [Cottlius, 1889], p. 143; Th. Ja. Treuland, *Sbornik materialov po etnografii izdavajenij pri Daškovskom etnografičeskom Muzeje*, V [Moscow, 1887], 148). Thompson's *Motif-Index* furnishes no references except to this text and its three imitators (C41.2, G423).

[46] In a letter to the first translator of *Kinder- und Hausmärchen* Scott expressed his delight at receiving the volume and added: "The Prince Paddock was ... a legend well known to me; where a princess is sent to fetch water in a sieve" (Edgar Taylor, trans. *German Popular Stories and Fairy Tales as Told by Gammer Grethel,* rev. ed. [London, 1878], p. 305). In accordance with this version of the tradition is a variant published by the Grimms in volume ii of their first edition but dropped from subsequent editions and never translated (Wilhelm Hansen, *Grimm's Other Tales,* trans. Ruth Michaelis-Jena and Arthur Ratcliff [Edinburgh, 1956], pp. 16–18, 152).

[47] Edgar Taylor's first translation was done in 1823 (*German Popular Stories Translated from the Kinder und Hausmärchen collected by M. M. Grimm,* 2 vols. [London, 1823]), with "The Frog Prince" appearing on pp. 205–210. A second edition followed in 1827, with "The Frog Prince" on pp. 206–211, and a third, entitled *Gammer Grethel,* with "The Frog Prince" on pp. 227–232, in 1839. The revised edition noted above (n. 46) was the fourth.

[48] Lucy Crane, trans., *Household Stories from the Collection of the Bros. Grimm* (London, 1882); "The Frog Prince," pp. 32–36.

[49] Mrs. H. B. Paull and Mr. L. A. Wheatley, Grimm's *Fairy Tales and Household Stories for Young People* (London, 1895); "The Frog Prince," pp. 9–12.

[50] Mrs. Edward Lucas, trans., *Fairy Tales of the Brothers Grimm* (London, 1902), "The Frog Prince," pp. 79–85.

[51] That is, in that on occasion a guiding ball or a lost ball leads to an encounter with the protagonist's future mate, which is a far different thing from prior loss of virginity. Other instances of golden balls in traditional materials illustrate the fluidity of the symbol: a golden ball rolls into a group of playing children to announce the appearance of an ogre bent upon mischief (*HDA*, V, 763–764); a girl makes her escape from a giant by putting his golden ball, entrusted to her care, inside a golden ring and wishing herself home (Addy, *Household Tales,* pp. 6–7); a political exile exhorts his sympathizers to "love not too much the golden ball, / But keep your conscience" (John Harland, *Ballads and Songs of Lancashire* [London, 1875], p. 54). All of these "golden balls" are obviously symbols of power; even this attribution, however, is less pervasive in European tradition than that proposed by Baring-Gould and lacking in all narrative significance, the yellow sphere as the sun (*HDA*, V, 754–755).

[52] E. F. Rimbault, *A Little Book of Songs and Ballads* (London, 1851), pp. 49–52.

[53] Károly Kerényi, *Essays on a Science of Mythology,* trans. R. F. C. Hull, rev. ed., (New York, 1963), pp. 18–24; Clyde Kluckhohn, "Recurrent Themes in Myths and Mythmaking," *Daedalus* 88 (1959), 268–279. Compare chap. i, n. 35.

[54] Neither Baring-Gould's version of the *cante-fable,* which utilized the golden-ball-as-gift-of-little-man of German and English legend, nor the remaining variants, which retained from the Grimm tale only the golden-ball-given-to-girl-by-father-and-lost motif, can really explain the relatively wide distribution of the linking of the latter motif with "The Gallows Tree." As we have seen, there is no evidence whatsoever for a traditional source for that motif. A possible solution lies in the huge and steady stream of inexpensive chapbook publications emanating from presses in Aberdeen, Paisley, Edinburgh, and Glasgow during the first half of the nineteenth century; according to F. J. Harvey Darton, "there is direct evidence that [such publications] penetrated Southern nurseries," and that they "contained all the popular literature of four centuries in a reduced and degenerate form: most of it in a form rudely adapted for use by children and poorly educated country folk. Who the adapters were no one can guess. They did not always make texts we should now choose for high moral tone" (*Children's Books in England: Five Centuries of Social Life* [Cambridge, Eng., 1932] pp. 79–82). It will be recalled that Baring-Gould had learned *KHM* 4 from such a chapbook; that some such adapter had grafted fragments of "The Gallows Tree" onto a manufactured tale involving the threat of death for the loss of the princess' golden ball borrowed from Taylor's translation, while perhaps incapable of proof, is at least a more credible hypothesis than that the convergence was spontaneous (see Walter Anderson, *Zu Albert Wesselski's Angriffen auf die finnische folkloristische Forschungsmethode, ACUT* [H] 38 [1936], 44–45).

[55] Collected from Seamus Mac a Baird, Innishigo, Co. Galway, 1960 (IFC MS 1607, pp. 251–253).

[56] William Andrews, "A Lancashire Ballad," *NQ* (ser. 6), 6 (1882), 269; Allan M. Trout, "Greetings," *LCJ,* January 30, 1958. Cf. discussions in William Chappell and J. Woodfall Ebsworth, *The*

Roxburghe Ballads, 8 vols. (Hertford, 1871–1899), I, 318–319, and *NQ* (ser. 4), 4 (1869), 294, 417, 525; 5 (1870), 95–96.

[57] "The English Merchant of Chichester," Chappell and Ebsworth, *Roxburghe Ballads,* I, 320–325.

[58] "Die Drei Gefangenen," Erk-Böhme 65c.

[59] "Erlösung von Galgen," *DVM* 22.

[60] "Die Bernauerin," *DVM* 65.

[61] "The Noble Lord," in H. F. Birch-Reynardson, *Sussex Songs* (London, [n.d.]), pp. 8–9, and "Constance of Cleveland," Chappell and Ebsworth, *Roxburghe Ballads,* VI, 572–575.

[62] Wilhelm Heiske, "Rechtsbrauch und Rechtsempfinden im Volkslied," *DJV* 2 (1956), 73–79; Hinrich Siuts, "Volksballaden—Volkserzählungen (Motiv- und Typenregister)," *Fabula* 5 1962), 72–89.

[63] For a variant of Laws Q 37 from American oral tradition with notes, see Bertha McKee Dobie, "Tales and Rhymes of a Texas Household," In *Texas and Southwest Lore, PTFS* 6 (1927), 56–65

[64] Logan, *Pedlar's Pack,* p. 157.

[65] W. W. Skeat, *The Lay of Havelok the Dane, EETS,* extra series 4 (London, 1868).

[66] Karl Brunner, *The Seven Sages of Rome (Southern Version),* EETS 191 (London, 1933), xx, 204–205.

[67] For a discussion of this theme in classical and medieval literature, see *HDM,* I, 350–351.

[68] Cosmo Innes, *Lectures on Scottish Legal Antiquities* (Edinburgh, 1872), p. 234; W. S. Holdsworth, *A History of English Law,* rev. ed., 14 vols. (London, 1956), II, 363. The tenacity of the concept is illustrated by the report of John A. and Alan Lomax that the father of Huddie Ledbetter "tried to buy him out of the penitentiary, and couldn't understand why Captain Flanagan wouldn't take his money and let his boy go home" (*Negro Folk Songs as Sung by Lead Belly* [New York, 1936], p. 20), and by such American murder ballads as Laws E10 "Wild Bill Jones," and Laws F6 "Rose Connolly," in which a death sentence for the protagonist is regularly accompanied by stanzas in which the relatives try to purchase his freedom.

[69] See, in addition to the examples cited above, an episode in *The Saga of Grettir the Strong,* trans. G. A. Hight (London, 1914, 1929), pp. 140–142, and AaT 451 (for a variant of AaT 451 from Scots oral tradition, see "The Three Shirts of Canach Down," John G. McKay, *More West Highland Tales* [Edinburgh and London, 1940], pp. 347–369). It is obvious that rescue from the gallows itself takes many variant forms, while rescue by payment of a large sum of money traditionally is effected (or attempted) before that stage of the narrative is reached.

[70] Anne Gilchrist and Lucy E. Broadwood, "Notes on Children's Game-Songs: The Prickly Bush (The Maid Freed from the Gallows) and Its Connection with the Story of the Golden Ball," *JFSS* 5 (1915), p. 234, and Dorothy Scarborough, *On the Trail of Negro Folk-Song* (Cambridge, Mass., 1925), p. 38. These assertions make no distinction between the hanging of "The Gallows Tree" and the burning of "Lady Maisry"; indeed, it is suggested that the "prickly bush" refrain constitutes a reference to the bonfire materials of the latter.

[71] A. Ewert, ed. *The Romance of Tristan by Béroul* (Oxford, 1939), pp. 26–27; Eugène Vinaver, ed. *The Works of Sir Thomas Malory,* 3 vols. (Oxford, 1947), III, 1165–1178; Jonas Balys, *Lithuanian Narrative Folksong* (Washington, D.C., 1954), p. 17; Heiske, "Rechtsbrauch und Rechtsempfinden," p. 76; Sir Frederick Pollock and F. W. Maitland, *The History of English Law before the Time of Edward I,* 2 vols. (Cambridge, 1895), II, 372, 542; William Andrews, *Bygone Punishments* (London, 1931), pp. 213–221. William E. Sellers ("Kinship in the British Ballads: The Historical Evidence," *SFQ* 20 (1956), 199–215) expressed doubt that the kinship system upon which such an offense would be based obtained very generally at the time of the composition of most of the British ballads (p. 204); a satirical treatise, *A Short Discourse why a law should pass in England, to punish Adultery with Death,* published April 17, 1675, refers to Cromwell's attempt to establish adultery as a civil offense (*The Harleian Miscellany,* 12 vols. [London, 1810], VIII, 66–68; see also X, 240–241). Seller's opinion may not go far enough, for the versions of *Tristan* and *Lancelot* cited above are exceptional in the two traditions even for the period 1150–1500.

[72] Ewert, *Tristan,* pp. 26–27; Vinaver, *Malory,* III, 1165–1178; Archer Taylor, "Themes Common to English and German Balladry," *MLQ* 1 (1940), 30–31; Child, II, 113; Karl von Amira, "Die germanischen Todesstrafen," *ABAW (P–H)* 21 (1922), 195–198. Andrews (*Punishments,* pp. 90–96) and John Laurence (*A History of Capital Punishment* [New York, 1960], pp 6, 9, 22) point out

that burning was until the end of the eighteenth century the preferred punishment for women regardless of offense, although drowning (the method preferred in Lithuanian ballads according to Balys) was also favored for them (Andrews, *Punishments*, pp. 87–89; Laurence, *Capital Punishment*, pp. 10–11; Innes, *Legal Antiquities*, p. 59).

[73] "Pwyll, Prince of Dyfed," in *The Mabinogion*, trans. Gwyn Jones and Thomas Jones (London, 1949, 1966), pp. 18–19 (a wife, not a maiden); Child 173 "Mary Hamilton"; Holdsworth, *English Law*, IV, 501; and Laurence, *Capitol Punishment*, p. 168 (extension of the crime to concealment of death of bastard child in seventeenth century). It is evident here how "The Gallows Tree" became attached to "Mary Hamilton": the latter's French and Hungarian analogues mention the possibility of ransom (Lajos Vargyas, *Researches into the Medieval History of Folk Ballad* [Budapest, 1967], p. 59). Needless to say, the crime imputed is murder, as it is in the majority of English and American ballads in which the circumstance arises, not fornication.

VI: THE TRADITION IN EUROPE

[1] Erik Pohl, *Die deutsche Volksballade von der "Losgekaufte,"* FFC 105 (Helsinki, 1934), p. 339; Hakon Grüner-Nielsen, *DGF*, VIII, 465; Julius Krohn, "Das Lied vom Mädchen, welches erlöst werden soll," *JSFO* 10 (1892), 125. The reasoning of all three is based in part upon Krohn's conclusion that the meter of the Finnish version was unknown in West Finland before the end of the seventeenth century.

[2] Biði Frísir og Frísir biði, Fraendur munu mig leysa.
Minn góði faðirinn og goði minn faðirinn,
Leystu mig frá Frísum!
"Minn goða dótterin og goða mín dótterin,
Með hverju á eg þig oð leysa?"
"Minn goði faðirinn og goði minn faðirinn,
Gjaltu þinn garðinn ut fyrir mig."
"Min goða dótterin og goða mín dótterin,
Betri þykir mér hann en þú."

Translation based on Falk and Torp, *NDEW*.

[3] Georg Heeger and Wilhelm Wüst, *Volkslieder aus der Rheinpfalz*, 2 vols. (Kaiserslautern, 1909), I, 61–63.

[4] Karl Simrock, *Die deutsche Volkslieder* (Frankfurt, 1851), pp. 55–56.

[5] Alexander Reifferscheid, *Westfälische Volkslieder im Wort und Weise* (Heilbronn, 1879), p. 138.

[6] Raimund and Elizabeth Zoder, "Das Volkslied," *Oesterreich und die angelsächsische Welt*, ed. Otto Hietsch (Vienna, 1961), pp. 384–407.

[7] Georgios A. Megas, "Die Ballade von der Losgekauften," *JVF* 3 (1932), 54–73.

[8] *Ibid.*, pp. 56–57; cf. chap. iv, n. 27. This version, characterized by the verb "verkaufe,' turning the ship rather than sinking it ("rumme gahn"), and the demand that the lover sell himself to the galleys, had as extraordinary circulation in print as did certain American texts of "The Gallows Tree." In the form published by Böhme, it was cited by Anne Gilchrist and Lucy E. Broadwood ("Notes on Children's Game-Songs: The Prickly Bush [The Maid Freed from the Gallows] and Its Connection with the Story of the Golden Ball," *JFSS* 5 (1915), 239) as having appeared in a popular song-book entitled *Der Zupfgeigenhansl*, ed. Hans Breuer (Leipzig, 1914). More frequently reprinted is von Droste-Hülshoff's composition, beginning "Lass du das Fähnlein rumme drehn, / lass du das Schiffen untergehn." It appeared in the collections of Ludwig Uhland, *Alte hoch- und niederdeutsche Volkslieder* (Stuttgart and Tübingen, 1844), No. 117; Franz Ludwig Mittler, *Deutsche Volkslieder* (Frankfurt, 1865), No. 61; A. F. C. Vilmar, *Handbüchlein für Freunde des deutschen Volkslieds* (Marburg, 1867), p. 207; G. Scherer, *Jungbrunnen* (Berlin, 1875), No. 13B; C. F. Aumer, *Ulmer Liederbuch* (Ulm, 1883), No. 88; V. Böckel, *Handbuch des deutsches Volkslieds* (Marburg, 1908), p. 153; and, of course, in the article by John Meier and Erich Seemann demonstrating its authorship ("Volksliedaufzeichnungen der Dichterin Annette von Droste-Hülshoff," *JVF* 1 (1928), 114). A text published by Simrock has "Lass das Schiff zu Lande gehn," a "sinken-ertrinken" rhyme, and the "verkaufe-ans-Ruder" motif, indicating that this mass-media-promoted version was not without its effect upon oral tradition (Simrock, *Deutschen Volkslieder*, pp. 90–91).

[9] Albert R. Frey, *A Dictionary of Numismatic Names* (New York, 1917), pp. 204, 213.

[10] *DW*, X, 661–662.

[11] Henry Sager, "Die Losgekaufte," *MP* 27 (1929), 129–145.

[12] Branford P. Millar, "Eighteenth-Century Views of the Ballad," *WF* 9 (1950), 124–135. See also Erik Dal, *Nordisk folkeviseforskning siden 1800* (Copenhagen, 1956).

[13] Text published in full by Felix Liebrecht, *Zur Volkskunde* (Heilbronn, 1879), pp. 223–226, from an earlier publication by Salvatore Struppa; résumé and reconstituted text, Giovanni B. Bronzini, *La Canzone Epico-lirica nell'Italia Centro-Meridionale*, 2 vols. (Rome, 1956), I, 271–276.

[14] The sporadic appearance of "lass das Schiff zu Lande gahn" in German tradition is in agreement, however.

[15] Ettore Rossi, "Scibilia Nobili e la leggenda maltese della Sposa della Mosta," *Lares* (N.S.), 3 (1932), 5–10; Antonio Cremona, "Is the Maid of Mosta a Myth?" *JMULS* 10 (1934).

[16] Francesch Pelay Briz., *Cansons de la Terra*, 5 vols. (Barcelona, 1864–1877), I, 117–118.

[17] Liebrecht, *Zur Volkskunde*, pp. 231–232 ("La Donzella," reprinted from *Die Balearen in Wort und Bild Geschildert* [Leipzig, 1871], II, 263 ff). Cited by Bronzini, *Canzone Epico-lirica*, p. 231, and Briz *Cansons*, IV, 15–17.

[18] Briz, *Cansons*, IV, 13–14. Cited by Iivar Kempinnen, *Lunastettava neito: Vertaileva Balladi-Tutkimus* (Helsinki, 1957), pp. 12–13, and Reifferscheid, *Westfälische Volkslieder*, p. 139.

[19] H. Neus, *Ehstnische Volkslieder*, 2 vols. (Reval, 1850), I, 109.

[20] Michele Barbi, "Scibilia Nobili e la Raccolta dei Canti Popolari," *Pallante*, 1 (1929), 1–73.

[21] This formulation supports the hypothesis of German provenance for the coin-differentiating syndrome, these coins appearing at a later date than "Ross" and "Schwert":"two pieces of money" ("Löwenpfennige"), "two of silver" ("Falkenthaler"), and "gold."

[22] Elvira Francello, "An Italian Version of 'Maid Freed from the Gallows,'" *NYFQ* 2 (1946), 139–140. Two other American variants, published in *La Calabria*, June 15, 1889, and September 15, 1890, have not been examined.

[23] Lutz Röhrich, "Die Volksballade von 'Herrn Peters Seefahrt' und die Menschenopfer-Sagen," *Märchen, Mythos, Dichtung*, eds. Hugo Kuhn and Kurt Schrier, *Festschrift Friedrich von der Leyen* (Munich, 1963), pp. 177–212.

[24] W. H. D. Rouse, "Sacrifice to Avoid Shipwreck," *Folk Lore* 12 (1901), 105.

[25] Basil Hall Chamberlain, trans. *Ko-ji-ki (Records of Ancient Matters)*, *TASJ* 10, supplement (1882), 212.

[26] Esther Lowell Hibbard, "The Ulysses Motif in Japanese Literature," *JAF* 59 (1946), 232.

[27] "The Story of Ginevra," purporting to date to the fifteenth century, and relating how a girl married against her will dies and is buried, but returns to life to seek shelter in turn from her husband, family members, and former lover, is a parallel but obviously independent tradition (see Felix Liebrecht, "Die Todten von Lustnau," *Germania* 13 [1868], 168–169.

[28] O. J. Brill, "Der Schäfer und der Edelmann," *PQ* 9 (1930), 43–50.

[29] Leopold Haupt and Johan Ernst Schmaler, *Volkslieder der Wenden in der Ober- und nieder-Lausitz*, 2 vols. (Grimma, 1841–1843), I, 297–298.

[30] Equivalent to a ducat; so named after the slang term for penny, "Fuchs." The word came into poetic use as a metaphor for a horse with a reddish-gold hide in the nineteenth century (Frey, *Numismatic Names*, p. 89; *DW*, IV, 775–776).

[31] It should no longer be possible to doubt that Erik Pohl's contention that the English ballad is a free and arbitrary reconstruction of the Spanish version ("*Losgekaufte*," pp. 315, 323) and that "gold and fee" antedates "silver" and "to set me free" in that ballad (pp. 50, 57) is inacceptable. Neither the theory of "convergence" nor the theory of "complex-demand" will satisfactorily account for the patterns that have emerged from this review.

[32] Anton Herrmann, "Beiträge zur Vergleichung der Volkspoesie: Liebesprobe," *EMU* 1 (1887), 42–43.

[33] Karl Ulmann, *Lettische Volkslieder übertragen im Versmasse der Originale* (Riga, 1874), pp. 168–169.

[34] Krohn, "Mädchen," p. 116.

[35] Anastasius Grün [Anton Alexander von Auersperg], *Volkslieder aus Krain* (Leipzig, 1850), pp. 30–33; reprinted by Reifferscheid, *Westfälische Volkslieder*, pp. 140–141, and cited by Child, II, 350.

[36] P. von Goetze, *Stimmen, des russischen Volks in Liedern* (Stuttgart, 1828), pp. 150–151. Another translation of the same text is to be found in Haupt and Schmaler, *Wenden*, I, 358, and in Joseph Wenzig, *Slawische Volkslieder* (Halle, 1830), pp. 151–152.

[37] Julius Altmann, *Die Balalaika: Russische Volks-Lieder* (Berlin, 1863), pp. 40–44.

[38] *DGF*, VIII, 461.

[39] Jonas Balys, *Lithuanian Narrative Folksong* (Washington, D.C., 1954), pp. 64–65 (résumé of Lithuanian type).

[40] Walter Ruben, *Ozean der Märchenströme, Teil I, FFC* 133 (Helsinki, 1944), 279 (résumé).

[41] Heinrich von Wlislocki, *Volksdichtungen der siebenbürgischen und südungarischen Zigeuner* (Vienna, 1890), pp. 119–121; cited by Kempinnen, *Lunastettava neito*, p. 51.

[42] P. von Goetze, *Serbische Volkslieder in's deutsch uebertragen* (Leipzig, 1827), pp. 48–49.

[43] In spite of Pohl's single Polish variant, it is doubtful that this version of the ballad cycle has had any wide circulation in Poland. Neither the collection of Jan Bystroń (see chap. iv, n. 29) nor that of Oskar Kolberg (*Lud: Jego zwyczaje, sposób zycia, mowa, podania, przsłowia, aberzedy, gusła, zabawy, pieśni, musyka, i tance*, 35 vols. [Krakow, 1857–1907]) yielded an example upon search. Types that do appear are the thirst motif, as has been mentioned, and two involving the loss of a girl's wreath and the beating of a wife by her husband (only her brother is willing to intervene), all three of which are also found in Lithuanian tradition (Erich Seemann, "Deutsche-litauische Volksliedbeziehungen," *JVF* 8 [1951], 197–198, and Balys, *Lithuanian Narrative Folksong*, pp. 57, 65).

[44] Seemann, "Volksliedbezehungen," pp. 197–199 (only Aa, Ba, and Ca "Befreiung aus Notlage" are considered here).

[45] This Spanish tradition has been identified only by means of two variants of "Delgadina" from the western hemisphere. One, published in *CFSB* 1 (April, 1962), 20–21, lacks the sequence of relatives: when she refuses to commit incest with him, a girl's father locks her in a dark room without food or water, and her mother learns of the reason for the punishment too late to save her from dying of thirst. The other version was kindly furnished me from New Mexico oral tradition by Professor John Robb of the University of New Mexico; the situation is the same, but on successive days the girl sees her sister combing her hair with a golden comb, her brother bouncing a golden ball (!), her mother putting on golden shoes, and her father sitting on golden pillows. She asks each one to give her water to quench her thirst, but in vain. In a comparable Greek version, the thirst motif is combined with the narrative tradition in which a mother kills her son's bride by poisoning her (Hermann Lübke, *Neugriechische Volks- und Liebslieder* [Berlin, 1895], pp. 235–236).

[46] It was remarked in chapter iii that the resemblance in narrative structure between variant C47 of "The Gallows Tree" and certain eastern European variants might be accounted for in terms of "complex-demand." No such explanation serves for the presence in Laws I20, a ballad of Black American provenance entitled "Willie Warfield," of stanzas whose narrative content is almost precisely identical to that of the Russian, Lithuanian, and Turkish variants demanding an unspecified ransom (notes 36, 37, 39, 40):

> I wrote my father a letter,
> "Oh, come and go my bail."
> He sent me back for answer,
> He had no land for sale.
> Every man ought to know when he loses.
>
> I wrote my girl a letter,
> "Oh, come and go my bail."
> She pawned her ring and diamonds,
> And now I'm out of jail.
> Every man ought to know when he loses.

(*Kentucky Folklore Record*, III [1957], 105). It appears that the degree of culture-contact in the United States between Black Americans and Americans of Slavic descent, to say nothing of those of Scots and Irish descent (as is abundantly attested in "Gallows Tree" variants), has been very much greater than official record or popular belief has heretofore allowed.

⁴⁷ See Franz Xaver Miklosich, "Über die Mundarten und die Wanderungen der Zigeuner Europas," *DKAW (P-H)* (Vienna, 1872–1881), XXI, 197–253; XXII, 21–102; XXIII, 1–46, 273–340; XXV, 1–68; XXVI, 1–66, 161–247; XXVII, 1–108; XXX, 159–208, 391–486; XXXI, 1–54, 55–114; Jean-Paul Clébert, *Les Tziganes* (Paris, 1961), pp. 51–55; Brian Vesey-Fitzgerald, *Gypsies of Britain: An Introduction to Their History* (London, 1944, 1946), pp. 12–20.

⁴⁸ See Charles G. Leland, *English Gypsy Songs* (Philadelphia, 1875), p. v; John Sampson, "English Gypsy Songs and Rhymes," *JGLS* 2 (1890–1891), 81; Anglo-Romani Songs," *JGLS* (N.S.) 3 (1909), 157–158; Moriz Rosenfeld, "Lieder der Zigeuner," *UR* (1882), p. 824 (reprint of "Die Zigeunerlieder und ihre Sänger," *AAW* 10 [1879], 362–367).

⁴⁹ A. F. Pott, *Die Zigeuner in Europa und Asien*, 2 vols. (Halle, 1844), I, 57; Vladislav Zielinski, "Notes on the Nomadic Gypsies of Poland," *JGLS* 3 (1891–1892), 108–109.

⁵⁰ Laura Smith, *Through Romany Songland* (London, 1889), pp. 124–125, 136–138, 135–136, 169–170.

⁵¹ Vesey-Fitzgerald, *Gypsies of Britain*, p. 12; Clébert, *Tziganes*, p. 108. The principal evidence for this early date is an Act declared in Scotland in 1449 directed against "sorners, overliers, and masterful beggars, with horse, hounds, or other goods."

⁵² "Early Annals of the Gypsies in England," *JGLS* 1 (1889), 6–7.

⁵³ Crofton, "Gypsies in England," pp. 8–13; Vesey-Fitzgerald, *Gypsies of Britain*, pp. 29–31; Clébert, *Tziganes*, pp. 83–108, passim.

⁵⁴ Clébert, *Tziganes*, pp. 108–111, passim; Hermann Aichele, *Die Zigeunerfrage mit besonderer Berücksichtigung Württembergs* (Stuttgart, 1911), pp. 53–54; Vladislav Zielinski, "Notes on the Gypsies of Poland and Lithuania," *JGLS* 2 (1891), 239.

⁵⁵ Eric O. Winstead, "Early Annals," *JGLS* (N.S.), 4 (1910–1911), 159–160.

⁵⁶ Crofton, "Gypsies in England," p. 24. A few others were reported to have been hanged at Stafford immediately after the Restoration; Vesey-Fitzgerald called this the last instance of Gypsy persecution, but confused it with the Suffolk hanging (*Gypsies of Britain*, p. 31).

⁵⁷ H. B. McKerrow, ed. *The Gull's Horne-Booke* (London, 1904).

⁵⁸ C. F. Tucker Brooke and Nathaniel Burton Paradise, *English Drama 1580–1642* (Boston, 1933), pp. 625–644.

⁵⁹ Henry T. Crofton, "Supplementary Annals of the Gypsies in England before 1700," *JGLS* (N.S.), 1 (1907–1908), 33.

⁶⁰ I do not regard this opinion as sacrosanct; the ballad could have been communicated and adapted to the local language at any time from the beginning of the fifteenth century in any European country. The failure to recover it in France, however, and the certainty that the Scandinavian versions are derived from antecedent traditions, coincide with the unusual amount of hostility toward Gypsies characteristic of those countries. Italy, where both the prison theme and the ransom-by-cash theme seem to have best been preserved on the Continent, was relatively hospitable to the invaders, according to Clébert.

VII: THE SOURCE

¹ Cecil J. Sharp, *English Folk Songs*, 2 vols. (London, 1959), II, v; reprinted from Cecil J. Sharp and Charles E. Marson, *Folk Songs from Somerset*, V (London, 1909), 88.

² Archer Taylor, "Some Recent Studies in Folksongs," *MF* 7 (1957), 232–233.

³ Alexander H. Krappe, "The Maid Freed from the Gallows," *Speculum*, 16 (1941), 240; Friedrich Ege, review of Kempinnen's *Lunastettava neito*, in *JAF* 72 (1959), 72. Kempinnen's conclusion that the ballad proper originated in the twelfth or thirteenth century in southern Europe does agree, if only roughly, with my own.

⁴ Bernhard Schmidt, *Das Volksleben der Neugriechen und das hellenische Alterthum* (Leipzig, 1871), pp. 236–237.

⁵ Bernhard Schmidt, *Griechische Märchen, Sagen, und Volkslieder* (Leipzig, 1877), p. 155.

⁶ The Greek appellations are related to German "Groschen" and Italian "Florin"; all are derived from Byzantine Greek γρῶσιον "small change, cash" and φλῶριον "gold coin" (Carolo du Fresne

DuCange, *Glossarium ad Scriptores Mediae et Infimae Graecitatis* [Graz, 1958], p. 1685; Appendix, p. 52).

[7] Notable, too, is the circumlocution for "never" found in one American variant of "The Gallows Tree" (see chap. iii, n. 43). This correspondence may be coincidental, although it is well to be cautious in this regard (see chap. vi, n. 46). The others, however, strongly suggest that the composer of this elegiac knew the ballad in the form that became attached to "Scibilia Nobili."

[8] Emile Legrand, *Recueil de chansons populaires grècques* (Paris, 1874), pp. 254–255. Here Charon is specified as the skipper, and the proffered ransom is gold, "gifts," and "keys" (perhaps to strongboxes?). Again, however, the influence is more likely to be that of the popular ballad upon the elegy than the other way around. In literary tradition, Charon's fee was cited often enough from the fifth century B.C. onward (see L. V. Grinsell, "The Ferryman and His Fee: A Study in Ethnology, Archaeology, and Tradition," *Folk-Lore*, 68 [1957], 261–262); but the fee was to guarantee safe passage to the other world, not to forestall it.

[9] Otto Waser, *Charon, Charun, Charos* (Berlin, 1898), passim; F. von Duhn, "Charonlekythen," *JDAI* 2 (1887), 240–243. On the basis of technique and style, von Duhn dated his examples around the beginning of the fourth century of the Christian era.

[10] Dirk Christian Hesseling, *Charos: Ein Beiträg zur Kenntnis des Neugriechischen Volksglaubens* (Leiden and Leipzig, 1897), pp. 11, 49; Julius Athanasius Ambrosch, *De Charonte Etrusco* (Bratislava, 1837), pp. 27–28, 63.

[11] Henry George Liddell and Robert Scott, *A Greek-English Lexicon*, rev. ed. (Oxford, 1940), p. 1981 and reference to p. 1980 (χαροπός).

[12] Kurt Heinemann, *Thanatos in Poesie und Kunst der Griechen* (Munich, 1913), pp. 58, 81; Alfred Maury, "Du personnage de la mort et de ses représ dans l'antiquité et au moyen âge," *RA* 4 (1847), 784–785; Otto Waser, "Thanatos," in W. H. Roscher, *Ausführliches Lexicon der griechischen und römischen Mythologie*, 6 vols. (Leipzig and Berlin, 1884–1937), V, 497.

[13] Karl Krumbacher, *Geschichte der byzantinischen Litteratur von Justinian bis zum Ende des oströmischen Reiches (527–1453)* (Munich, 1891), pp. 406–408; Schmidt, *Neugriechen*, pp. 225–228.

[14] Schmidt, *Griechische Märchen*, pp. 159–161. Again "gold and silver" appears as a ransom against death, without the shipboard setting this time.

[15] *Diodorus of Sicily* (trans. C. H. Oldfather et al., 11 vols., Loeb Classical Library [London and New York, 1933–1957], I, 92, 96) is the authority for the borrowing of the figure, together with the rites of Osiris and Isis. Unlike the latter, however, which found popular expression in the cult of Dionysus and Demeter, Charos as ferryman is to be met with only as a convention in literature. Three "Charon" ballads in the Roxburghe collection (Chappell and Ebsworth, *Roxburghe Ballads*, V, 24–25, 34–35; VII, 521–522) may be compared with the Greek *Myrologia* cited above in this respect.

[16] Hesseling observed (*Charos*, p. 49) that such images, although lacking a mythic or traditional foundation, may well in the course of time become genuine oral traditions; however, just as there was no evidence that ballad singers in England and the United States who incorporated golden balls into their variants of "The Gallows Tree" ever ascribed sexual significance to them, so there is little evidence that 2500 years of literary allusion to Charon as the ferryman to the other world has been sufficient to supplant the Etruscan armed-horseman figure in the popular imagination, even in Greece. The quasi-professional mourners who compose *Myrologia*, of course, might be expected to draw upon both learned and popular sources.

[17] David Grene and Richmond Lattimore, eds. *The Complete Greek Tragedies*, 4 vols. (Chicago, 1959–1960), III, 7. All references to Greek drama will be to this edition.

[18] Mary Grant, trans. *The Myths of Hyginus*, University of Kansas Publications, Humanistic Studies, 34 (Lawrence, Kans., 1960), 58 (fabula li).

[19] James G. Frazer, trans. *The Library of Apollodorus*, 2 vols., Loeb Classical Library (Cambridge, Mass., 1961), I, 90–93 (I. ix. 15–16).

[20] Grene and Lattimore, *Greek Tragedies*, I, 161. The Chorus reproaches Apollo: "Such was your action in the house of Pheres. Then / you beguiled the Fates to let mortals go free from death.... You won the ancient goddesses over with wine / and so destroyed the orders of an older time."

[21] Benjamin Jowett, trans. *The Dialogues of Plato*, 4th ed., 5 vols. (Oxford, 1937), I, 549.

Phaedrus is speaking: "Love will make men dare to die for their beloved; and women as well as men. Of this, Alcestis, the daughter of Pelias, is a monument to all Hellas; for she was willing to lay down her life on behalf of her husband, when no one else would, although he had a father and mother; but the tenderness of her love so far exceeded theirs, that they seemed to be as strangers to their own son, having no concern with him; and so noble did this action of hers appear, not only to men, but also to the gods, that among the many who have done virtuously she was one of the very few to whom the gods have granted the privilege of returning to earth, in admiration of her virtue; such exceeding honor is paid by them to the devotion and virtue of love."

[22] Albin Lesky, *Alkestis, der Mythus und das Drama, SAWW (P–H)* 103 (Vienna, 1925).

[23] Georgios A. Megas, "Die Sage von Alkestis," *AR* 30 (1933), 1–2.

[24] The three fairies who customarily invoke curses and blessings upon the newborn infant in modern tale tradition are traceable to the μοῖραι of Greek tradition; but these figures, like Apollo in the Alcestis legend, are less likely to be "mythical" than reflections of an already well-established popular tradition, since Μοῖρα (singular) is independently attested as the acknowledged goddess of destiny (see Maury, "Personnage de la mort," p. 691).

[25] See Dirk Christian Hesseling, "Euripides' Alcestis en de Volkspoëzie," *VMKAW (L)* (Reeks 4), 12 (1914), 1–32.

[26] Wolfram Eberhard and Pertev N. Boratev, *Typen türkischen Volksmärchen* (Weisbaden, 1953), p. 134 (no. 113).

[27] Walter Ruben, *Ozean der Märchenströme, FFC* 133 (Helsinki, 1944), I, 230. See also another variant type, pp. 230–231. The denouement here is identical with that of Anglo-American variant E20, discussed in chapter v, and thus provides another bit of evidence for unsuspected culture contacts.

[28] Moses Gaster, "Fairy Tales from Inedited Hebrew MSS of the Ninth and Twelfth Centuries," *Folk-Lore*, 7 (1896), 240–241; reprinted in Moses Gaster, *Studies and Texts in Folklore, Magic, Medieval Romance, Hebrew Apocrypha and Samaritan Archaeology*, 3 vols. (London, 1925–1928), II, 919–920, 931–932, and summarized in Moses Gaster, *The Exempla of the Rabbis* (London, 1924), p. 85. According to Dov Noy, variants have been collected recently in Israel ("The First Thousand Folktales in the Israel Folktale Archives," *Fabula*, 4 [1961], 107).

[29] Gaster, *Exempla*, pp. 104, 115–116.

[30] Schmidt, *Griechische Märchen*, pp. 68–70.

[31] Edmund Kurt Heller, "The Story of the Sorcerer's Serpent," *Speculum*, 15 (1940), 338–347. See also Child 301 "The Queen of Scotland," which tells a similar story.

[32] Paul G. Brewster, "A Rumanian Analogue of 'The Maid Freed from the Gallows,'" *SFQ* 5 (1941), 25–28. Other variants are reported by Heinrich von Wlislocki, *Volksdichtungen der siebenbürgischen und südungarischen Zigeuner* (Vienna, 1890), p. 109; Gaster, "Fairy Tales," p. 229; Marcu Beza, *Paganism in Roumanian Folklore* (London, 1928), pp. 148–149; Ninon A. Leader, *Hungarian Classical Ballads and Their Folklore* (Cambridge, Mass., 1967), pp. 251–254; Iivar Kempinnen, *Lunastettava neito: Vertaileva Balladi-Tutkimus* (Helsinki, 1957), p. 47.

[33] Although it is admittedly a dangerous procedure to rely too heavily upon scattered materials isolated from their own contexts, not only my own closer study of verbal units in the Western tradition of "The Gallows Tree," but the experience of Megas ("Die Sage von Alkestis"), Lajos Vargyas *(Researches into the Medieval History of Folk Ballad* [Budapest, 1967], Holger Nygard *(The Ballad of Heer Halewijn, FFC* 169 [Helsinki, 1958]), and Schmidt *(Griechische Märchen)* has shown that it is precisely this kind of fragmentary dissociation of motifs that is to be expected in oral tradition; see the comments of Vargyas (p. 62) and Schmidt (p. 6).

[34] W. R. S. Ralston, *Russian Folk-Tales* (London, 1873), pp. 360–361.

[35] Leopold Haupt and Johan Ernst Schmaler, *Volkslieder der Wenden in der Ober- und nieder-Lausitz*, 2 vols. (Grimma, 1841–1843), I, 357–358.

[36] Olive Lodge, "Džamutra, or the Bridegroom: Some Marriage-Customs in the Villages around Tetovo in Serbian Macedonia or Southern Serbia (Part II)," *Folk-Lore*, 46 (1935), 311.

[37] W. R. S. Ralston, *The Songs of the Russian People* (London, 1872), pp. 198–199.

[38] Auguste Dozon, *Chansons populaires bulgares* (Paris, 1875), pp. 98–99, 288. Jonas Balys re-

ports this version in Lithuanian tradition *(Lithuanian Narrative Folksong* [Washington, D.C., 1954], p. 65); Kempinnen cites one from Poland *(Lunastettava neito,* pp. 105–106).

[39] Alexander Reifferscheid, *Westfälische Volkslieder im Wort und Weise* (Heilbronn, 1879), p. 140.

[40] Vargyas *(Medieval History,* pp. 12–17) gives at least one example of a French ballad, "The Two Captives," which acquired a sequential refusal of relatives to come to the assistance of the victims only when it became part of the Hungarian tradition; it is their mother who finally responds. Is it not at least a tenable hypothesis, considering this phenomenon together with my own findings, that all "incremental repetition" in western European balladry is traceable to the transmission of eastern European materials by Gypsies rather than to the innate tendencies of the savage mind?

BIBLIOGRAPHY

Aarne, Antti. *Leitfaden der vergleichenden Märchenforschung. FFC* 13. Hamina, 1913.

———. *Verzeichnis der Märchentypen. FFC* 3. Helsinki, 1910. This was revised and enlarged by Stith Thompson, as *The Types of the Folktale, FFC* 184 (Helsinki, 1961) [AaT].

Abrahams, Roger D. "Patterns of Structure and Role Relationships in the Child Ballads in the United States," *JAF* 79 (1966), 448–462.

Abrahams, Roger D., and George Foss. *Anglo-American Folksong Style.* Englewood Cliffs, N.J., 1968.

Adams, William Forbes. *Ireland and Irish Emigration to the New World from 1815 to the Famine.* New Haven, 1932.

Addy, Sidney O. "A Folk Song," *Athenaeum,* 3510 (February 2, 1895), 148–149.

———. *Household Tales, Collected in the Counties of York, Lincoln, Derby, and Nottingham.* London, 1895.

Aichele, Hermann. *Die Zigeunerfrage mit besonderer Berücksichtigung Württembergs.* Stuttgart, 1911.

Altmann, Julius. *Die Balalaika: Russische Volks-Lieder.* Berlin, 1863.

Ambrosch, Julius Athanasius. *De Charonte Etrusco.* Bratislava, 1837.

Ames, Russell. "Art in Negro Folklore," *JAF* 56 (1943), 242–254.

Amira, Karl von. "Die germanischen Todesstrafen," *ABAW (P-H)* 21 (1922), 195–198.

Anderson, Geneva. "A Collection of Ballads and Songs from East Tennessee." M.A. thesis, University of North Carolina, 1932.

Anderson, Walter. *Kaiser und Abt. FFC* 42. Helsinki, 1923.

———. *Eine neue Arbeit zur experimentellen Volkskunde. FFC* 167. Helsinki, 1956.

———. *Zu Albert Wesselski's Angriffen auf die finnische folkloristische Forschungsmethode. ACUT (H)* 38 (1936).

———. "Geographische-historische Methode," *HDM,* II.

Andrews, William. *Bygone Punishments.* London, 1931.

———. "A Lancashire Ballad," *NQ* (ser. 6), 6 (1882), 269.

"Anglo-Romani Songs," *JGLS* (N.S.), 3 (1909), 157–160.

Arlt, Gustave O. "The Status of Research in Folk Melodies." M.A. thesis, University of Chicago, 1929.

Arnim, Ludwig Achim von. *Des Knaben Wunderhorn.* 3 vols. Heidelberg, 1808.

Arnold, Byron. *Folksong of Alabama.* University of Alabama, 1950.

Asch, Moses, and Alan Lomax. *The Leadbelly Songbook: The Ballads, Blues, and Folksongs of Huddie Ledbetter.* New York, 1962.

Aumer, C. F. *Ulmer Liederbuch.* Ulm, 1883.

Balys, Jonas. *Lithuanian Narrative Folksong.* Washington, D.C., 1954.

Bandinel, J. "A Folk Song," *Athenaeum,* 3509 (January 26, 1895), 118.

Barbi, Michele, "Scibilia Nobili e la Raccolta dei Canti Popolari," *Pallante* 1 (1929), 1–73.

Baring-Gould, Sabine. *Curiosities of Olden Times.* Edinburgh, 1896.

———. "The Story of the Golden Ball," in William Henderson, *Notes on the Folk Lore of the Northern Counties of England and the Borders.* London, 1866. Pp. 333–335.

Baring-Gould, Sabine, and H. Fleetwood-Sheppard. *Songs and Ballads of the West.* London, 1892.

Barry, Phillips. "American Folk Music," *SFQ* 1 (1937), 29–47.

———. "The Part of the Folksinger in the Making of Folk Balladry," in MacEdward Leach and Tristram P. Coffin, eds. *The Critics and the Ballad.* Carbondale, Ill., 1961. Pp. 59–76.

Barry, Phillips, Fanny H. Eckstrom, and Mary W. Smyth. *British Ballads from Maine.* New Haven, Conn., 1929.

Bascom, William. "The Main Problems of Stability and Change in Tradition," *JIFMC* 11 (1959), 7–12.

Bayard, Samuel P. "American Folksongs and Their Music," *SFQ* 17 (1953), 122–139.

———. "Ballad Tunes and the Hustvedt Indexing Method," *JAF* 55 (1942), 248–254.

———. "Two Representative Tune Families of British Tradition," *MF* 4 (1954), 13–33.

Beckwith, Martha. "The English Ballad in Jamaica," *PMLA* 39 (1924), 455–483.

157

Beit, Hedwig von. *Symbolik des Märchens*. 2 vols. Bern, 1957.

Belden, Henry M. *Ballads and Songs Collected by the Missouri Folklore Society*. Columbia, Mo., 1940, 1955.

Belden, Henry M., and Arthur Palmer Hudson, eds. *Folk Ballads from North Carolina*. Frank C. Brown Collection of North Carolina Folklore, II. Durham, N.C., 1952.

———. *Folk Songs from North Carolina*. Frank C. Brown Collection of North Carolina Folklore, III. Durham, N.C., 1952.

Bell, John. *Rhymes of Northern Bards*. Newcastle, 1812.

Ben-Amos, Dan "The Situation-Structure of the Non-Humorous English Ballad," *MF* 13 (1963), 163–176.

Beza, Marcu. *Paganism in Roumanian Folklore*. London, 1928.

Birch-Reynardson, H. F. *Sussex Songs*. London, [n.d.].

Boberg, Inge. *Motif-Index of Early Icelandic Literature*. Copenhagen, 1966.

Böckel, V. *Handbuch des deutsches Volkslieds*. Marburg, 1908.

Böhme, Franz Magnus. *Volksthümliche Lieder der Deutschen im 18. und 19. Jahrhundert*. Leipzig, 1895.

Bokelman, Marina. " 'The Coon-Can Game': A Blues Ballad Tradition." M.A. thesis, University of California at Los Angeles, 1968.

Bolte, Johannes, and Georg Polívka. *Anmerkungen zu den Kinder- und Hausmärchen der Brüder Grimm*. 5 vols. Leipzig, 1912–1932.

Bolton, Ethel Stanwood. "Immigrants to New England, 1700–1775," *Essex Institute Historical Collections*, LXIII (1927), 177–192, 269–284, 365–380; LXIV (1928), 25–32, 257–272; LXV (1929), 57–72, 113–128, 531–546; LXVI (1930), 411–426, 521–536; LXVII (1931), 89–112, 201–224, 305–328.

Boswell, George. "Reciprocal Controls Exerted by Ballad Texts and Tunes," *JAF* 70 (1967), 169–174.

———. "Some Characteristics of Folksongs in Middle Tennessee," *TFSB* 15 (1949), 63–69.

Botkin, Benjamin A. *The American Play-Party Song*. *USUN* 37 (1937).

———. "The Play-Party in Oklahoma," in *Follow the Drinkin' Gou'd*. *PTFS* 7 (1928), 7–24.

———. *A Treasury of American Folklore*. New York, 1944.

Boulton, Harold. *Songs of the Four Nations*. London, 1893.

Breuer, Hans, ed. *Der Zupfgeigenhansl*. Leipzig, 1914.

Brewster, Paul G. *Ballads and Songs of Indiana*. Bloomington, Ind., 1940.

———. "A Rumanian Analogue of 'The Maid Freed from the Gallows,' " *SFQ* 5 (1941), 25–28.

———. "Traditional Ballads from Indiana," *JAF* 48 (1935), 295–317.

Brill, O. J. "Der Schäfer und der Edelmann," *PQ* 9 (1930), 43–50.

Briz, Francesch Pelay. *Cansons de la terra*. 5 vols. Barcelona, 1864–1877.

Broadwood, Lucy. *English Traditional Songs and Carols*. London, 1908.

Broadwood, Lucy, and J. Fuller-Maitland. *English County Songs*. London, 1893.

Bronson, Bertrand H. "About the Commonest British Ballads," *JIFMC* 9 (1957), 22–27.

———. "Folksong and the Modes," *MQ* 22 (1964), 37–49.

———. "The Interdependence of Ballad Tunes and Texts," *CFQ* 3 (1944), 185–207.

———. "Mechanical Help in the Study of Folk Song," *JAF* 62 (1949), 81–86.

———. "Melodic Stability in Oral Transmission," *JIFMC* 3 (1951), 50–55.

———. "The Morphology of the Ballad Tunes," *JAF* 67 (1954), 1–13.

———. "Mrs. Brown and the Ballad," *CFQ* 4 (1945), 129–140.

———. "On the Union of Words and Music in the 'Child' Ballads," *WF* 11 (1952), 233–249.

———. *The Traditional Tunes of the Child Ballads*. 3 vols. Princeton, N.J., 1962–1967.

Bronzini, Giovanni B. *La Canzone Epico-lirica nell'Italia Centro-Meridionale*. 2 vols. Rome, 1956.

Brooke, C. F. Tucker, and Nathaniel Burton Paradise. *English Drama 1580-1642*. Boston, 1933.

Bruce, J. Collingwood, and John Stokoe. *Northumbrian Minstrelsy*. Newcastle, 1882; Hatboro, Pa., 1965.

Brunner, Karl. *The Seven Sages of Rome (Southern Version)*. EETS 191. London, 1933.

Burstein, Sona Rosa. "Moses Gaster and Folklore." *Folk-Lore* 68 (1957), 288–290.

Bystroń, Jan St. *Pieśni Ludowe z Polskiego Ślaska*. Vol. I. Krakow, 1934.

Cambiaire, Celestin Pierre. *East Tennessee and Western Virginia Mountain Ballads*. London, [n.d.].

Campbell, John Gregorson. *The Fians: Stories, Poems, and Traditions*. Argyllshire Series, IV. London, 1891.

Campbell, Marie. "The Gallows Tree," *TFSB* 3 (1937), 95.

Campbell, Olive Dame, and Cecil J. Sharp. *English Folk Songs from the Southern Appalachians.* New York and London, 1917. (See Sharp, Cecil J., and Maud Karpeles, *English Folk Songs from the Southern Appalachians,* 2 vols. [London, 1932, 1951, 1960].)

Carney, James. *Studies in Irish Literature and History.* Dublin, 1955.

Carrothers, W. A. *Emigration from the British Isles.* London, 1929.

Chamberlain, Basil Hall, trans. *Ko-ji-ki (Records of Ancient Matters) TASJ* 10, supplement (1882).

Chappell, Louis W. *Folk-Songs of Roanoke and the Albemarle.* Morgantown, W.Va., 1939.

Chappell, William, and J. Woodfall Ebsworth. *The Roxburghe Ballads.* 8 vols. Hertford, 1871–1899.

Charters-Maitland, H. M. Communication in *Athenaeum,* 3511 (February 9, 1895) 184.

Child, Alice M. "Folk Ballads and Folk Songs of the South." M.A. thesis, University of Missouri, 1929.

Child, Francis James. *English and Scottish Popular Ballads.* 5 vols. Boston, 1882–1898; New York, 1965.

Christie, W. *Traditional Ballad Airs.* 2 vols. Edinburgh, 1876.

Clark, Andrew, ed. *The Shirburn Ballads.* Oxford, 1907.

Clébert, Jean-Paul. *Les Tziganes.* Paris, 1961.

Coffin, Tristram P. "The 'Braes of Yarrow' Tradition in America," *JAF* 63 (1950), 328–335.

———. *The British Traditional Ballad in North America.* Philadelphia, 1963.

———. "The Folk Ballad and the Literary Ballad: An Essay in Classification," *MF* 9 (1959), 5–18.

———. "The Golden Ball and the Gallows Tree," in D. K. Wilgus, ed. *Folklore International: Essays in Traditional Literature, Belief, and Custom in Honor of Wayland Debs Hand.* Hatboro, Pa., 1967. Pp. 23–28.

———. "An Index to Borrowing in the Child Ballads of America," *JAF* 62 (1949), 156–161.

———. " 'Mary Hamilton' and the Anglo-American Ballad as an Art Form," *JAF* 70 (1957), 208–214. (Reprinted in *The Critics and the Ballad,* ed. MacEdward Leach and Tristram P. Coffin [Carbondale, Ill., 1961], pp. 245–256.)

———. "The Murder Motive in 'Edward,' " *WF* 8 (1949), 314–319.

———. "Remarks Preliminary to a Study of Ballad Meter and Ballad Singing," *JAF* 78 (1965), 149–153.

———. "Six Unusual Texts from Mildred Haun's 'Cocke County Ballads and Songs,' " *SFQ* 29 (1965), 179–187.

Coirault, Patrice. *Formation de nos chansons folkloriques.* 4 vols. Paris, 1953–1963.

Coleman, Satis N., and Adolph Bregman. *Songs of American Folks.* New York, 1942.

Conot, Robert. *Rivers of Blood, Years of Darkness.* New York, 1967.

Cox, John Harrington. *Folk-Songs of the South.* Cambridge, Mass., 1925.

———. *Traditional Ballads Mainly from West Virginia.* AFP III. New York, 1939.

Craigie, W. A., and A. J. Aitken. *A Dictionary of the Older Scottish Tongue.* 4 vols. Chicago and London, 1963.

Craigie, W. A., and J. R. Hulbert. *A Dictionary of American English on Historical Principles.* 4 vols. Chicago, 1938–1944.

Crane, Lucy, trans. *Household Stories from the Collection of the Bros. Grimm.* London, 1882.

Cremona, Antonio. "Is the Maid of Mosta a Myth?" *JMULS* 10 (1934).

Crofton, Henry T. "Early Annals of the Gypsies in England," *JGLS* 1 (1889), 5–24.

———. "Supplementary Annals of the Gypsies in England, before 1700," *JGLS* (N.S.), 1 (1907–1908), 31–34.

Cross, Tom Peete, *Motif-Index of Early Irish Literature. PIU (F)* 7. Bloomington, Ind., [n.d.].

Cross, Tom Peete, and C. H. Slover, *Ancient Irish Tales.* New York, 1936.

Dal, Erik. *Nordisk Folkeviseforskning siden 1800.* Copenhagen, 1956.

Damant, M. "The Three Golden Balls," *Folk-Lore* 6 (1895), 306–307.

Darton, F. J. Harvey. *Children's Books in England: Five Centuries of Social Life.* Cambridge, Eng., 1932.

Davis, Arthur Kyle. *More Traditional Ballads from Virginia.* Chapel Hill, N.C., 1960.

———. *Traditional Ballads from Virginia.* Cambridge, Mass., 1929.

Dimock, James F., ed. *Itinerarium Kambriae. Giraldus Cambrensis Opera,* Vol. VI. London, 1868.

Dixon, J. H. *Ballads and Songs of the Peasantry of England. PSP* 17. London, 1946.

Dobie, Bertha McKee, "Tales and Rhymes of a Texas Household," in *Texas and Southwestern Lore. PTFS* 6 (1927), 23–71.

Dorson, Richard M. "A Theory for American Folklore," *JAF* 72 (1959), 197–215.

Dozon, Auguste. *Chansons populaires bulgares.* Paris, 1875.

DuCange [Carolo du Fresne]. *Glossarium ad Scriptores Mediae et Infimae Graecitatis.* Graz, 1958.

Duhn, F. von. "Charonlekythen," *JDAI* 2 (1887), 24–43.

Duncan, Ruby. "Ballads and Folk Songs Collected in Northern Hamilton County." M.A. thesis, University of Tennessee, 1939.

d'Urfey, Thomas. *Wit and Mirth, or Pills to Purge Melancholy.* 6 vols. London, 1719.

Eberhard, Wolfram, and Pertev N. Boratev. *Typen türkischen Volksmärchen.* Wiesbaden, 1953.

Eddy, Mary O. *Ballads and Songs from Ohio.* New York, 1939.

Ege, Friedrich. Review of Iivar Kempinnen, *Lunastettava neito: Vertaileva Balladi-Tutkinus,* in *JAF* 72 (1959), 71–72.

Elliott, Scott. "Pulling the Heather Green," *JAF* 48 (1935), 352–361.

Emmett, Thomas Addis. "Irish Emigration during the Seventeenth and Eighteenth Centuries," *JAIHS* 2 (1899), 56–70.

Entwistle, William J. "Notation for Ballad Melodies," *PMLA* 55 (1940), 161–172.

Erk, Ludwig, and Franz Magnus Böhme. *Deutscher Liederhort.* 3 vols. Leipzig, 1893–1894.

Ewert, A., ed. *The Romance of Tristan by Béroul.* Oxford, 1939.

Falk, H. S., and Alf Torp. *Norwegisch-dänisches etymologisches Wörterbuch.* 2 vols. Oslo and Bergen, 1960.

Farmer, John S. *Merry Songs and Ballads prior to the Year A.D. 1800.* 5 vols. [London?], 1897.

Feldmann, Susan. *African Myths and Tales.* New York, 1963.

Fishwick, H., communication in *NQ* (ser. 6), 6 (1882), 415.

Flanders, Helen Hartness. *Ancient Ballads Traditionally Sung in New England.* 3 vols. Philadelphia, 1960–1963.

Flügel, Ewald. "Zur Chronologie der englischen Balladen," *Anglia,* 21 (1899), 312–358.

Folkard, Richard. *Plant Lore, Legends, and Lyrics,* 2nd ed. London, 1892.

Foss, George. "The Transcription and Analysis of Folk Music," in *A Good Tale and a Bonnie Tune. PTFS* 32 (1964), 237–265.

Fowke, Edith, "British Ballads in Ontario," *MF* 13 (1963), 133–162.

Fowler, David C. "Toward a Literary History of the Popular Ballad," *NYFQ* 21 (1965), 123–141.

Francello, Elvira. "An Italian Version of 'Maid Freed from the Gallows,'" *NYFQ* 2 (1946), 139–140.

Frazer, James G., trans. *The Library of Apollodorus.* 2 vols. Loeb Classical Library. Cambridge, Mass., 1961.

Frey, Albert R. *A Dictionary of Numismatic Names.* New York, 1917.

Friedman, Albert B. "The Formulaic Improvisation Theory of Ballad Tradition—A Counterstatement," *JAF* 74 (1961), 113–115.

———. *The Viking Book of Folk Ballads of the English-Speaking World.* New York, 1956.

Frobenius, Leo. *Volkserzählungen und Volksdichtungen aus dem Zentralsuden. Atlantis* 9. Jena, 1924.

Fuller-Maitland, J. A. "A Folk Song," *Athenaeum,* 3509 (January 26, 1895), 119.

Fuson, Harvey H. *Ballads of the Kentucky Highlands.* London, 1931.

Gardner, Emelyn Elizabeth, and Geraldine Jenks Chickering. *Ballads and Songs of Southern Michigan.* Ann Arbor, 1939.

Gaster, Moses. *The Exempla of the Rabbis.* London, 1924.

———. "Fairy Tales from Inedited Hebrew MSS of the Ninth and Twelfth Centuries," *Folk-Lore* 7 (1896), 217–250.

———. *Studies and Texts in Folklore, Magic, Medieval Romance, Hebrew Apocrypha and Samaritan Archaeology.* 3 vols. London, 1925–1928.

Geijer, E. G., and A. A. Afzelius. *Svenska Folkeviser.* Stockholm, 1880.

Gerould, Gordon Hall. *The Ballad of Tradition.* New York, 1932, 1957.

Gewehr, Wesley M. *The Great Awakening in Virginia, 1740–1790.* Durham, N.C., 1930.

Gilbert, Allan, trans. *The Orlando Furioso of Ariosto.* 2 vols. New York, 1954.

Gilchrist, Anne. "Conventional Ballads," *JFSS* 3 (1907), 61–76.

———. "A Note on the Modal System of Gaelic Tunes," *JFSS* 4 (1911), 150–153.

Gilchrist, Anne, and Lucy E. Broadwood. "Notes on Children's Game-Songs: The Prickly Bush (The Maid Freed from the Gallows) and Its Connection with the Story of the Golden Ball," *JFSS* 5 (1915), 228–239.

Goetze, P. von. *Serbische Volkslieder in's deutsche uebertragen*. Leipzig, 1827.

———. *Stimmen des russischen Volks in Liedern*. Stuttgart, 1828.

Gordon, Jean. *The Pageant of the Rose*. New York, 1953.

Gordon, Philip. "The Music of the Ballads," *SFQ* 6 (1942), 143–148.

Gordon, R. W. In *Adventure Magazine*, December 20, 1925; July 23, 1926.

Gower, Herschel M. "How the Scottish Ballads Flourished in America." *SR* 6 (1960), 7–11.

Graham, George Farquhar. *The Songs of Scotland*. 3 vols. Edinburgh, 1861.

Grant, Mary, trans. *The Myths of Hyginus*. *PUK* (*H*) 34. Lawrence, Kans., 1960.

Grauer, Victor A. "Some Song-Style Clusters—A Preliminary Study," *Ethnomusicology* 9 (1965), 265–271.

Graves, Robert, and Raphael Patai. *The Hebrew Myths*. New York, 1963.

Greenway, John. "The Flight of the Grey Goose: Literary Symbolism in the Traditional Ballad," *SFQ* 18 (1954), 165–174.

———. "Folksong as an Anthropological Province: The Anthropological Approach," in *A Good Tale and a Bonnie Tune*. *PTFS* 32 (1964), 209–217.

Greig, Gavin. *Folk Song of the North-East*. 2 vols. Peterhead, 1914.

———, and Alexander Keith. *Last Leaves of Traditional Ballads and Ballad Airs*. Aberdeen, 1925

Grene, David, and Richmond Lattimore, eds. *The Complete Greek Tragedies*. 4 vols. Chicago, 1959–1960.

Grimm, Jacob and Wilhelm. *Kinder- und Hausmärchen*. 2 vols. Munich and Leipzig, 1812.

———, et al. *Deutsches Wörterbuch*. 16 vols. Leipzig, 1854–1954.

Grinsell, L. V. "The Ferryman and His Fee: A Study in Ethnology, Archaeology, and Tradition," *Folk-Lore* 68 (1957), 157–269.

Grün, Anastasius [Auersperg, Anton Alexander von]. *Volkslieder aus Krain*. Leipzig, 1850.

Grundtvig, Svend, et al., eds. *Danmarks gamle Folkeviser*. 11 vols. Copenhagen, 1853–1935.

Gubernatis, Angelo de. *La mythologie des plantes*. 2 vols. Paris, 1872–1882.

Guillet, Edwin C. *The Great Migration: The Atlantic Crossing by Sailing-Ship since 1770*. London, 1937.

Gummere, Francis B. *The Popular Ballad*. Boston, 1907.

Gutmann, Bruno. *Volksbuch der Wadschagga*. Leipzig, 1914.

Hahn, J. G. von. *Griechische und albanesische Märchen*. Munich, 1868, 1918.

Hainworth, W. "A Folk Song," *Athenaeum*, 3509 (January 26, 1895), 119.

Halliwell, James O. *The Yorkshire Anthology*. London, 1851.

Halpert, Herbert J. "The Cante-Fable in Decay," *SFQ* 5 (1941), 191–200.

———. "The Cante-Fable in New Jersey," *JAF* 55 (1942), 133–143.

———. "The Folksinger Speaks," *HF* 3 (1944), 29–35.

Hansen, Wilhelm. *Grimm's Other Tales*, trans. Ruth Michaelis-Jena and Arthur Ratcliff. Edinburgh, 1956.

Harland, John. *Ballads and Songs of Lancashire*. London, 1875.

The Harleian Miscellany, or, a Collection of scarce, curious and entertaining Pamphlets and Tracts, as well in manuscript as in print, found in the late Earl of Oxford's library, interspersed with historical, political, and critical Notes. 12 vols. London, 1810.

Hartland, E. S. *The English Fairy and Other Folktales*. London, 1890.

Haun, Mildred. "Cocke County Ballads and Songs." M.A. thesis, Vanderbilt University, 1937.

Haupt, Leopold, and Johan Ernst Schmaler. *Volkslieder der Wenden in der Ober- und nieder-Lausitz*. 2 vols. Grimma, 1841–1843.

Heeger, Georg, and Wilhelm Wüst. *Volkslieder aus der Rheinpfalz*. 2 vols. Kaiserslautern, 1909.

Heinemann, Kurt. *Thanatos in Poesie und Kunst der Griechen*. Munich, 1913.

Heiske, Wilhelm. "Rechtsbrauch und Rechtsempfinden im Volkslied," *DJV* 2 (1956), 73–79.

Heller, Edmund Kurt. "The Story of the Sorcerer's Serpent," *Speculum* 15 (1940), 338–347.

Hendren, Joseph W. "The Scholar and the Ballad Singer," *SFQ* 18 (1954), 139–146.

———. *A Study of Ballad Rhythm, with Special Reference to Ballad Music*. PSE 4, Princeton, N.J., 1936.

Henry, Mellinger. "Ballads and Songs of the Southern Highlands," *JAF* 42 (1929), 254–300.

———. *Folk-Songs from the Southern Highlands*. New York, 1938.

———. "Two Ballad Fragments," *American Speech*, I (1925), 247.

Henry, Mellinger, and Maurice Matteson. *Beech Mountain Folk-Songs and Ballads*. New York, 1936.

Herrmann, Anton. "Beiträge zur Vergleichung der Volkspoesie: Liebesprobe," *EMU* 1 (1887), 34–50.

Herzog, George. "Musical Typology in Folksong," *SFQ* 1 (1937), 49–55.

———. "The Study of Folksong in America," *SFQ* 2 (1936), 59–64.

Hesseling, Dirk Christian. *Charos: Ein Beiträg zur Kenntnis des neugriechischen Volksglaubens*. Leiden and Leipzig, 1897.

———. "Euripides' Alcestis en de Volkspoezie," *VMKAW* (L) (Reeks 4), 12 (1914), 1–32.

Hibbard, Esther Lowell. "The Ulysses Motif in Japanese Literature," *JAF* 59 (1946), 221–246.

Hight, G. A., trans. *The Saga of Grettir the Strong*. London, 1914, 1929.

Hill, Ellen M. "A Folk Song," *Athenaeum*, 3509 (January 26, 1895), 119.

Hoffmann-Krayer, E., and Hans Bächtold-Stäubli. *Handwörterbuch des deutschen Aberglaubens*. 10 vols. Berlin, 1926–1942.

Holdsworth, W. S. *A History of English Law*. Rev. ed. 14 vols. London, 1956.

Hotten, John Camden. *The Original Lists of Persons of Quality; Emigrants; Religious Exiles; Political Rebels; Serving Men Sold for a Term of Years; Apprentices; Children Stolen; Maidens Pressed; and Others Who went From Great Britain to the American Plantations 1600–1700*. London, 1874.

Hudson, Arthur Palmer. "Ballads and Songs from Mississippi," *JAF* 39 (1926), 93–194.

———. *Folksongs of Mississippi and Their Background*. Chapel Hill, N.C., 1936.

———. *Folk Tunes from Mississippi*. New York, 1937.

———. *Specimens of Mississippi Folklore*. Ann Arbor, 1928.

Hughes, Herbert. *Irish Country Songs*. 4 vols. London, 1909.

Hustvedt, Sigurd Bernhard. *Ballad Books and Ballad Men*. Cambridge, Mass., 1930.

———. "A Melodic Index of Child's Ballad Tunes," in *PUCLALL* 1 (1936), 51–78.

Hutchison, Percy Adams. "Sailors' Chanties," *JAF* 19 (1906), 16–28.

Hyde, Douglas. *Beside the Fire*. London, 1910.

Hyman, Stanley Edgar. "The Child Ballad in America: Some Aesthetic Criteria," *JAF* 70 (1957), 235–239.

Innes, Cosmo. *Lectures on Scottish Legal Antiquities*. Edinburgh, 1872.

Jackson, Kenneth. *The International Popular Tale and Early Welsh Tradition*. Cardiff, 1961.

Jacobs, Joseph. *English Fairy Tales*. London, 1895.

———. *More English Fairy Tales*. London, 1894.

Jacobs, Melville. "A Look Ahead in Oral Literature Research," *JAF* 79 (1966), 413–427.

Jacobus, Donald Lines. "The Irish in New England before 1700," *NEHGR* 90 (1936), 165–167.

Jamieson, John. *An Etymological Dictionary of the Scottish Language*. 4 vols. Edinburgh, 1840–1841.

Jekyll, Walter. *Jamaican Song and Story*. PFS 55 (1907).

Jewitt, Llewellyn, ed. *The Ballads and Songs of Derbyshire*. London, 1867.

Johnny Bond Compositions (For professional use only). [n.p.], [n.d.].

Johnson, Stanley C. *A History of Emigration from the United Kingdom to North America 1763–1912*. London, 1913.

Jones, Gwyn, and Thomas Jones, trans. *The Mabinogion*. London and New York, 1949, 1966.

Jones, James H. "Commonplace and Memorization in the Oral Tradition of the English and Scottish Ballads," *JAF* 74 (1961), 97–112.

Joret, Charles. *La Rose dans l'antiquité et au moyen âge*. Paris. 1892.

Journal of the Irish Folk Song Society, 13 (1913).

Jowett, Benjamin, trans. *The Dialogues of Plato*. 4th ed. 5 vols. Oxford, 1937.

Joyce, Patrick W. *Old Celtic Romances: Tales from Irish Mythology*. New York, 1962.

———. *A Short History of Ireland.* London, 1894.

Kapper, S. *Die Gesänge der Serben.* 2 vols. Leipzig, 1852.

Keightley, Thomas. *The Fairy Mythology.* London, 1873.

Kempinnen, Iivar. *Lunastettava neito: Vertaileva Balladi-Tutkimus.* Helsinki, 1957.

Kentucky Folklore Record, III (1957), 104–105.

Kerényi, Károly (with C. G. Jung). *Essays on a Science of Mythology,* trans. R. F. C. Hull. Rev. ed. New York, 1963.

Kidson, Frank, and Mary Neal. *English Folk-Song and Dance.* Cambridge, Eng., 1915.

Kirkland, Edwin Capers, and Mary Neal. "Popular Ballads Recorded in Knoxville, Tennessee," *SFQ* 2 (1936), 65–80.

Kittredge, George Lyman. "Ballads and Songs," *JAF* 30 (1917), 318–322.

———. "Two Popular Ballads," *JAF* 21 (1908), 54–56.

———. "Various Ballads," *JAF* 26 (1913), 175.

Kluckhohn, Clyde. "Recurrent Themes in Myths and Mythmaking," *Daedalus* 88 (1959), 268–279.

Knight, A. Communication in *Athenaeum,* 3508 (January 19, 1895), 86.

Kolberg, Oskar. *Lud: Jego zwyczaje, sposób zycia, mowa, podania, przysłowia, oberzedy, gusła, zabawy, pieśni, muzyka, i tance.* 35 vols. Krakow, 1857–1889.

Kolinski, Mieczyslaw. "The Structure of Melodic Movement: A New Method of Analysis," in *Miscelanea de estudios dedicados a Fernando Ortiz.* 3 vols. Havana, 1956. Vol. II, pp. 879–918.

Koller, Oswald. "Die beste Methode, Volks- und Volksmässige Lieder nach ihrer melodischen Beschaffenheit lexicalisch zu ordnen," *SIM* 4 (1902–1903), 1–15.

Krappe, Alexander H. "The Maid Freed from the Gallows," *Speculum* 16 (1941), 236–241.

Krohn, Julius. "Das Lied vom Mädchen, welches erlöst werden soll," *JSFO* 10 (1892), 111–129. (Translated from *Virittäjä* 2 [n.d.], 36–50.)

Krohn, Kaarle. *Die folkloristische Arbeitsmethode.* Oslo. 1926.

Krumbacher, Karl. *Geschichte der byzantinischen Literatur von Justinian bis zum Ende des oströmischen Reiches (527–1453).* Munich, 1891.

Kühn, E. *Der Spreewald und seine Bewohner.* Cottlius, 1889.

Kurath, Hans, and Sherman H. Kuhn. *Middle English Dictionary.* 4 vols. to H. Ann Arbor, 1954–1967.

Landeroin, Moïse A., and Marie A. J. Tilho. *Grammaire et contes Haoussas.* Paris, 1909.

Laurence, John. *A History of Capital Punishment.* New York, 1960.

Laws, G. Malcolm, Jr. *American Ballads from British Broadsides.* PAFS (B) 8. Philadelphia, 1957.

———. "Anglo-Irish Balladry in America," in Horace P. Beck, ed. *Folklore in Action.* Philadelphia, 1962. Pp. 172–183.

———. *Native American Balladry.* PAFS (B) 1. Philadelphia, 1950.

Leach, MacEdward. *The Ballad Book.* New York, 1955.

Leach, MacEdward. "The Singer or the Song," in *Singers and Storytellers.* PTFS 30 (1961), 30–45.

Leader, Ninon A. *Hungarian Classical Ballads and Their Folklore.* Cambridge, Mass., 1967.

Leahy, A. H. *Heroic Romances of Ireland.* 2 vols. London, 1905.

Legrand, Emile. *Recueil de chansons populaires qrècques.* Paris, 1874.

Leland, Charles G. *English Gypsy Songs.* Philadelphia, 1875.

Lesky, Albin. *Alkestis, der Mythus und das Drama. SAWW* (P-H) 103. Vienna, 1925.

Liddell, Henry George, and Robert Scott. *A Greek-English Lexicon.* Rev. ed. Oxford, 1940.

Liebrecht, Felix. "Die Todten von Lustnau," *Germania* 13 (1868), 161–172.

———. *Zur Volkskunde.* Heilbronn, 1879.

Liestøl, Knut. "Scottish and Norwegian Ballads," *SN* 1 (1946), 3–16.

List, George. "An Approach to the Indexing of Ballad Tunes," *FFMA* 6 (1963), 7–16.

———. "An Ideal Marriage of Ballad Text and Tune, *MF* 7 (1957), 95–112.

Lodge, Olive. "Džamutra, or the Bridegroom: Some Marriage Customs in the Villages around Tetovo in Serbian Macedonia or Southern Serbia (Part II)," *Folk-Lore* 46 (1935), 306–330.

Logan, William Hugh. *A Pedlar's Pack of Ballads and Songs.* Edinburgh, 1869.

Lomax, John A. and Alan. *Leadbelly: A Collection of World-Famous Songs by Huddie Ledbetter.* New York, 1959.

———. *Negro Folk Songs as Sung by Lead Belly.* New York, 1936.

————. *Our Singing Country.* New York, 1941.

Lübke, Hermann, *Neugriechische Volks- und Liebslieder.* Berlin, 1895.

Lucas, Mrs. Edward, trans. *Fairy Tales of the Brothers Grimm.* London, 1902.

Lüthi, Max. *Die Gabe im Märchen und in der Sage.* Zurich, 1943.

McDowell, Lucien L., and Flora Lassiter. *Memory Melodies: A Collection of Folk Songs from Middle Tennessee.* Smithville, Tenn., 1947.

McIntosh, David S., "My Golden Ball," *HF* 7 (1948), 97–100.

McKay, John G. *More West Highland Tales.* Edinburgh and London, 1940.

Mackensen, Lutz, and Johannes Bolte. *Handwörterbuch des deutschen Märchens.* 2 vols. to Gyges. Berlin and Leipzig, 1930–1933.

McKerrow, H. B., ed. *The Gull's Horne-Booke.* London, 1904.

MacLean, J. P. *An Historical Account of the Settlements of Scotch Highlanders in America prior to the Peace of 1783.* Glasgow, 1900.

McNeil, Brownie. "The Child Ballad in the Middle West and Lower Mississippi Valley," in *Mesquite and Willow. PTFS* 27 (1957), 23–77.

Mannhardt, Wilhelm. *Wald- und Feldkulte.* 2nd ed. 2 vols. Berlin, 1904–1905.

Marzell, Heinrich. *Die Pflanzen im deutschen Volksleben.* Jena, 1925.

Mason, Robert. "Folk-Songs and Folk-Tales of Cannon County, Tennessee." M.A. thesis, George Peabody College, 1939.

————. "Ten Old English Ballads in Middle Tennessee," *SFQ* 11 (1947), 119–137.

Matthews, Mitford. *A Dictionary of Americanisms on Historical Principles.* 2 vols. Chicago, 1951.

Maury, Alfred. "Du personnage de la mort et de ses reprẽs dans l'antiquité et au moyen âge," *RA* 4 (1847), 305–339.

Megas, Georgios A. "Die Ballade von der Losgekauften," *JVF* 3 (1932), 54–73.

————. "Die Sage von Alkestis," *AR* 30 (1933), 1–33.

Meier, John, and Erich Seemann. "Volksliedaufzeichnungen der Dichterin Annette von Droste-Hülshoff," *JVF* 1 (1928), 79–118.

Meier, John, et al. *Deutsche Volkslieder mit ihren Melodien, I. Balladen.* 4 vols. Leipzig, 1935–1959.

Meyer, Kuno, and Alfred Nutt. *The Voyage of Bran Son of Febal.* Grimm Library, IV. London, 1895.

Miklosich, Franz Xaver. "Über die Mundarten und die Wanderungen der Zigeuner Europas," *DKAW* (P-H) (Vienna, 1872–1881), XXI, 197–253; XXII, 21–102; XXIII, 1–46, 273–340; XXV, 1–68; XXVI, 1–66, 161–247; XXVII, 1–108; XXX, 159–208, 391–486; XXXI, 1–54, 55–114.

Millar, Branford P. "Eighteenth-Century Views of the Ballad," *WF* 9 (1950), 124–135.

Miller, E. Joan Wilson. "The Rag-Bag World of Balladry," *SFQ* 24 (1960), 217–225.

Mittler, Franz Ludwig. *Deutsche Volkslieder.* Frankfurt, 1865.

Mlotek, Eleanor Gordon. "International Motifs in the Yiddish Ballad," in *For Max Weinrich on His Seventieth Birthday.* The Hague, 1964. Pp. 208–228.

Montgomerie, William. "Sketch for a History of the Scottish Ballad," *JEFDSS* 8 (1956), 40–43.

Moore, Ethel and Chauncey. *Ballads and Folksongs of the Southwest.* Norman, Okla., 1964.

Moore, John Robert. "Omission of the Central Action in English Ballads," *MP* 11 (1914), 391–406.

Morris, Alton C. *Folksongs of Florida.* Gainesville, Fla., 1950.

Muir, Willa. *Living with Ballads.* London, 1965.

Murray, James, et al., eds. *A New English Dictionary on Historical Principles.* 10 vols. Oxford, 1888–1928.

Musick, Ruth Ann. "Folklore from West Virginia," *HF* 6 (1947), 41–49.

Neus, H. *Ehstnische Volkslieder.* 2 vols. Reval, 1850.

Nicholson, Frank, trans. *Old German Love Songs.* Chicago, 1907.

Notes and Queries (ser. 4), IV (1869), 294, 417, 525; V (1870), 95–96.

Noy, Dov. "The First Thousand Folktales in the Israel Folktale Archives," *Fabula* 4 (1961), 99–110.

Nutt, Alfred. "An Old Ballad," *FJ* 6 (1888), 144.

Nygard, Holger. *The Ballad of Heer Halewijn.* FFC 169. Helsinki, 1958.

————. "Ballads and the Middle Ages," *TSL* 5 (1960), 85–96.

O'Keeffe, J. G. *Buile Suibne* [*The Frenzy of Suibne*]. *ITS* 12. London, 1913.

Oldenburg, Hermann. *Die Literatur des alten Indien.* Stuttgart and Berlin, 1903.

Oldfather, C. H., et al., trans. *Diodorus of Sicily.* 11 vols. Loeb Classical Library. London and New York, 1933–1957.

O'Sullivan, Donal. *Songs of the Irish.* Dublin, 1960.

Owen, Mary Alicia. *Old Rabbit the Voodoo and Other Sorcerers.* London, 1893.

Owens, William A. *Swing and Turn: Texas Play-Party Games.* Dallas, 1936.

———. *Texas Folk Songs.* Austin, 1950.

Parsons, Elsie Clewes. *Folk-Lore of the Sea Islands, South Carolina.* MAFS 16. Cambridge, Mass., 1923.

———. *Folk Tales from the Andros Islands.* MAFS 13. New York, 1918.

Patch, Hyder Rollins. *The Other World According to Descriptions in Medieval Literature.* Cambridge, Mass., 1950.

Paull, Mrs. H. B., and Mr. L. A. Wheatley. *Grimm's Fairy Tales and Household Stories for Young People.* London, 1895.

Perry, Henry Wocaster. "A Sampling of Folklore from Carter County, Tennessee." M. A. thesis, George Peabody College, 1938.

Pittman, J., Colin Brown, and Myles B. Foster. *Songs of Scotland.* 3 vols. London, 1877.

Pohl, Erik. *Die deutsche Volksballade von der "Losgekaufte."* FFC 105 Helsinki, 1934.

Pohl, Marta. *Gemeinsame Themen englisch-schottischer und französischer Volksballaden.* SVF 4 Berlin, 1940.

Poladian, Sirvart. "The Problem of Melodic Variation in Folk Song," *JAF* 55 (1942), 204–211.

Pollock, Sir Frederick, and F. W. Maitland. *The History of English Law before the Time of Edward I.* 2 vols. Cambridge, Eng., 1895.

Porter, Kenneth. "Some Examples of 'The *Cante-Fable* in Decay,'" *SFQ* 21 (1957), 100–103.

Pott, A. F. *Die Zigeuner in Europa und Asien.* 2 vols. Halle, 1844.

Pound, Louise. *American Ballads and Songs.* New York, 1922.

———. "New-World Analogues of the English and Scottish Popular Ballads," *MWQ* 3 (1916), 171–187.

———. "On the Dating of the English and Scottish Ballads," *PMLA* 47 (1932), 10–16.

Pressel, Gustav. "Die Musik der Ungarn," *NZM* 36 (1852), 213–217, 225–227.

Propp, Vladimir. *The Morphology of the Folk-Tale,* trans. Laurence Scott. Bloomington, Ind., 1958.

Quellmaltz, Fred. "Die Melodie zur ballade von der Losgekauften," *JVF* 3 (1932), 74–86.

Ralston, W. R. S. *Russian Folk-Tales.* London, 1873.

———. *The Songs of the Russian People.* London, 1872.

Randolph, Vance. *Ozark Folksongs.* 4 vols. Columbia, Mo., 1946–1950.

———. In *Ozark Life,* 6 (1930), 34.

Rands, Robert L., and Carroll L. Riley. "Diffusion and Discontinuous Distribution," *AA* 60 (1958), 274–297.

Ranke, Friedrich. *Der Erlöser in der Wiege.* Munich, 1911.

Rattray, R. S. *Akan-Ashanti Folktales.* Oxford, 1930.

Reeves, James. *The Everlasting Circle.* London, 1960.

———. *The Idiom of the People.* London, 1958.

Reifferscheid, Alexander. *Westfälische Volkslieder im Wort und Weise.* Heilbronn, 1879.

Reinsberg-Düringsfeld, Otto von, and Ida Düringsfeld. *Sprichwörter der germanischen und romanischen Sprachen.* 2 vols. Leipzig, 1872–1875.

Reynolds, W. B. "The Irish Folk Scale," *JIFSS* 10 (1911), 12–15.

Richmond, W. Edson. "The Comparative Approach: Its Aims, Techniques, and Limitations," in *A Good Tale and a Bonnie Tune.* PTFS 32 (1964), 217–227.

———. "Romantic-Nationalism and Ballad Scholarship: A Lesson for Today from Norway's Past," *SFQ* 25 (1961), 91–100.

Rimbault, E. F. *A Little Book of Songs and Ballads.* London, 1851.

Ritchie, Jean. *Singing Family of the Cumberlands.* New York, 1956.

Ritson, Joseph. *The Bishoprick Garland.* [London?], 1784. (Republished in *Northern Garlands* [Edinburgh, 1887], pp. 17–26.)

Robbins, Harry, trans. *The Romance of the Rose by Guillaume de Lorris and Jean de Meun.* New York, 1962.

Roberts, Morley. "A Folk Song," *Athenaeum,* 3506 (January 5, 1895), 16.

Rockham, H. et al., trans. *Natural History of Pliny the Elder.* 10 vols. Loeb Classical Library. London, 1938–1942.

Rodway, Allan. Review of James Reeves, *The Idiom of the People* and *The Everlasting Circle,* in *EC* 11 (1961), 215–219.

Röhrich, Lutz. "Die Volksballade von 'Herrn Peters Seefahrt' und die Menschenopfer Sagen," in Hugo Kuhn and Kurt Schier, eds. *Märchen, Mythos, Dichtung (Festschrift Friedrich von der Leyen).* Munich, 1963. Pp. 177–212.

Rolland, Eugène. *Recueil de chansons populaires.* Paris, 1883.

Rooth, Anna Birgitta. *The Cinderella Cycle.* Lund, 1951.

———. *Loki in Scandinavian Mythology.* Lund, 1961.

———. "Scholarly Tradition in Folktale Research," *Fabula* 1 (1957–1958), 193–200.

Roscher, W. H. *Ausführliches Lexicon der greichischen und römischen Mythologie.* 6 vols. Leipzig and Berlin, 1884–1937.

Rose, J. Holland, et al. *The Cambridge History of the British Empire.* Vol. I: *The Old Empire from the Beginnings to 1783.* New York, 1929.

Rosenfeld, Moriz. "Leider der Zigeuner," *UR* (1882), pp. 823–832. (Reprinted from *AAW* 10 [1879], 362–367.)

Rossi, Ettore. "Scibilia Nobili e la leggenda maltese della Sposa della Mosta," *Lares* (N.S.), 3 (1932), 5–10.

Rouse, W. H. D. "Sacrifice to Avoid Shipwreck," *Folk-Lore* 12 (1901), 105.

Ruben, Walter. *Ozean der Märchenströme, Teil I.* FFC 133. Helsinki, 1944.

Russell, Edward R. "A Folk Song." *Athenaeum,* 3510 (February 2, 1895), p. 248.

Sackett, S. J. "Metaphor in Folksong," *FFMA* 6 (1963), 6–15.

Sager, Henry. "Die Losgekaufte," *MP* 27 (1929), 129–145.

Sampson, John. "English Gypsy Songs and Rhymes," *JGLS* 2 (1890–1891), 80–93.

Sandburg, Carl. *The American Songbag.* New York, 1927.

Sargent, Helen Child, and George Lyman Kittredge. *English and Scottish Popular Ballads.* Boston, 1904, 1932.

Scarborough, Dorothy. *On the Trail of Negro Folk-Song.* Cambridge, Mass., 1925.

———. *A Song Catcher in the Southern Mountains.* New York, 1937.

Scherer, G. *Jungbrunnen.* Berlin, 1875.

Schinhan, Jan. *The Music of the Ballads.* Frank C. Brown Collection of North Carolina Folklore, IV. Durham, N.C., 1957.

Schleiden, M. J. *Die Rose: Geschichte und Symbolik.* Leipzig, 1873.

Schmidt, Bernhard. *Griechische Märchen, Sagen, und Volkslieder.* Leipzig, 1877.

———. *Das Volksleben der Neugriechen und das hellenische Alterthum.* Leipzig, 1871.

Schultze, Leonhard. *Aus Namaland und Kalahari.* Jena, 1907.

Scouten, A. H. "On Child 76 and 173 in Divers Hands," *JAF* 64 (1951), 131–132.

Seemann, Erich. "Deutsche-litauische Volksliedbeziehungen," *JVF* 8 (1951), 142–211.

Sellers, William E. "Kinship in the British Ballads: The Historical Evidence," *SFQ* 20 (1956), 199–215.

Seward, Barbara. *The Symbolic Rose.* New York, 1960.

Sharp, Cecil J. *English Folk Song: Some Conclusions,* ed. Maud Karpeles. 4th ed., rev. Belmont, Calif., 1965.

———. *English Folk Songs.* 2 vols. London, 1959.

———. *One Hundred English Folk Songs.* London, 1916.

Sharp, Cecil J., and Maud Karpeles. *English Folk Songs from the Southern Appalachians.* 2 vols London, 1932, (rev. ed.) 1952, (rev. ed.) 1960.

Sharp, Cecil J., and Charles E. Marson. *Folk Songs from Somerset.* 5 vols. London, 1904–1909.

Sheppard, Muriel Early. *Cabins in the Laurel.* Chapel Hill, N.C., 1935.

Shepperson, George. "Writings in Scottish-American History: A Brief Survey," *WMQ* (ser. 3), 11 (1954), 163–178.

Shipton, Clifford K. "Immigration to New England, 1680–1740," *JPE* 44 (1936), 225–239.

Simrock, Karl. *Die deutsche Volkslieder.* Frankfurt, 1851.

Siuts, Hinrich. "Volksballaden-Volkserzählungen (Motiv- und Typenregister)," *Fabula* 5 (1962), 72–89.

———. "Die Volkslieder unserer Tage," *ZV* 55 (1959), 67–84.

Skeat, W. W. *The Lay of Havelok the Dane. EETS* extra series 4. London, 1868.

Skinner, Charles M. *Myths and Legends of Flowers, Trees, Fruits, and Plants.* Philadelphia, 1911

Smith, C. Alfonso. "Ballads Surviving in the United States," *MQ* 2 (1916), 109–129.

Smith, G. Elliott, Bronislaw Malinowski, Herbert J. Spinden, and Alex Goldenweiser. *Culture: The Diffusion Controversy.* New York, 1927.

Smith, J. Oates. "The 'Fifth Act' and the Chorus in the English and Scottish Ballads," *DR* 12 (1962), 329–340.

Smith, Laura. *Through Romany Songland.* London, 1889.

Smith, Reed. "La balada tradicional," *BLAM* 5 (1941), 275–284.

———. *South Carolina Ballads.* Cambridge, Mass., 1928.

———. *The Traditional Ballad and Its South Carolina Survivals. USCB* 182. Columbia, S.C., 1925.

Smith, Reed, and Hilton Rufty. *American Anthology of Old-World Ballads.* New York, 1937.

Stephenson, R. C. "Dialogue in Folktale and Song," in *Mesquite and Willow. PTFS* 27 (1957), 129–137.

Stewart, George R., Jr. "The Meter of the Popular Ballad," *PMLA* 40 (1925), 933–962.

Stokes, Whitney H., and E. Windisch. *Echtra Cormac.* Irische Texte (ser. 3, vol. I), III. Leipzig, 1891.

Stokoe, John, and Samuel Reay. *Songs and Ballads of Northern England.* London, 1899.

Swahn, Jan-Öjvind. *The Tale of Cupid and Psyche.* Lund, 1955.

Sydow, Carl W. von. "Folksagorforskningen," *FF* 14 (1927), 105–137.

Taylor, Archer. "Una comparación tentativa de temas de baladas inglesas y españoles," *FA* 4 (1956), 5–27.

———. *"Edward" and "Sven i Rosengård."* Chicago, 1931.

———. "German Folksongs in Spain," *HR* 27 (1959), 49–55.

———. "The Pertinacious Cobold," *JEGP* 31 (1932), 1–9.

———. "Precursors of the Finnish Method of Folk-Lore Study," *MP* 25 (1927–1928), 481–491.

———. "Some Recent Studies in Folksongs," *MF* 7 (1957), 229–236.

———. "Themes Common to English and German Balladry," *MLQ* 1 (1940), 23–35.

Taylor, Edgar, trans. *German Popular Stories Translated from the Kinder und Hausmärchen collected by M. M. Grimm.* 2 vols. London, 1823.

———. *German Popular Stories Translated from the Kinder und Hausmärchen collected by M. M. Grimm.* London, 1827.

———. *Gammer Grethel, or German Fairy Tales and Popular Stories from the Collection of Mm. Grimm, and other sources; with illustrative notes.* London, 1839.

———. *German Popular Stories and Fairy Tales as Told by Gammer Grethel.* Rev. ed. London, 1878.

Thomas, Jean. *Devil's Ditties.* Chicago, 1931.

Thompson, Harold. *Body, Boots, and Britches.* Philadelphia, 1940.

Thompson, Kate. "A Lancashire Ballad," *NQ* (ser. 6), 10 (1884), 354.

Thompson, Stith. *A Motif-Index of Folk Literature.* 6 vols. Bloomington, Ind., 1955–1958.

———. *The Types of the Folktale. FFC* 184. Helsinki, 1964.

Toelken, J. Barre. "An Oral Canon for the Child Ballads: Construction and Application," *JFI* 4 (1967), 75–101.

Tremearne, A. J. N. *Hausa Superstitions and Customs.* London, 1913.

Treuland, Th. Ja. In *Sbornik materialov po etnografii izdavajenij pri Daškovskom etnografičeskom Muzeje,* V. Moscow, 1887.

Trout, Allan M. "Greetings," *LCJ* December 19, 1957; January 30, 1958.

Uhland, Ludwig. *Alte hoch- und niederdeutsche Volkslieder.* Stuttgart and Tübingen, 1844.

Ulmann, Karl. *Lettische Volkslieder übertragen im Versmasse der Originale.* Riga, 1874.

Urica, Ingeborg. "The Gallows and the Golden Ball: An Analysis of 'The Maid Freed from the Gallows' (Child 95)," *JAF* 79 (1966), 463–468.

Vaïsänen, A. O. "Suggestions for the Methodical Classification and Investigation of Folk Tunes," *JIFMC* 1 (1949), 34–35.

Vargyas, Lajos. *Researches into the Medieval History of Folk Ballad.* Budapest, 1967.

Veckenstedt, E. *Wendische Sagen, Märchen und abergläubische Gebräuche.* Graz, 1880.

Venables, Edmund. "A Folk Song," *Athenaeum*, 3508 (January 19, 1895), 86.

———. "A Lancashire Ballad," *NQ* (ser. 6), 7 (1883), 275.

Verwijs, E., and J. Verdam. *Middelnederlandsch Woordenboek.* 7 vols. to S. Gravenhage, 1885–1912.

Vesey-Fitzgerald, Brian. *Gypsies of Britain: An Introduction to Their History.* London, 1944, 1946.

Vilmar, A. F. C. *Handbüchlein für Freunde des deutschen Volkslieds.* Marburg, 1867

Vinaver, Eugène, ed. *The Works of Sir Thomas Malory.* 3 vols. Oxford, 1947.

Violanti y Simorra, Ramon. *La Rosa segons la tradició popular.* Barcelona, 1956.

Wander, Karl. *Deutsches Sprichwörterlexicon.* 5 vols. Leipzig, 1867–1880.

Waser, Otto. *Charon, Charun, Charos.* Berlin, 1898.

Wells, Evelyn. *The Ballad Tree.* New York, 1950.

Wentworth, Harold, and Stuart Berg Flexner. *Dictionary of American Slang Based Upon Historical Principles.* New York, 1960, 1967.

Wenzig, Joseph. *Slawische Volkslieder.* Halle, 1830.

Wesselski, Albert. *Das Märchen des Mittelalters.* Berlin, 1925.

"W. F." "A Lancashire Ballad," *NQ* (ser. 6), 6 (1882), 476.

Wilgus, D. K. *Anglo-American Folksong Scholarship since 1898.* New Brunswick, N. J., 1959.

———. "Ballad Classification," *MF* 5 (1955), 95–100.

———. "The Rationalistic Approach," in *A Good Tale and a Bonnie Tune.* PTFS 32 (1964), 227–237.

———. "Shooting Fish in a Barrel: The Child Ballad in America," *JAF* 71 (1958), 161–164.

Williams, Alfred. *Folksongs of the Upper Thames.* London, 1923.

Wilson, Epiphanius, ed. *Turkish Literature.* New York, 1901.

Winkelman, Donald. "Musicological Techniques of Ballad Analysis," *MF* 10 (1960–1961), 197–205.

Winstead, Eric O. "Early Annals," *JGLS* (N.S.) 4 (1910–1911), 159–160.

Wlislocki, Heinrich von. *Volksdichtungen der siebenbürgischen und südungarischen Zigeuner.* Vienna, 1890.

Wolford, Leah Jackson. *The Play-Party in Indiana.* Indianapolis, 1916.

Woodall, James R. " 'Sir Hugh': A Study in Balladry," *SFQ* 19 (1955), 77–84.

Wright, Joseph. *The English Dialect Dictionary.* 6 vols. London, 1923.

Wyman, Loraine, and Howard Brockway. *Lonesome Tunes.* New York, 1916.

Yeatts, Eunice. In *Grapurchat* (East Radford, Virginia, State Teachers' College), August 25, 1932, p. 3.

Zielinski, Vladislav. "Notes on the Gypsies of Poland and Lithuania," *JGLS* 2 (1891), 237–240.

———. "Notes on the Nomadic Gypsies of Poland," *JGLS* 3 (1891–1892), 108–109.

Zoder, Raimund and Elizabeth. "Das Volkslied," in Otto Hietsch, ed. *Oesterreich und die angelsächsische Welt.* Vienna, 1961. Pp. 384–407.

DISCOGRAPHY

Allen, Vernon, "Ropes-i-man," 1941 (LC-AFS 5100 A).

Ball, Bentley, "The Gallows Tree," 1919 (Columbia Records A3084).

Blue Sky Boys [Bill and Earl Bolick], "Poor Boy," in *Presenting the Blue Sky Boys,* 1965 (Capitol Records T/ST 2483 [12-inch LP]).

Brewer, Pearl, "Hangman, Hangman," 1958 (LC-AFS 11,905 B4).

Browning, Bradley, "The Man Made Free from the Gallows," 1937 (LC-AFS 1387 A2, B1).

Cagle, C. J., "Hangman, Hangman," 1954 (LC-AFS 11,893 A2).

Crimes, Roy, "Mr. Brakeman," 1953 (LC-AFS 11,891 A21).

Drain, Mary, "Hangman, Hangman," 1942 (LC-AFS 5394 B1).

Driftwood, Jimmie [James Morris], "Slack Your Rope," in *The Wilderness Road of Jimmie Driftwood.* 1959 (RCA Victor LPM-1994 [12-inch LP]).

Gerlach, Fred, "Gallows Pole," 1962 (LC-AV 102; in *Twelve-String Guitar,* Folkways Records FG 3529 [12-inch LP]).

Hewett, Fred, "The Prickle-holly Bush," 1955 (BBC 21859).

Jackson, Harry, "The Hangman's Song," in *Harry Jackson the Cowboy: His Songs, Ballads, and Brag Talk,* ed. Kenneth Goldstein, 1959 (Folkways Records FH 5723 [12-inch LP]).

Keen, Ted, "The Prickly Bush," 1952 (BBC 18140).

Leadbelly [Huddie Ledbetter], "The Gallis Pole"/"Mama, Did You Bring Me Any Silver?" 1938 (LC-AFS 2501 A; in *Leadbelly: The Library of Congress Recordings, recorded by John A. and Alan Lomax,* ed. Lawrence Cohn, Elektra Records EKL-301/2 [12-inch LP]).

Lester, the Highwayman [Lester "Pete" Bivins], "The Highwayman," ca. 1937 (Decca Records 5559 [64412-A]).

Lucas, Walter C., "The Prickly Bush," 1949 (BBC 9467, and LC-AFS 9917 A; in *Columbia World Library of Folk and Primitive Music, III: English Folk Songs,* Columbia Records KL-206 [12-inch LP]).

Lunsford, Bascom Lamar, "The Hangman's Tree," 1935 (LC-AFS 1782 B1).

———. "The Hangman's Tree," 1949 (LC-AFS 9474 A3).

McAllister, Mary Bird [?], "The Maid Freed from the Gallows," 1956 (LC-AFS 11,305 A18, and BBC 16206).

McCord, May Kennedy, "The Hangman's Rope," 1941 (LC-AFS 5334 B1).

———, "Hangman," 1952 (LC-AFS 11,457 A1).

McDonald, Laura [Mrs. H. L.], "Hangman, Hangman"/"The Hangman," 1942 and 1958 (LC-AFS 5418 B1, LC-AFS 11,904 A9).

Marlor, Nate, "The Little Silver Cup," 1936 (LC-AFS 3169 A).

Martin, Mrs. W. L., "The Hangman's Song," 1939 (LC-AFS 2757 B4).

Monroe, Jane, "The Maid Freed from the Gallows," 1935 (LC-AFS 481 B2, LC-AFS 482 A1, and BBC 13877).

Parker, Carroll Wayne, "The Hangman's Tree," 1958 (LC-AFS 11,908 A11).

Poole, Charlie, and his North Carolina Ramblers, "The Highwayman," 1926 (Columbia Records 15160-D [142659]).

———, "Hangman, Hangman, Slack that Rope," 1928 (Columbia Records 15318-D [146772]).

Riddle, Almeda, "The Hangman," in *Badman Ballads (Southern Journey 9),* 1959 (Prestige/International Records INT 15009 [12-inch LP]).

———, "The Hangman," in *Traditional Music at Newport,* 1964 (Vanguard Records VRS-9183/VSD-79183 [12-inch LP]).

Ritchie, Jean, "Hangman," 1951 (LC-AFS 10,089 A9; in *British Traditional Ballads in the Southern Mountains,* Folkways Records FA 2301 [12-inch LP]).

Scaddon, Julia, "The Prickly Bush," 1952 (BBC 18694; in *The Folk Songs of Britain, IV,* eds. Peter Kennedy and Alan Lomax (Caedmon Records TC-1145B [12-inch LP]).

Shiflett, Robert, "Hangman," 1961 (LC-AFS 12,004 A5).

Smith, Hobart, "Hangman, Swing the Rope," 1942 (LC-AFS 6723 B1).

Spencer, Sadie, "Wait, Hangman," 1962 (LC-AFS 13,138 A12).

Thurston, Gertrude, "The Maid Saved from the Gallows," 1935 (LC-AFS) 388 B3, and BBC 13877).

Turbyfill, Lena Bare, "Hold Up Your Hand, Old Joshua, She Cried," 1939 (LC-AFS 2844 B).
Ward, Mr. and Mrs. Crockett, "Gallows Tree," 1940 (LC-AFS 4083 B2).
Wilburn, Jo, "Beneath the Gallows Tree," 1958 (LC-AFS 12,050 B17).

This discography in its entirety has been placed in deposit in the Archives of California and Western Folklore, University of California at Los Angeles.